(Un)Like Subjects

(Un)Like Subjects deals with the relationship between women and writing, mothers and daughters, the maternal and history. Gerardine Meaney addresses the questions about language, writing and the relations between women which have preoccupied the three most influential French feminists and three important contemporary British women novelists. Treating both fiction and theory as texts, the author traces the connections between the theorists – Hélène Cixous, Luce Irigaray and Julia Kristeva – and the novelists – Doris Lessing, Angela Carter and Muriel Spark.

Gerardine Meaney's reading of the work of these six major women writers explores new forms of women's identity, subjectivity and narrative and demonstrates how theoretical and literary texts can illuminate each other to bridge the gap between theory and literary criticism. *(Un)Like Subjects* is a book which will provide readers with a new way forward, opening up a relatively unexplored method of argument with verve and originality.

Gerardine Meaney is a lecturer in English at University College, Dublin. She writes fiction as well as criticism and her work on Irish women's writing includes a pamphlet, *Sex and Nation: Women in Irish Culture and Politics.*

...ture, Difference

... editor: Catherine Belsey

(Un)Like Subjects

Women, theory, fiction

Gerardine Meaney

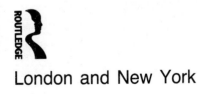

London and New York

First published 1993
by Routledge
11 New Fetter Lane, London EC4P 4EE

Simultaneously published in the USA and Canada
by Routledge Inc.
29 West 35th Street, New York, NY 10001

© 1993 Gerardine Meaney

Phototypeset by Intype, London

Printed in Great Britain by
T. J. Press (Padstow) Ltd, Cornwall

British Library Cataloguing in Publication Data:
Meaney, Gerardine
  (Un)Like Subjects: Women, Theory, Fiction. – (Gender, Culture,
  Difference Series)
  I. Title II. Series
  809

Library of Congress Cataloging in Publication Data:
Meaney, Gerardine
    (Un)like subjects: women, theory, fiction / Gerardine Meaney.
      p. cm. — (Gender, culture, difference)
    Includes bibliographical references and index.
    1. Fiction—Women authors—History and criticism. 2. Feminist
literary criticism. 3. Women and literature. 4. Feminism and
literature. 5. Women in literature. 6. Mothers in literature.
  I. Title II. Title: Unlike subjects. III. Series.
  PN3401.M43 1993
  809.3′0082—dc20
                                    92–36699

ISBN 0–415–07098–8
    0–415–07099–6 (pbk)

Contents

General editor's preface

Feminism has now reached a point where it is possible to produce a series of books written with the explicit aim of bringing together the politics of gender, cultural analysis and theoretically informed ways of reading. *Gender, Culture, Difference* offers a new kind of cultural history, which investigates the topics feminism has foregrounded, and takes the full range of cultural documents as its material.

Gender

Feminism attends to the power relations inscribed in the areas patriarchal history treats as incidental: sexuality, private life and personal relations, cultural difference itself. At the same time, it also recognizes transgression of the existing conventions as a mode of resistance, and therefore takes an interest in behaviour traditionally classified as perverse or dangerous. Above all, it is able to identify the differences within the relationships and practices it explores, treating them not as unified and homogeneous, but as contradictory to the degree that they participate in the uncertainties, incoherences, and instabilities of the cultures where they are found. The series addresses the topics politicized by feminism, analyzing them as sites where power is contested.

Culture

It is in culture that hierarchies of power are defined and specified. Recent theory urges that the material of cultural analysis is always textual. We have no access to 'experience,' past or present, but only to the differential meanings in circulation within a culture.

And these meanings reside in the existing documents, which can be read in order to make a history that refuses the injustices perpetrated by conventional patriarchal histories.

The documents of culture include, of course, every kind of material that it is possible to interpret: images, design and fashion, maps and domestic architecture, as well as philosophy, law, medicine. . . . But the project also involves attention, perhaps special attention, to fiction, since it is in stories, legends, plays, and poems that many cultures have tended to treat most freely and most precisely the relations between the sexes. (This in itself is a matter of some interest to feminism: fiction is what a patriarchal culture identified as 'not true,' not serious, not real and important. But to the extent that life follows art, in practice fiction returns to haunt the 'real' history which marginalizes it).

Difference

Cultural contradictions, incoherences, and instabilities are pressure points for feminism, because they constitute evidence that existing power relations are always precarious. In this respect the interests of feminism coincide with recent modes of interpretation which specifically seek out instances of uncertainty, of difference within the text. For this reason, the series takes advantage of a range of theoretical developments which promote a differential practice of reading.

At the same time, feminism avoids the closed mode of address that sets out to deflect criticism and forestall debate. *Gender, Culture, Difference* is a speculative series that sets out to enlist readers in the process of discussion, and does not hesitate to engage with questions to which it has no final answers.

A New Direction

The series brings together a differential reading practice and the construction of a cultural history which celebrates difference. In this respect *Gender, Culture, Difference* also offers a new model for literary studies. The epoch of the Author is over; few teachers and virtually no students now want to hear about maturity and the organic society, or about ambiguity and balance; and Elizabethan and other world pictures are totally played out. Meanwhile, English departments are looking for a way forward. It would not be at all surprising if feminism proved itself to be responsible for identifying one of the most exciting among the possible new directions.

Catherine Belsey
Centre for Critical and Cultural Theory
University of Wales, Cardiff

Acknowledgements

My particular thanks are due to Seamus Deane for his encouragement of new modes of research and new ways of thinking and for his scholarly and insightful comments on this work as it developed. My thanks also to Catherine Belsey, who, as general editor of this series, contributed so helpfully to the final stages of the book.

I would also like to acknowledge the help of the following, my present and former colleagues at University College Dublin: Karen Corrigan, Thomas Docherty, Alan Fletcher, Marion Gunn, Mairéad Hanrahan, J. C. C. Mays and Helen Meaney. I would like to thank the Institute of Irish Studies, Queen's University, Belfast, for its support and to express my gratitude to my former colleagues there and at the School of English, Trinity College Dublin, for their patience and interest while I worked with them. I am particularly indebted to Jennifer Fitzgerald, Dympna MacLoughlin and Jane Moore. I would also like to thank all of the past and present members of UCD Women's Studies Forum, UCD Feminist Literary Theory Group, QUB Women's Studies Forum and Trinity College Women's Studies Group for creating a context in which work of this kind can develop. And I acknowledge, with some sadness, the considerable help I received from Angela Carter in the course of an interview with her.

My particular and personal thanks to Gerry Dowling and to Mary and Norah Meaney.

Extracts from **The Kristeva Reader**, edited by Toril Moi, are reprinted with the kind permission of Columbia University Press.

Introduction

CONTEXTS

In 1984, at the time when I first undertook this research, Elaine Showalter published an article entitled 'Women's time, women's space'. It attempted to summarize and describe the history of feminist criticism to that point in time and to project the future directions feminist criticism might take. Directions, not direction, because Showalter could not define feminist criticism and saw nothing to be gained from trying to impose on it a uniformity to which in any case it would never submit. Feminist criticism has mirrored feminist politics in its acceptance of diversity; its ability to accommodate often divergent and occasionally contradictory views is one of its political and intellectual strengths:

> There is no Mother of Feminist Criticism, no fundamental work against which one can measure other feminisms. Feminist criticism has been rather a powerful movement than a unified theory, a community of women with a shared set of concerns but with a complex and resourceful variety of methodological practices and theoretical affiliations. In addition to having a broad social and intellectual base, feminist criticism is unusually wide in scope. It is not limited or even partial to single national literature, genre or century; it is interdisciplinary in theory and practice; it can handle Harlequin Books as well as *Paradise Lost*.
>
> (Showalter, 1984: 303)

This affirmation of harmony in diversity is ironically also a catalogue of submerged conflict. There is a mother of feminist criticism or at least a mother text. There can be few feminist critics who have never had cause to refer to, quote, ponder on, or attack

A Room of One's Own (Woolf, 1977 [1928]). Showalter's influential rejection of that mother (1982 [1978]) has been fairly successfully challenged, particularly by Toril Moi (1985: 1–8). Showalter's repudiation of Woolf was always compromised and ambivalent: the title of the work of feminist literary history in which she attacks Woolf is *A Literature of Their Own.*

The 'community of women' which has shaped feminist criticism has been a strife-torn community. The often conflicting claims of Marxist, lesbian, theoretical, anti-theoretical, separatist and anti-separatist movements in feminist politics and criticism have defined and repeatedly redefined it. The accusation of ethnocentrism[1] remains the strongest challenge to Showalter's vision of a coherent movement. Access to a variety of methodologies has sometimes been blocked by distrust and dissension. But then a distrust of any methodology and of methodology itself happily remains intrinsic to feminism. Method, along with reason, judgement, 'understanding', and so many of the values close to the heart of the academy, has too often been the agent of denial of women's perspectives, experience and even existence: 'Under patriarchy, Method has wiped out women's questions so totally that even women have not been able to hear and formulate our own questions, to meet our own experience' (Daly, 1973: 12–13). Yet Showalter's claim that feminist scholarship is uniquely interdisciplinary and broad in scope is irrefutable. The nature of its links with feminist activism endows feminist criticism with a vitality which itself gives to feminist criticism and women's studies the only kind of cohesion acceptable to it. Beneath the intellectual diversity there is a common, though not a single, political purpose. The community of feminist scholarship is not achieved under the sign of denial of difference, but through the activation of difference into political and intellectual energy.

Feminist research has its origins outside the universities and academic systems. Campaigns for changes in legislation and in social and economic practice necessitated research which would turn women's perspectives and experiences into forms which rendered their knowledge powerful. Reports, documents, statistics and studies of all sorts on the condition of women proliferated throughout the 1960s and 1970s and were the well-spring of the proliferation of courses and programmes in women's studies in the 1980s. Its more obvious usefulness in effecting social and political change would appear to privilege sociological feminist scholarship over other forms:

> Literary criticism was hardly a central factor in the early period of the new women's movement. Much like any other radical critic, the feminist critic can be seen as the product of a struggle mainly concerned with social and political change; her specific role within it becomes an attempt to extend such general political action to the cultural domain.
>
> (Moi, 1985: 22–3)

Unlike other radical movements, however, the movement which proclaimed that the personal is political has increasingly focused on the cultural domain as an area with the potential for wide-ranging changes which will have an impact in every other domain of power.

At least one of the subjects of this study sees the coming of women to writing as not merely revolutionary, but necessary to revolutionary change in the nature of gender and power: 'Writing is precisely *the very possibility of change*, the space that can serve as a springboard for subversive thought, the precursory movement, of a transformation of social and cultural structures' (Cixous, 1976: 879).[2] The response of feminist criticism to Cixous's fervour has been mixed. For some its valorization of writing (as the site of revolution) and its celebration of the revolutionary body have been exhilarating. For others it constitutes an evasion of the complex ways in which gender is intertwined with class and race and with the internalization by women of the mind-set and language of patriarchy (Moi, 1985: 121–6). The once widespread view that Cixous's writing postulates an essentialist view of sexual identity is now losing ground, but the distrust of French feminist theory persists (Christian, 1989) and still focuses on those same issues. With regard to Irigaray and Kristeva the distrust of any valorization of the 'feminine' has been complicated by a distrust of academic 'elitism'. There is an apparent incompatibility between their complex work and writing practice, and the demystification and democratization of knowledge which were and remain an important project of feminism and have shaped its attitudes to education, research and even literary style.[3] An increasing awareness of the difficulties and dangers inherent in the use of 'plain' or 'common-sense' gender-loaded terminologies and strategies has mitigated that distrust. But in 1984 Showalter was still talking about two distinct categories within feminist criticism, though the distinction, she was happy to report, was beginning to blur:

> Since 1975, feminist criticism has taken two theoretical directions, that of the Anglo-American focus on the specificity of women's writing I have called *gynocritics*, and that of the French exploration of the textual consequences and representations of sexual difference that Alice Jardine has named *gynesis*. These ought not to be taken as oppositional or exclusive terms either; in fact they describe tendencies within feminist critical theory rather than absolute categories. As such, however, they represent different emphases and perceptions of the role of feminist inquiry. Gynocritics is, roughly speaking, historical in orientation; it looks at women's writing as it has actually occurred and tries to define its specific characteristics of language, genre, and literary influence, within a cultural network that includes variables of race, class, and nationality.
>
> Gynesis rejects, however, the temporal dimension of women's experience . . . and seeks instead to understand the space granted to the feminine in the symbolic contract. . . . The problematic of women's space has had practical meanings, of course, for Anglo-American feminist inquiry as well. . . . Gynesis goes beyond these, however, to repossess as a field of inquiry all the space of the Other, the gaps, silences and absences of discourse and representation, to which the feminine has traditionally been relegated.
>
> (Showalter, 1984: 36)

There is misrepresentation or at least confusion here of the Kristevan concept of 'women's time'. As presented in Kristeva's article of that name it is not an ahistorical realm of the feminine but an other, disruptive order of time which Kristeva sees as *anti*-historical where history is understood as masculine-defined linear history. The dynamic potential of using women's space to refuse to adopt a predetermined role in such a history is ignored by Showalter. None the less her description of these two 'tendencies' in feminist criticism is valuable and provides a whole series of openings for the complementary practice of both. Showalter's own work is increasingly a gynocritics informed by gynesis.[4]

'Women's time, women's space' does raise one fundamental

objection to gynesis, possibly the most fundamental and persistent objection to it: 'its dependence on male masters and male theoretical texts' (37). The first 'wave' of feminist criticism, identified now almost solely with Kate Millett (1970) and Mary Ellman (1968), was followed by the emergence of an 'images of women' school of feminist criticism. The depressing exercise of pointing out the misogyny of the existing canon is a form of criticism now little practised by Anglo-American feminism. It is generally perceived to have been a necessary first step, but no longer of enabling value for feminist criticism and the feminist movement. As it addressed itself to 'images of women' in women's fiction and their relationship to the corresponding 'images' in literature by men, this school gradually built up the basis on which later criticism devoted to the specificity of women's writing could build. Gynocritics had effectively replaced it as the dominant force in Anglo-American feminist criticism by the middle of the 1970s. (Though by that time French feminist literary theory began to make its influence felt in English-language feminist circles. *Signs* emerged as one of the most influential feminist journals and, between 1976 and 1980, carried translations of work by Kristeva, Irigaray and Cixous.) The publication of *A Literature of Their Own* (Showalter, 1982 [1978]) and of the influential *The Madwoman in the Attic* (Gilbert and Gubar, 1979) crystallized the growing awareness of the specificity of women's writing and gave that writing its own history. Gilbert and Gubar postulated that the history of women's writing had a continuity and a thematic and stylistic unity. *The Madwoman in the Attic* established the idea of nineteenth-century women's writing as a literature defined by the problematic nature of the relation between sexual and artistic identity for the woman writer. The effectiveness with which it tackled that problem displaced more traditional modes of evaluating these writers' work. In short, in the process of uncovering a counter-tradition to an English literature dominated by the 'great men of letters', Gilbert, Gubar, Showalter and others created a tradition, that of women's writing. Wollstonecraft, Austen, Shelley, the Brontës, Gaskell and Eliot certainly meant something before feminist criticism read them, but it was feminist criticism which gave them a collective meaning and identity and which produced the narrative or history of women's writing.

Perhaps it is the nature of every revolutionary movement to postulate a long tradition to which that movement can be the inevitable and long-awaited apotheosis. Feminist scholarship, whether in history, archaeology, or literature, has not simply uncovered the past of women and of the women's movement. It has for the first time postulated that the past of women has meaning. Within the context of 'women's time', it has taken women's past and made it into women's history.

It is not surprising that Anglo-American feminism at first reacted defensively to the challenge which European critical theory posed for these newly emerging modes of understanding women's experience. 'They are afraid that if the theory is perfected the movement will be dead', commented Elaine Showalter in 1979 (1986: 128). Greater familiarity must have assuaged the fear of perfection. It is an indication of the intellectual and institutional flourishing of feminist criticism in the decade which has passed since then that the challenge of theory has been met, not defensively, but by taking advantage of the opportunities it affords for greater insight into the symbolic construction of sexual identity. That insight has been developed in the context of the historical and sociological framework which continues to be elaborated.

The integration of theoretical and historical analysis had already begun with the publication of a collection of essays, edited by Mary Jacobus, entitled *Women Writing and Writing about Women* (1979). Margaret Homans's *Women Writers and Poetic Identity* (1980) did for nineteenth-century women poets what Gilbert and Gubar had done for the novelists and to critique contemporary formulations of women's poetic 'identity' in the light of poststructuralist views of language in general and the work of Luce Irigaray in particular.

There have been two major consequences of this integration. The first has been a redefinition of the tradition of women's writing. Woolf, for example, has been reread and transformed by a more subtle and theoretically informed criticism. The second has been the adaptation and translation of the work of Cixous, Irigaray, Kristeva and, to a lesser extent, Wittig and Clément into the Anglo-American defined tradition of women's writing.

The excitement and pitfalls of this two-way process are exemplified by the way in which Sandra Gilbert presented Cixous and Clément's *The Newly Born Woman* to an English and American readership in 1986:

For an American feminist – at least for this American feminist – reading *The Newly Born Woman* is like going to sleep in one world and waking in another – going to sleep in a world of facts where one must labour to theorize, and waking in a world of theory where one must strive to (f)actualize.

(Gilbert, 1986: x)

Gilbert's introduction to the translation of *The Newly Born Woman*, and her adoption in that introduction of some of the fluidity and linguistic play of the text, was itself significant. One of the most influential of feminist literary historians was giving her imprimatur to the 'apocalyptic vision that energizes Hélène Cixous's brilliant and mystical tarantella[5] of theory' (xiv). There were obviously reservations: 'Of course, to represent the historical range and variety of female experience chiefly in terms of such extreme figures as the sorceress and the hysteric may seem on the one hand, hyperbolic and, on the other hand, reductive' (xii). Gilbert integrates Cixous and Clément's work into Anglo-American feminism on two fronts. First she dismisses the 'reasonable' objections to *The Newly Born Woman* mentioned above by 'factualizing' the dominant textual images: 'The paradigms of sorceress and hysteric become increasingly convincing when one contextualizes them with contemporary anthropological theory about – to use the scholar Gayle Rubin's phrase – "sex-gender" systems' (xiii). Gilbert moves from this one scholarly phrase to a whole series of them, briefly mentioning Lévi-Strauss before moving on to make analogies between *The Newly Born Woman* and Sherry Ortner's influential and controversial 'Is female to male as nature is to culture?' (1974). Gilbert uses Ortner to render Cixous and Clément intelligible in terms familiar to an Anglo-American feminist criticism strongly defined by an interdisciplinary relationship with feminist sociology, history and anthropology. She then integrates them into that mode of feminist criticism. This process of integration is typified in a long paragraph which is worth quoting in full as it raises several key issues. What is the nature of the tradition of women's writing, who defines it, how and why? What is buried beneath this constructed tradition?

A sorceress and a hysteric – that is, a displaced person – everywoman must inevitably find that she has no home, no *where*. Central to Cixous's thinking, and to Clément's, this sense of metaphysical alienation, symbolized by geographical dispossession, has also been important in the Anglo-American feminist tradition. Indeed, Cixous's reiteration of points made earlier in England and America seems almost uncanny. 'I can never say the word "patrie", "fatherland",' she confesses at one point, 'even if it is provided with an "anti",' adding later that 'I, revolt, rages, where am I to stand? What is my place if I am a woman? I look for myself throughout the centuries and don't see myself anywhere' (p. 75). Her words echo those of Virginia Woolf in the twentieth century ('As a woman I have no country. As a woman I want no country' [*Three Guineas*]) and those of Elizabeth Barrett Browning in the nineteenth century ('I look everywhere for grandmothers and find none' [*Letters*]). We too have been seeking the other country as well as 'the other history' for hundreds of years now. 'Hysterics', intermittently mad (Woolf) or addicted to opium (Barrett Browning), our ancestresses were also sorceresses who transmitted to us what Dickinson, speaking of Barrett Browning, called 'Tomes of solid Witchcraft' in which they too, though not so explicitly, fantasized about a new heaven and a new earth.

(Gilbert, 1986: xvi)

A realignment emerges here. The contrasting tendencies are now Anglo-American and Franco-American, which latter relationship appears to be first mediated through the English tradition (Woolf and Barrett Browning, in the exotic guises of madwoman and opium addict), but finally endorsed by the one nineteenth-century American woman writer who made her way into the old-style canon. What is apocalyptic in Cixous becomes millenarian in Gilbert. Cixous and Clément become twin messiahs, with Woolf, Barrett Browning, Dickinson and later H.D., Gertrude Stein and Sylvia Plath (xviii) as their prophets. Even in its most emphatic insistence on the status of woman as dispossessed, of no one country or culture, the passage gives evidence of cultural difference. Gilbert assimilates Cixous and Clément not just into Anglo-American feminist culture, but into American culture, and specifically white American culture. Cixous's

Story of a girlhood as a dispossessed female Algerian French Jew is one with which almost any immigrant – Jewish-, black-, Chicana-, Italian-, Polish-American – woman can identify. In

fact even if we were, like Dickinson, WASPS, Yankee prin-
cesses, couldn't we at least sympathize?

(Gilbert, 1986: xvi)

Gilbert evades the problem that while as women we are all dispossessed some women are more dispossessed than others. She may
be right in commenting that it must mean something that Dickinson 'didn't need either the Algerian revolution or the Vietnam
war, either the Paris barricades or the New York ghettoes, to
say "Good Morning – Midnight/I'm coming home" ' (xvi). It is
perhaps more to the point that in women's various ghettoes or
wars or on their barricades, Dickinson's lines will mean different
things to different women. Paradoxically it is the American feminist critic who is rendering the supposedly ahistorical French feminism apolitical. Cixous and Clément's sorceresses are being turned
into practitioners of nice, white magic:

> As culture has constructed her, 'woman' *is* 'the dark continent'
> to which *woman* must return.
> But returning, a sorceress and a hysteric – that is a displaced
> person – everywoman must inevitably find that she has no
> home, no *where*.[6]
>
> (Gilbert, 1986: xvi)

Nowhere. Utopia. The power of the feminine imaginary and the
woman's word is withdrawn from the world of politics and
history into an eternal realm where unity is preserved at the price
of submerging whole continents of difference.

Sandra Gilbert's genuine attempt to bring together gynocritics
and gynesis is limited by its assumption of the identity of women
rather than their difference and specificity. That does not detract
from either the validity of attempts to integrate the two
approaches or Gilbert's own contribution in endorsing and
attempting to practise such an integration. It does alert us to the
dangers of generalization and the necessity of paying close attention to the detail of textual practice in both the theoretical and
literary writings of women.

(Un)Like Subjects reads contemporary women's theory and
fiction in an attempt to fuse gynocritical and gynetical practice.
It focuses on the specificity of women's writing, attempting to
identify common concerns and practices in six texts – three novels
and three 'theoretical' essays[7] – and to explore the 'gaps, silences

and absences' which emerge. Such an attempt to combine gyno-critical and gynetic practice in this way must confront two questions. The first is the one raised by Gilbert's introduction to *The Newly Born Woman*. What approach will be taken to the concept of a distinct tradition of women's writing? The second is that raised by Elaine Showalter in 'Women's time, women's space'. How does one deal with the 'dependence on male masters and male theoretical texts' (37) which besets gynesis?

Any engagement with contemporary theories and practices of women's writing must take place within the context of the history of women's writing elucidated by gynocritics. While I make considerable reference to that context, my emphasis here is synchronic, focusing on six texts, all of which were first published in a twelve-year period (1965–77) during which the social and symbolic function of 'Woman' and the lives and self-concept of women were undergoing very significant changes.

Doris Lessing, in an afterword to *The Making of the Representatives for Planet 8* (1982), has commented on the life and death of ideas, the cultural processes in which we are all entangled, which every writer inscribes, negatively or positively. These assume the force of 'natural' and eternal truths at the time, yet are in hindsight, she points out, clearly the product of their era. Analysing the common ground of contemporary theories and practices of women's writing is an attempt to explore the cultural crisis produced by and producing a new form of feminine subjectivity. The three novelists discussed in this book are extremely diverse both in their writing practices and their expressed views of the functions of that work. Muriel Spark in particular has never been associated with the feminist movement. Commentary on her novels has praised their capacity to push fiction to its self-reflexive limits and simultaneously to insist on fiction's right and ability to reflect on that which is outside fiction and even language. Spark's novels, like those of Carter and Lessing, are involved in a radical interrogation of the novel form and the assumptions which underlie it. This interrogation of western culture – the relentless revision, the rewriting and undoing of myth, of history, above all of wilful consciousness and the fictions (societies, languages, selves) it supports – is not only a practice shared by these diverse novelists with the equally diverse 'theorists'. It is a process in which women writers are now almost inevitably engaged, whether or not they engage in it as self-conscious feminists. This does not imply that there is an 'essential' difference between the writing of men and that of women. It does mean that the inscription of difference, sexual and otherwise, is in process in a culture which has functioned on the assumption of identity.

The second problem for an attempt to integrate gynocritical and gynetic strategies is less easily resolved. Many feminists object strongly to what they perceive as feminist literary theory's deference to figures like Lacan, Derrida and Althusser. Obviously the emergence of structuralism, poststructuralism and Lacanian psychoanalysis forms a vital context for the emergence of current trends in feminist criticism and cannot be disregarded. Yet it is necessary to maintain a certain critical distance from those movements in assessing their impact on the reading and writing of feminist theory. The complexity, divergence and prolific output of those movements has sometimes threatened to obscure the specificity of feminist criticism. Feminist literary theory can occasionally be perceived as a distant goal reached only after 'a long apprenticeship to the male theoretician, whether he be Althusser, Barthes, Macherey or Lacan; and then an application of the theory of signs or myths or the unconscious to male texts or films' (Showalter, 1986: 130). Showalter points out that 'the temporal and intellectual investment one makes in such a process increases resistance to questioning it and to seeing its historical and ideological boundaries'. It also obscures the historical and ideological context in which such theories are elaborated. In particular it obscures the extent to which changing theories of the subject, for example, may be a *response to* rather than a *precondition of* the feminist challenge. Showalter sceptically reviews the way in which literary theorists first 'attempted to make the study of literature more serious and manly by structuring its principles scientifically like the laws of physics, biology, mathematics' (1984: 40) and more recently 'have begun to acknowledge that feminist criticism offers a paradigm for the kind of criticism they really want to do' (41):

> It may well turn out that in the critical histories of the future, these years will not be remembered as the Age of Structuralism or the Age of Deconstruction, but as the Age of Feminism. Wouldn't it be a surprise if, without having realized it, we have all been living in women's time?
>
> (Showalter, 1984: 42)

It was Hélène Cixous who remarked that now, for women, 'Il est urgent d'anticiper' (1976 [1975]: 39).[8] In so far as it is possible my reading of contemporary women's writing anticipates. 'I do not deny that the effects of the past are still with us. But I refuse to strengthen them by repeating them, to confer upon them an irremovability the equivalent of destiny' (1976: 875). In common with a great many of those now interested in feminist literary theory, I came to theory through feminism and to literary theory through feminist literary theory. The priorities implicit in that process and the anticipated precedence of feminist over other kinds of literary theory inform and shape this work. There is no attempt to exclude male writers and thinkers. Neither is there any attempt to introduce extraneous material by them to validate points made in relation to the women writers who are the sole focus of this work. The texts of Engels, Rousseau, Lacan, Freud and others are introduced and discussed. They are part of the literary and political culture which any woman writing both challenges and inherits. In all cases they are introduced because they are of specific relevance to the key texts under discussion. Where, for example, concepts such as 'the feminine Imaginary' or 'identity' are adequately expounded in the key texts, I see no reason to supplement those expositions by detailed reference to other 'authorities'.

In the course of my research and writing, the theoretical writings of Julia Kristeva have become central to this work. There are a variety of reasons for this. While Kristeva has not written extensively on women writers,[9] readings of Spark and Carter in conjunction with Kristeva's texts prove particularly productive. Her work on the sublime is especially illuminating in relation to *The Hothouse by the East River* and though it has occasioned some criticism is highly relevant to the current debate on the role of feminist aesthetics (Ecker, 1985: Yaeger, 1989; Edelman, 1989). Paradoxically, the more structured 'theoretical' framework of Kristeva's work makes it easier to integrate within a gynocritical approach to women's writing. Irigaray's very effective deconstructions of western metaphysical discourse constitute a practice which has limited value in relation to a tradition of women's writing still in process of construction. Cixous is more concerned to set a precedent for a new type of fiction or poetic prose.

My project is not, however, the application of a ready-made theory to docile novels. If reading Kristeva offers interesting insights into the fiction of Spark and Carter, it is equally the case that Kristeva's texts can be read with more illumination and provocation in the context of the fiction than they might be read in the context of writing by other theorists.[10]

A NOTE ON STRUCTURE AND TERMINOLOGY

I have chosen to deal with three novelists (Doris Lessing, Angela Carter and Muriel Spark) and three theorists (Hélène Cixous, Luce Irigaray and Julia Kristeva). Each section focuses on one novel and one theoretical essay, though obviously other texts by the relevant authors are integrated into the discussion where appropriate. The somewhat complex structure serves two purposes. It forestalls generalization and facilitates engagement with a range of theoretical and literary discourses without losing sight of the detail of textual practice. It also avoids any privileging of theory over fiction. Both the theoretical writings and the novels are treated as primary texts. In the interplay between texts, each comments on and puts the other into question.

Any study which attempts to deal with cultural process must of necessity immerse itself in intertextual relations. It has therefore been necessary, for example, to look at Angela Carter's reading and rewriting of Rousseau in *Heroes and Villains*, to examine R. D. Laing's radical psychiatry in the context of Doris Lessing's exploration of madness and to compare Hélène Cixous's treatment of the myth of the Medusa with that of predecessors as diverse as Freud and Hesiod.

Certain terms frequently used in this study remain contentious. Cixous's use of the term 'feminine' has often proved problematic, particularly when it is understood in its English-language context where it has come to mean conformity to the social confinement and denigration of women. The French *'féminin'* indicates both female and feminine and is used by Cixous to refer to the challenging and subversive aspects of 'feminine' biology, creativity, writing and a 'different' subjectivity. This kind of femininity is by no means exclusive to those who have female bodies, although 'The laugh of the Medusa' declares 'woman must write woman. And man, man' (889). Cixous's present position appears to be that it is possible that female biology may be better able to sustain a feminine libidinal economy, but that we cannot know whether this is so.[11] Cixous has clarified and extended her conception of the feminine into that of a feminine libidinal economy (Sellers, 1988). This economy is fluid, differential, disturbing: it diffuses, it affirms, it writes and it empowers. It is engaged in a dialectical conflict with a masculine libidinal economy which centralizes, organizes under the law of the One and the same. It denies, possesses and takes power. This version is obviously quite different from what is usually implied by the English term 'feminine'.

A distinction is drawn in this work between 'Woman', the socio-symbolic generality, and women, specific and diverse.

The use of the term 'subject' is more problematic. It can indicate any possible position of subjectivity available within the symbolic order. This study is, however, concerned with the erosion and change of that order and the emergence of an other, different discourse of feminine specificity as a foundation for a different kind of subjectivity. So 'the subject' and 'subjectivity' are terms which gain and lose different shades of meaning within the text.

Such fluidity of meaning cannot be confined to just one term, of course. The confusion with regard to the term 'feminine', discussed above, cannot now be banished from any English-language discussion of the subject. None of the texts dealt with permits the postulation of any stable meaning within or about them and an instability of terminology is inevitable in a text which seeks to engage with them.

Chapter 1

Between the mother
and the Medusa

'The laugh of the Medusa' was the first of Hélène Cixous's texts to be translated into English. That translation and Luce Irigaray's 'When our lips speak together' were published in the first issue of *Signs* (1976) and were thus the first 'French feminist' texts to be widely available to a women's studies and critical readership in English. Although Cixous is a prolific novelist and dramatist as well as a theorist it is on 'The laugh of the Medusa' that I wish to focus. Its place in the history of feminist criticism is only one reason for such a focus. The essay is also a good starting-place for an attempt to integrate contemporary women's 'literary theory' and fiction because its poetic and visionary nature immediately makes nonsense of any distinction between 'theory' and 'literature'. 'The laugh of the Medusa' is a celebration and an exploration of central images of women, less an analysis of women's writing than a sustained exhortation: 'And why don't you write? Write! Writing is for you, you are for you; your body is yours, take it' (Cixous, 1976: 876).

The tone of Doris Lessing's work is in marked contrast to Cixous's exuberance, as her distrust of the feminine in language makes clear. Lessing has exclaimed her disappointment that her most famous novel, *The Golden Notebook* (1962), has been read as a feminist tract and attempted in her preface to the second edition (1972) to focus attention on the formal experiment which she considers central. Cixous, for whom writing is 'the anti-logos weapon' (1976: 880), insists that 'a feminine text cannot fail to be more than subversive' (888).

The Doris Lessing novel which will be discussed with 'The laugh of the Medusa' is quite different in tone. *Landlocked* (1965) is a novel about a pause in history, a period of personal and political paralysis in the life of the heroine, Martha Quest. *Landlocked* marks a pause in Lessing's fiction also. It was written after the formally experimental *The Golden Notebook*, and immediately before the novel which marked Lessing's dramatic move away from 'realism' and into speculative fiction, *The Four-Gated City*.

Lessing considers the women's movement to be obsolete and parochial in the face of impending global disaster (1972: 9). Her grave reservations about maternity and her insistence on the universal, human significance of *The Golden Notebook* contrast sharply with Cixous's insistence that a transformation in female identity is a potential revolution of 'a force never yet unleashed and equal to the most forbidding of suppressions' (1976: 886) which 'will bring about a mutation in human relations, in thought, in all praxis . . . the staggering alteration in power relations' (882).

It is in their analysis of the relation between sexual identity and language that *Landlocked* and 'The laugh of the Medusa' overlap. For both writers, the maternal and, specifically, the mother-daughter relationship are central to this analysis. In the *Children of Violence* series the relationship between Martha Quest and her mother has a nightmarish intensity which has attracted much comment from critics.[1] A fresh perspective on this relationship and its implications for the formal development of Lessing's fiction can be gained by looking at it in the context of 'The laugh of the Medusa' and also of Luce Irigaray's lyrical essay on mother-daughter bonding, 'And the one doesn't stir without the other' (1981). Lessing's treatment proves to have many similarities to Irigaray's. Both contrast sharply with Cixous's celebration of the life-affirming maternal.

In Lessing's fiction the Medusa is an implicit figure for the dangers of the maternal, language and feminine madness. These implicit dangers are made explicit in work which has had a major influence on Lessing, that of R. D. Laing. Considerable note has been taken of the influence of Laing on Lessing's work.[2] A number of similarities are apparent between the fictional case history of Lynda Coleridge in *The Four-Gated City* and the actual case of 'Julie' in *The Divided Self* (1960). Lessing's most overt borrowing from Laing is that of the voyage into 'inner space' of Charles *Watkins* in *Briefing for a Descent into Hell*: in *The Politics of Experience* (1967) Laing reports the 'ten day voyage' into 'inner space and time' (136) of a sculptor friend, Jessie *Watkins*. Laing himself appears to be the prototype of the radical and sympathetic psychiatrists, Dr Yn2 (Lessing, 1969) and Doctor Y (Lessing, 1971).

Laing provides a provocative link between Cixous and Lessing by his use of the Medusa myth in his key text, *The Divided Self*. Laing considers schizophrenia to be rooted in ontological insecurity and a fear of petrification and engulfment. An analysis of his use of the Medusa myth shows that the schizophrenic subject is a fearful Perseus, and what Perseus most fears is the mother and the maternal. This proves to have considerable significance for a reading of Lessing's later work.

In both *Landlocked* and 'The laugh of the Medusa' engulfment by the maternal can be traced as the fate of the feminine subject. In both cases language is both the agent of engulfment and the residue of resistance to that engulfment. Early versions of the story of Medusa provide us with a figure who cannot easily be assimilated to the fiction of the 'mother goddess' or of the mother as 'womb and tomb of the world' (Campbell, 1974: 25). Through this other Medusa one can explore that which exceeds representation and which re-presents the woman in the texts of Cixous and Lessing.

IN SEARCH OF THE ETRUSCANS

The Medusa myth is not directly cited in Lessing's fiction, but the revulsion at the maternal which is an important aspect of that myth is crucial to the development of that fiction. The Medusan aspect of the mother-daughter relationship is central in both Cixous's and Lessing's writing.

In Lessing it is the image of 'the overbearing, clutchy "mother" ' (Cixous, 1976: 880), 'the accomplice to a sociality' (888), which dominates. The relationship of Martha Quest to her mother, May, throughout the *Children of Violence* series is antagonistic and sometimes paralysing. May Quest is perceived, not only as the epitome of all that Martha rejects in the feminine role, but also as a powerful agent of assimilation to that role. May Quest symbolizes the paralysing force of the family, in its structuration of personality and limitation of potential.

Cixous acknowledges that the mother-daughter relationship as agent of repression exists, just as she acknowledges that the ideology behind the Medusa myth has succeeded in frightening women away from themselves and their own bodies: 'They have made for women an anti-narcissism! A narcissism which loves women only for what they haven't got! They have constructed the infamous logic of anti-love.'[3] Within the general denunciation of patriarchal ideology there is a specific objection to the Freudian construction of feminine identity in terms of castration and penis-envy. In mapping feminine sexuality and development on to the Oedipal model Freud denies feminine difference and translates woman into not-man. Before going on to analyse the role of feminine difference in Lessing's and Cixous's writing it will be useful to outline Freud's theory of 'femininity' and introduce the challenge to that form of femininity in Cixous's work. The key lecture, 'Femininity', in which this theorization of the feminine in masculine terms occurs has been the focus of considerable attention from feminist critics and analysts, notably Juliet Mitchell (1974), Jane Gallop (1982), Alice Jardine (1985), Luce Irigaray (1985a), Mary Jacobus (1986). Freud renders explicit in the essay the implicit denial of feminine experience in western culture. 'Femininity' is to a large extent a rationalization and 'justification' (Freud, 1981b: vol. 22, 131) of that denial. The second reason for the concentrated critical attention on the essay on 'Femininity' is that it marks the point where justification becomes necessary, which is to say that it marks the point at which denial has ceased to be effective and where the clamour of hysterics and feminists is threatening enough to require silencing. In this context, Freud's imposition of the Oedipal model on feminine development had the double function of reinforcing the idea of women's sexual inferiority on the one hand and their moral inferiority on the other. Having introduced the little 'girl' to the Oedipal stage, Freud abandons her there without hope of resolution:

> In the absence of fear of castration the chief motive is lacking which leads boys to surmount the Oedipus complex. Girls remain there for an indeterminable length of time; they demolish it late and, even so, incompletely. In these circumstances the formation of the super-ego must suffer; it cannot attain the strength and independence which give it its cultural significance, and feminists are not pleased when we point out to them the effect of this factor upon the average feminine character.
>
> (Freud, 1981b: vol. 22, 129)

Grafting the new quasi-science of psychology on to age-old preju-
dice is not quite enough to reinstate the old masculine assurance,
however: 'If you reject the idea[4] as fantastic and regard my belief
in the influence of lack of a penis on the configuration of femininity as an *idée fixe*, I am of course defenceless' (132). Perhaps this
defencelessness on Freud's part also stems from the awareness
that feminine dependence on desire for *'l'homme père'*. (Irigaray,
1974: 47) may be secondary and derivative, a displacement of a
frustrated desire for the mother:

> The number of women who remain till a late age tenderly
> dependent on a paternal object, or indeed on their real father,
> is very great. We have established some surprising facts about
> these women with an intense attachment of long duration to
> their father. We know, of course, that there had been a prelimi-
> nary stage of attachment to the mother, but we did not know
> that it could be so rich in content and so long-lasting, and
> could leave behind so many opportunities for fixations and
> dispositions. During this time the girl's father is only a trouble-
> some rival. . . . Almost everything that we find later in her
> relationship to her father was already present in this earlier
> attachment and had been transferred subsequently on to her
> father. In short, we get an impression that we cannot under-
> stand women unless we appreciate this phase of their pre-
> Oedipus [*sic*] attachment to their mother:
>
> (Freud 1981b: vol. 22, 119)

It is in its foregrounding of the pre-Oedipal relation of the female
child to her mother that Freud's essay ceases to be a useful target
for feminist criticism and becomes of use to feminism. As Luce
Irigaray point outs, the emphasis of Freud's essay is on how very
difficult it is to become a woman (Irigaray, 1985a). Freud finds
that a mature 'woman' 'often frightens us by her psychical rigidity
and unchangeability' (Freud, 1981b: vol. 22, 135). 'The little girls
and their ill-mannered bodies immured, well preserved, intact
unto themselves, in the mirror. Frigidified' (Cixous, 1976: 877).
Cixous identifies paralysis as the fate of women in patriarchal
culture; 'They riveted us between two horrifying myths: between
the Medusa and the abyss' (1976: 883). Irigaray depicts the stale-
mate of the conventional mother – daughter relationship in similar
terms: 'Et l'une ne bouge pas sans l'autre' (1981 [1979]).

THE NIGHTMARE OF REPETITION

Landlocked is a novel of paralysis. Political paralysis grips Zambesia in the wake of the Second World War. In *A Ripple from the Storm* Lessing's protagonists had perceived themselves as agents of history. Their constant historical and social analysis was the means by which they asserted their control over the historical processes they formulated. In *Landlocked* the protagonists are trapped by the logic of history and analysis merely confirms their paralysis.

Personal history also becomes inexorable and predetermined. In *A Ripple from the Storm* politics offered Martha Quest a way out of her socially determined role as wife and mother. In *Landlocked* social and sexual roles are seen to reproduce themselves in characters whose 'analysis' of themselves and their situation is far in advance of their emotional responses. In *A Proper Marriage* the ferris wheel came to symbolize for Martha the nightmare of her life as a trapped housewife. Her wartime political activism proves an abortive escape. Her affair with Thomas Stern in *Landlocked* briefly offers an alternative way out of her lethargic submissiveness. When she finally physically escapes the repressive Zambesian state, the wheel comes full circle. In *The Four-Gated City* Martha will once again become a house-bound observer of history as housekeeper and mistress to Mark Coleridge. She and Lynda Coleridge mark the disintegration of Martha's quest for identity into the classic polarity of 'madwoman in the attic',[5] (or in this case the basement) and her sane surrogate, the wife and mother. Escaping her own family, Martha is merely appropriated by another. The role of nurturer assumes the force of an inevitable doom as *Children of Violence* develops. This concept of maternity as 'inevitable trap' (Cixous, 1976: 890) is heavily reinforced in *Landlocked* by the treatment of May Quest. For the first time in *Children of Violence* Martha's mother becomes a 'character ' rather than a malignant force exerting an almost occult influence on her daughter's life. A fuller picture of May Quest serves to introduce the idea that that influence is not only inevitable, but is the product of an endless cycle of repetition, a cycle of mother–daughter antagonism stretching back through the generations.

It is important to realize how thoroughly doom-laden the mother–daughter relationship is for Lessing. An understanding of her presentation of that relationship is vital to an understanding of the development of her fiction, her formal experiments and her move to speculative fiction. The contours of the mother–daughter relationship in Lessing's fiction are illuminated in the context of Luce Irigaray's 'And the one doesn't stir without the other' (1981). This relationship which is so crucial to the development of Lessing's fiction is also crucial to the cultural definition of femininity and to feminism's attempt to redefine womanhood. Against its backdrop the scandalous extent of the rewriting of maternity by Cixous becomes apparent.

THE MOTHER

> The beautiful young woman had leaned down, smiling, from heaven, and handed the daughter she had scarcely known three red roses, fresh with bright water. Mrs. Quest, weeping with joy, her heart opening to her beautiful mother, had looked down and seen that in her hand the roses had turned into – a medicine bottle.
>
> Yes, the dream had the quality of sheer brutality. Nothing was concealed, nothing was glossed over for kindness' sake. . . . The beautiful woman had been unkind. Yes, that was it, she had been pretty and reckless – and unkind.
>
> (Lessing, 1965: 70)

Mrs Quest weeps at the cruelty of the dream and thinks, 'Medicine bottles, yes; that was her life, given her by a cruel and mocking mother'.

The nightmare of motherhood portrayed in *Landlocked* is not yet complete. Mrs Quest remembers earlier nightmares. 'As a small girl she had started up in bed from a nightmare screaming: "They wanted her to die" ' for her dead mother was beautiful, 'and with the sort of beauty not easily admitted by that house whose chief virtue had been respectability, described as "a sense of proportion" and "healthy" ' (69). An invincible determinism traps each succeeding generation of mothers and daughters in a cycle of rejection, self-denial and cruelty as unbreakable as any hereditary curse. *The Memoirs of a Survivor* takes up this motif, tracing the neglect of Emily and her much-traumatized psychic landscape, to the rejection experienced by her mother in her own childhood.

You look at yourself in the mirror. And already you see your own mother there. And soon your daughter, a mother. Between the two, what are you? What space is yours alone? In what frame must you contain yourself? And how to let your face show through, beyond all the masks?

(Irigaray, 1981: 63).

Luce Irigaray's poetic essay, 'And the one doesn't stir without the other', like *Landlocked*, encapsulates in its title the impasse of the mother – daughter relation it describes.

Irigaray shares the accursed nightmare of Martha Quest and Cixous's wish to transform it. 'Frozen' (60) by mother's milk – which here is certainly not the metaphor for fluid expression it becomes for Cixous – the daughter is 'immobile, rooted . . . paralysed by emotion'. Irigaray adopts the voice of the daughter transfixed by the 'absence', the 'non-existence' (64) that is the only nurture offered by the mother, 'I received from you only your obliviousness of your self' (65). This is in many ways the voice of Martha Quest, but it is also the voice of May Quest, the little girl who dreams of her cruel, beautiful, powerful mother. The relation of mother and daughter in Irigaray's text is reciprocal. Neither has the power to change it yet both are its agents. For the daughter is also, perhaps, responsible, not simply forced into the role of 'the stand-in for your absence?', but also 'the guardian of your non-existence?'. The voice of the embittered daughter dominates Irigaray's essay. Yet the voices of mother and daughter are presented as interchangeable. Each occupies an intra-subjective space and plays out overlapping roles and desires. The daughter's voice in this context must of necessity be that of the mother also. There is a positive interplay as well as a fear of the amorphous and undifferentiated identities of mother and daughter, 'Of the two of us, who was the one, who was the other?' (63). Irigaray concludes, 'And what I wanted from you, Mother, was this: that in giving me life you still remain alive' (67).

It seems as if Lessing shares such an understanding of the plight of the mother through the plight of the daughter in *The Four-Gated City*. In the earlier novels, there was a terrifying and despairing acknowledgement that 'she couldn't help herself'. In the final novel of *Children of Violence*, Lessing includes instances of May Quest helping herself, to the extent of her undoubtedly limited abilities. For the first time we see her independently of her relationship to Martha and the Quest family. More importantly, in the battle of nerves waged by the two women in Martha's London home, Martha becomes agent as well as victim of her mother's paralysis.

HER MOTHER'S DAUGHTER

The spectre of motherhood, that nightmare of repetition, looms over Martha from the very first page of *Martha Quest*. She sits, reading Havelock Ellis, deliberately establishing in herself an opposite to her mother and Mrs Van Rensberg, who gossip nearby. Martha's horrified contemplation of Mrs Van Rensberg's scarred and varicose legs will recur in various guises in the course of *Children of Violence*: 'Martha was thinking with repugnance, Her legs are like that because she has had so many children' (Lessing, 1952: 9). Martha's horror of motherhood and horror of her mother are indistinguishable throughout. She thinks of May Quest as 'the eternal mother', but this mother does not give life, only 'sleep and death' (37).

It is not surprising that the daughter is petrified. In this economy the mother is monstrous, either a 'phallic mother' or a 'castrated one' (Freud, 1981b: vol. 22, 126). She is, in effect, a Medusa. The mother who had seemed all-powerful, a guarantor of nurture and safety, is not so: 'Girls hold their mothers responsible for their lack of a penis and do not forgive her for their being thus put at a disadvantage' (124). The fear that accompanied infantile dependence conquers (though never fully) the powerful attachment to the mother, and the mother appears as the one who deprived the little girl of access to (phallic) power, as castrator and as a premonition of the powerless fate of the not-man: 'The turning away from the mother is accompanied by hostility: the attachment to the mother ends in hate' (121). It is not surprising that Freud is frightened by feminine libidinal paralysis and observes that it is 'as though the difficult development to femininity had exhausted the possibilities of the person concerned' (135). The development to 'femininity' is predicated on rejection of the mother, not only the primary love-object, but also the parent with whom the female child must identify. It is a development into 'anti-narcissism' (Cixous, 1976:878), towards rejection of one's self as woman and acceptance of the blankness of 'not-man'. Martha Quest experiences her mother as a denial of herself and rightly so: 'For thoughts of Martha always filled her with such violent emotions that she could not sustain them; she began to pray for Martha . . . *please let her be like her brother*. Mrs. Quest fell asleep soothed by tender thoughts of her son' (Lessing, 1952: 69). Mrs Quest hates Martha because Martha is not her brother, because she is a woman *like herself*. Very much later, in *The Four-Gated City*, it will become obvious how much this hatred of Martha is hatred of herself. Mrs Quest becomes very fond of a young girl who is travelling on the same ship to England, but her affection is immediately transformed into utter repugnance ('Mrs. Quest seethed, raged, suffered') when she notices the girl is menstruating and is reminded of the 'long story of humiliation and furtiveness' (277) which her own youthful body had imposed.

Mrs Quest, who so detests the female, is something of an anti-mother. She and her elderly companions on the ship to England sit watching 'the young people flirting, the young married couples with their children' (Lessing, 1969: 227). Like a clutch of pathetic yet malevolent witches the old women mutter, "Yes, but they don't know, do they?" It was like a curse or a spell' (227). There are numerous references to the fact that her mother unwittingly half-starved Martha as an infant and the nightmare of repetition indeed seems to come true when Martha, following the advice of the 'authorities', similarly starves her own daughter. The real and persisting starvation which Martha imposes on Caroline is that of emotional deprivation, again precisely repeating her own relationship with her mother.

THE DAUGHTER AS MOTHER

> Her inability to enjoy Caroline simply filled her with guilt. Yet she could not relax with Caroline; that would be a disloyalty and even a danger to herself.
>
> (Lessing, 1954: 224)

The danger of motherhood to the integrity of the self is acknowledged by Lessing in *A Proper Marriage*, when, describing Martha giving birth, she emphasizes that 'the pain had swallowed *her* up' (162).[6]

When Martha finally leaves her own daughter to 'set her free', she in fact only abandons Caroline to the nightmare. The child is mothered by Elaine (whom Douglas marries after his divorce from Martha) who follows all the correct 'authorities'. Secondary mothering is supplied by May Quest herself who brings the child into her house of death, the house where Martha's father lies dying. May Quest torments Martha with the fact that she has access to Caroline, denied to the child's actual mother. This theft of the child by the eternal mother, despite the individual woman's best intentions, exemplifies the nightmare of repetition which mocks individual intentions and free will. 'Immanence' and 'confinement and restriction to a narrow round of uncreative or repetitious duties' (de Beauvoir, 1972: 63, translator's note) seem inescapable and Martha's every effort to escape seems to reinforce her paralysis.

Martha's quest is very much a quest for a subjectivity which is neither a capitulation to nor a reaction against her mother. Her relation with her mother is summarized in the title and central metaphor of *Landlocked*. That Mrs Quest shares Martha's predicament is indicated by the fact that she, who loves the sea, is even more landlocked than her daughter. At the end of the novel she moves further inland to live with her son. She too had a cruel mother and lives in a nightmare from which there is no awakening, only bitter acknowledgement of its truth (Lessing, 1965: 68–70; see p. 21).

'The laugh of the Medusa' presents the re-establishment of a positive relationship with the mother and the maternal as central to women's repossession of their bodies, their voices, writing and power. The economy of castration cuts woman off from the primary source of nurture and from the ability to nurture, esteem and enjoy herself. Against this 'infamous logic of anti-love', Cixous asserts a (m)other:

> There is hidden and always ready in woman the source; the locus for the other. The mother too is a metaphor. It is necessary and sufficient that the best of herself be given to woman by another woman for her to be able to love herself and return in love the body that was 'born' to her.
>
> (Cixous, 1976: 881)

'The laugh of the Medusa' unravels the 'prehistory of woman' (Freud, 1981b: vol. 22, 130) and finds a different Medusa, more than a mother, no longer petrifying except to those who fear to look on uncastrated woman:

Too bad for them if they fall apart upon discovering that women aren't men, or that the mother doesn't have one. But isn't the fear convenient for them? Wouldn't the worst be, isn't the worst, that women aren't, that they have only to stop listening to the Sirens (for the Sirens were men) for history to change its meaning. You have only to look at the Medusa straight on to see her. And she's not deadly. She's beautiful and she's laughing.

(Cixous, 1976: 885)

The following is an attempt to look at the Medusa straight on.

DISPLACEMENT OF ACCENT

In an interesting discussion of the Medusa myth, Joseph Campbell (1974) identifies the Medusa as a 'Great Mother' goddess. Medusa's name means 'mistress', 'ruler', 'queen' (153). She is 'the womb and tomb of the world: the primal, one and only ultimate reality of nature' (25–6). May Quest, whose attributes are 'sleep and death' (Lessing, 1952: 32), is a Medusa in this sense. Campbell draws attention to those elements of the myth of Medusa which show the traces of an earlier mythology in which the Medusa and not Perseus was of primary importance. According to Campbell the story of Perseus's slaying of the Medusa marks the overthrow of that earlier mythology and culture and the relegation of the 'female principle' to a secondary position.

In recent years a number of feminist writers have re-examined the mythology of ancient Greece and in particular of the Middle East in an attempt to unravel this process of mystifying displacement. The idea of a matriarchal religious sensibility which preceded and ought to have precedence over later patriarchal religions has influenced proponents of feminist spirituality, such as Mary Daly (1973, 1979). The danger for all these writers is that of return to a facile essentialism, an acceptance of a valorized 'eternal feminine' and the mystification of the female body. The myth of 'the Goddess' is satirized by Angela Carter in *The Sadeian Woman* and *The Passion of New Eve*, and implicitly warned against in *Heroes and Villains*. The regressive dangers implicit in this myth should not foreclose the possibility of rewriting and revising it, for it has a powerful hold on the imagination of western culture. Campbell comments in relation to the story of Perseus that

> The connotations of female personages in a patriarchal mythology is generally obscured by the device that Sigmund Freud termed with reference to the manifest content of dreams, 'displacement of accent'. A distracting secondary theme is introduced around which the elements of a situation are regrouped; revelatory scenes are omitted, reinterpreted, or only remotely suggested.
>
> (Campbell, 1974: 157)

This interpretation is as applicable to Laing and indeed Lessing as to ancient Greek propagandists. The 'distracting secondary theme' to which Campbell refers is that of the quest and heroic stature of Perseus. The quest in this light is an evasion of the conflict with the mother.

Martha reviews her own long quest in *The Four-Gated City*. She thinks of the veld, her political involvements, her lover Thomas Stern, her father, 'her mother – ah yes, here it was and she knew it. She had been blocking off the pain and had blocked off half her life with it' (Lessing, 1969: 227). Campbell warns that the more the power of the mother is feared and repressed the more certain and terrible is her return and recurrence as the nightmare of her offspring. The 'Great Mother' 'is there to be dealt with all the time and the more sternly she is cut down, the more frightening will her Gorgoneum be' (Campbell, 1974: 153).

THE OTHER MEDUSA

In examining the Medusa myth as it appears in early sources, traces of a lost or submerged mythos emerge from beneath the dominant modern interpretations, of which Campbell's reading is a relatively sympathetic variant. Hesiod's 'Theogany' provides one of the very earliest surviving references to the myth. Medusa as she is described in that 'Theogany' and even in the much later *Metamorphoses* of Ovid is quite distinct from the standard mother and death goddess to which twentieth-century readings of the myth homogenize her.

According to twentieth-century interpretations Medusa was a mother goddess; in the early accounts she was unable to give birth. Her offspring, Chrysaor and Pegasus, were born at her death, emerging from her severed neck. Not fertile, then, but as Cixous reminds us, the Medusa was described by all these writers as once beautiful, perhaps laughing, also dangerous (1976: 885). Many versions explain her petrifying visage as a punishment for sacrilege or rebellion. Literary versions, such as Ovid's, identify this sacrilege as defilement of the temple of Minerva (Ovid, 1955: 115).[7]

The most startling attribute of Medusa is the one to which Hesiod gave most attention and to which modern commentators have given least. Medusa was granddaughter of the Earth goddess, Gaea, but she herself, unlike her Gorgon sisters or any of the other divinities and monsters listed in the 'Theogany', was mortal.

Neither immortal nor 'eternal', Medusa died ignominiously at the hands of a cheating adventurer (Campbell, 1974: 156). Perseus killed her by trickery, avoiding her eyes and observing her image in his shield. This hero's Oedipal credentials are impeccable: his quest was instigated by Polydectes, a suitor to Perseus's mother Danaë, who hoped thus to be rid of the boy. Gazing at the dead Medusa's head is as lethal as looking at the live Medusa. The epilogue to the quest involves Perseus's use of Medusa's head as a weapon to kill his enemies (Ovid 1986: 121). In the course of these adventures he rescues a princess, Andromeda, and the story becomes a very conventional one of rewarded valour. Jupiter had ordered that Andromeda be sacrificed to a sea-monster to 'pay the penalty for the boastful utterances of her mother the queen' (112). There are connections between Andromeda's story and Medusa. The Gorgons lived 'beyond glorious Ocean' (Hesiod, 1982: 99) and Medusa is a kind of sea-monster.

The exposure of a daughter to terrible and oceanic dangers through the fault of the mother/Medusa is a motif which runs through the *Children of Violence* series. Lessing's presentation of a very negative view of the mother–daughter relationship contrasts with Cixous's positive revision of the Medusa myth. Both writers nonetheless explore the significance of the Medusa myth for women as mothers and daughters, and the implications of a culturally prevalent quest myth which posits the heroic search for adult identity in terms of annihilation of the power of woman. The writings of R. D. Laing, so influential for Lessing's treatment of issues of identity, offer a version of the Medusa myth which at first seems to postulate the quest in classic patriarchal and

Oedipal terms. The mother–daughter relationship proves, however, to be the repressed and decisive factor in Laing's version
of the Medusa, the problematics of identity and the quest for
selfhood.

PETRIFICATION AND ENGULFMENT

The myth of the Medusa provides a crucial metaphor in Laing's
work. The focus of Laing's discussion of insanity is on schizophrenia.[8] In so far as Lessing assimilates Laing's theories into her
exploration of the irrational, it is his description of schizophrenia
which must be most influential.[9] Laing diagnoses schizophrenia
as 'ontological insecurity', concomitant with a fear of petrification
and engulfment by external factors which in most cases are identified as the powerful personalities of others. In *The Divided Self*
(1960) he describes the techniques used by schizophrenics to
defend themselves against these threats and establish a sense of
'being' (the later extension of his theory would suggest such
techniques to be widespread among alienated contemporary man):
attempting to preserve their 'existence', schizophrenics divorce
their 'real' selves from the personality and circumstances of their
everyday life (46).

Lessing's *Memoirs of a Survivor* (1974) can be read as a fictional-
ized version of the schizophrenic's survival strategy, as can
Briefing for a Descent into Hell (1971). *Memoirs of a Survivor* is set
in the near future.[10] A mystical realm (beyond the wall of her
room) allows the narrator to escape the disintegrating society and
threatening environment in which she lives. Gradually, the mystical realm becomes more 'real' to the narrator than her everyday
experience. Finally conventional reality (as it is constructed in the
novel) is abandoned and the protagonists break through into the
new realm at the novel's problematic conclusion. In *Briefing for a
Descent into Hell*, Charles Watkins has already forgotten his
'normal' self at the beginning of the novel. The discovery of his
identity, as society defines it, is merely a sub-plot as the novel
progresses. The real quest is for an original self or soul which he
lost long ago in the process of socialization.

In 1960 Laing was arguing that such recourse to alternative
realities was a doomed device of schizophrenia, a symptom, but
his later invocations of 'transcendental experience' would
appear to allow the possibility that the self postulated by the

schizophrenic as the inviolable 'real' self may indeed be more real than the apparent circumstance of life. In this respect his theory follows the course of the disease it describes.

Laing very emphatically rejects the concept of the 'schizophrenegenic' mother as a distortion and a sexist one. Yet in the case from which he derives the concept of 'petrification' (the case of a young man named David), it is petrification by the mother which is feared (Laing, 1960: 79). Laing invokes the story of Perseus as a metaphor for the danger experienced. He makes use of this myth as 'the myth of Perseus and the Medusa's head' (117). Medusa is not admitted into Laing's text until safely decapitated by the hero. Laing moves from a discussion of a particular patient's fear of engulfment by his mother to the adoption of the term 'petrification' as a fear experienced in general by the schizophrenic. He then links this term to the myth without ever mentioning the identification of the Medusa with terror of the female and of the mother in particular in scholarly works on classical mythology and in the work of Freud (1955: vol. 18, 273–4). (Freud is as unwilling as Laing to entertain the notion of live and complete Medusas: his essay is entitled 'Medusa's head'.)

The displacement of emphasis practised by Laing is far more extreme than anything described by Campbell. Not only does he make Perseus agent rather than potential victim, but Medusa becomes no more than an instrument of the hero's will: 'Petrification, we remember, was one of Perseus' means of killing his enemies. By means of the eyes in Medusa's head, he turned them into stones' (Laing, 1960: 79). Reducing the Medusa herself to her appropriated head in this way is part of a more general confusion of agency in Laing's use of the term 'petrification'. At first it appears to be the form of the feared attack. Then – and this is where Perseus is introduced – petrification is portrayed as a defence against 'being a thing in someone else's eyes . . . to the schizoid individual every pair of eyes is in a Medusa's head which he feels has power actually to kill or deaden something precariously vital in him. He tries therefore to forestall his own petrification by turning others into stones' (79–80). Laing refuses to specify that it is the mother who petrifies, and transfers the petrifying power of the Medusa to any subject ('to the schizoid individual every pair of eyes is in a Medusa's head') hoping perhaps to dilute her power by such diffusion.

In *The Divided Self* Laing ignores that it is fear of possession by the personality of his mother that petrifies David. In *Sanity, Madness and the Family*, written with A. Esterson, the omissions are even more glaring. All the eleven cases dealt with are those of women patients. Laing and Esterson declare their intention of restricting their study to female subjects, with no explanation. In all these cases (with one possible exception) the relationship of the women to their mothers is crucial to their 'illness'.[11]

Fear of petrification and engulfment is fear of 'the mother'. For the female protagonist it is also fear of motherhood: Martha Quest's experience of childbirth is described as drowning in 'the dark *engulfing* sea' (Lessing, 1954: 162).[12]

MEDUSA'S HEAD

Freud's much earlier reading of the Medusa myth differs from Laing's by explicitly identifying the Medusa's head as a symbol of terrifying but desirable female difference. His emphasis is on the head *after* it has been appropriated by Athene: 'This symbol of horror is worn upon her dress by the virgin goddess, Athene. And rightly so, for thus she becomes a woman who is unapproachable, and repels all sexual desires since she displays the terrifying genitals of the mother' (Freud, 1955: vol. 18, 273–4). This reading is better supported than Laing's by that earlier texts. It is a fairly convincing account of the significance of the Medusa's *head*. Decapitation partially assimilates the Medusa to the mythology of the 'Great Mother' and the eternal feminine. It becomes clearer why it is only the severed head which can safely be admitted to authoritative discussions of the nature of identity.

The Medusa represents a complex of contradictory attributes as well as a disturbing, rebellious and turbulent persona. She can be made to signify the unity of life and death in some sort of eternal immanence, but she is herself mortal.[13] The myth may be plausibly interpreted as the manifestation of a male trauma, but also as the dramatization of a female struggle to escape the assimilation signified by the simultaneous end of Medusa's own life and the persistence and appropriation of her power by others.

In relation to the Oedipal tangle, Medusa is great-grandmother of the Sphinx.[14] It is hardly surprising that though Medusa can be heard in the texts of Lessing and Cixous, her utterances remain cryptic.

THE GAZE OF THE OTHER

The connection between the petrifying Medusa and the blinding Sphinx opens up another reading of the myth and casts light on its interpretations. Referring to the Sphinx, Irigaray comments: 'This (so-called) female sexuality will blind anyone taken up in its question' (Irigaray, 1985a: 80). To look upon the woman is dangerous. The Medusa's own gaze is deadly. It is 'the gaze of the other which is necessarily threatening because of its different viewpoint' (81). The displacement of accent described by Campbell and the confusion of agency practised by Laing are ways of denying the 'difference of view' (Woolf, 1966: 204; Jacobus, 1986: 27–40) is denied. The story of Medusa becomes the story of Perseus. Woman is denied the power of observation. It is she, rather than Oedipus, who is truly blinded: her different view will become no view at all. The moves in this blindfolding game are very similar to the stages of sexual maturation observed by Freud which turn the woman into a castrated man. This is hardly surprising. Within a sexual economy where nothing to be seen becomes nothing to see (Irigaray, 1985a: 48), blindness and impotence are indistinguishable. Medusa becomes the object of the gaze which she cannot return.

The denial and appropriation of Medusa's power are done with mirrors. One glance from Medusa petrifies, so Perseus cannot look at her 'straight on' (Cixous, 1976: 885). He fights and kills her by looking only on her reflection in the shield given him by Athene.[15] Her glance is not deadly if it is mediated, if it is experienced only as a reflection. Control of her image, her reflection in his shield, allows Perseus to appropriate Medusa's power. The live Medusa killed by *seeing*: the Medusa's head kills when *seen*. She loses the power of the gaze: Perseus seizes the power of representation. The mirror of representation becomes the site of that displaced 'feminine' which renders womanhood impossible.[16] The mirror image is 'the false woman that prevents the live one from breathing' (Cixous, 1976: 880).

RESISTANCE: THE DARKNESS WITHIN

Anxious to separate the concept of mother from the processes of sociality and to disclaim female collusion in female repression, Cixous represents the mother 'in terms of immense pleasure and violence' (1976: 882). She proclaims that the 'feminine affirms' (884).

Yet a shadowy figure emerges in the midst of her assertions, 'old grandmother ogresses, servants of their father-sons' (890). The image of 'grand/great mother' as opposed to the mother who gives 'me myself as myself' (882) persists. (In an earlier essay by Cixous, 'The character of character' (1974), this monster dominated the metaphorical landscape.) Once the mother as monster has been admitted to 'The laugh of the Medusa' the image immediately recurs of the mother as the upholder and affirmation of the male – 'the maternal mistresses of their little pocket signifier' (890) – and as enemy and denial of the female, like Athene and Mrs Quest. The spectre of reproduction as an inevitable trap (rather than the other without violence or separation) begins to hover over the 'feminine' affirmations of 'The laugh of the Medusa': 'It is impossible to *define* a feminine practice of writing. . . . It will be conceived of only by subjects who are breakers of automatisms, by peripheral figures that no authority can ever subjugate' (883). Multiple images of monstrous females begin to appear round the peripheries of the one, almost overwhelming, authoritative image of the 'good mother' in 'The laugh of the Medusa'. These images break through the impulse towards rigid definition and subjugating essentialism. The extreme, grotesque images, which run counter to the text's positive affirmations, put the bravura of the rhetoric into perspective. Such extravagance cannot parade long in the guise of authority and certainty.

The negative imagery gives force to the promise that 'the mother too is a metaphor'. The 'grandmother ogresses' are testament not only to the persistence of the culturally sanctioned version of the Medusa myth even in a text which proposes to subvert that version. That imagery also brings into play the truly subversive nature of the text. The ambivalent Medusa, the woman who is less than all, not only affirming, more than a mother, the mother as death as well as life: all of these rush back into Cixous's text. The contrariness of the myth explodes in her text, wrecks 'partitions, classes, and rhetorics, regulations and codes' and indeed proves 'equal to the most forbidding of suppressions' (886). Cixous's subject-matter and style prohibit the imposition of a 'unified' interpretation. Her espousal of inconsistency as subversive strategy combines with the ambiguity of her imagery to ensure that within 'The laugh of the Medusa' no capitulation can be final.

THE DARK STRANGER

In *Landlocked* the conflict between mother and daughter, May and Martha Quest, gathers unbearable momentum. The novel also contains the crucial relationship between Martha and Thomas Stern. Thomas Stern forcefully embodies those aspects of herself which may finally wake Martha from or finally imprison her in the nightmare of repetition. This male 'character' becomes the focus of all that is dangerous and threatening for Martha in her own sexuality. He marks the point at which a culturally defined femininity is exceeded, a point at which madness, maternity and death meet. He also marks the limit of Lessing's fiction, the point at which it encounters and attempts to vanquish the irrational. It is at this limit-point that a relationship can be established between the development of Lessing's fiction and Hélène Cixous's exploration and revision of the territory of otherness and irrationality which is symbolized by Thomas Stern in *Landlocked*.

Cixous speaks of the 'dark', that dark which patriarchy has been trying to make women accept as their attribute (1976: 876): 'Your continent is dark. Dark is dangerous. You can't see anything in the dark . . . we have internalized this horror of the dark' (877–88). *Landlocked* echoes not only the word, but also the reiterative technique. After a long absence, 'reporting on conditions' among the tribes of the Zambesi valley, Thomas's face was 'dark, austere . . . burned to a dark, glistening bronze . . . dark, proud' (Lessing, 1965: 230). The resonance might be no more than coincidental were it not for the association of Thomas with the 'dark continent' of Africa and with a type of writing which is almost an organic part of that continent. His papers and writings 'were in a dreadful state; for the ink had run where rain water had dripped on them. . . . Ants had left half a hundred pages looking like red-edged lace paper' (276). The destabilization of sexual identity in 'The laugh of the Medusa' is paralleled by the destabilization of sexual identity implicit in the assumption of feminine difference by the libidinal 'male' figure in *Landlocked*.

In his madness, Thomas becomes alien, other. He 'sounded – not like himself' (183). 'Martha realized that meeting him in the street she would not have known him' (207). 'Martha saw a stranger looking out of the window into Founder's Street. When he turned, it was Thomas' (229). He becomes, again like Cixous's conventional Woman, 'silent' (177, 179). And his darkness and strangeness and silence from the beginning cast a shadow over the other male characters in the novel, notably Martha's husband, Anton Hesse. When Martha begins her affair with Thomas, she finds that Anton 'had suddenly become a frightening unknown country' (118).

Thomas is one of a series of dark strangers to be found in women's writings over a considerable period. Emily Brontë's Heathcliff is not the prototype of the species though he is its epitome (Showalter, 1982 [1978]: 133–43; Gilbert and Gubar, 1979: 249–308). According to Angela Carter,[17] Heathcliff was a prototype for Jewel in *Heroes and Villains*.

The idyll of union with this fabulous creature is always short-lived in women's fiction. So it is in *Landlocked*. For a brief period Martha finds a way of living with the dark within: 'from this centre she now lived' (Lessing, 1965: 103). None the less both Martha and Thomas admit that 'this experience was unforeseen and therefore not entirely desired? . . . no, it was too strong, it was not what she wanted . . . much easier to live deprived, to be resigned, to be self-contained. No, she did not want to be dissolved and neither did he' (1965: 103–4). It seems that the author also finds this situation 'too painful': the description of their idyll is restricted to some eight pages and an uncharacteristic one-year break in the narrative transforms these two from lovers to silent dinner partners (179). Martha draws back from the darkness and Thomas descends into it. He goes native, goes mad and dies in the jungle. The logic of the narrative is to project the 'Woman' in the text (darkness, sexuality, irrationality, the unconscious . . .) on to a male character in order to kill her off.

Thomas's relation to the conflict between woman and mother can be illuminated by reference to *A Proper Marriage*. In that novel Martha experiences childbirth as drowning in 'the dark engulfing sea' (162). An African hospital cleaner for a few moments offers Martha a positive mothering and a positive induction into the dark which is immediately interrupted and forbidden by the hospital regime. That a nurse denies Martha a positive mothering and motherhood is hardly surprising: May Quest was, to her great pride, a nurse before she married. A self-affirming and life-giving relation with the dark had been hinted at earlier in *A Proper Marriage* when Martha and her friend, also pregnant, go swimming during a rainstorm, identifying themselves (again in a way that foreshadows Thomas Stern) with the overpowering fertility of the jungle (153). That it is the fear that the (anti-) mother lurks there that keeps Martha out of 'the forest' (Cixous, 1976: 879) is made obvious by her reaction when she comes home from this adventure and contemplates with disgust the violation of her bodily integrity by her pregnancy (Lessing, 1965: 155). Martha establishes a positive relation with the darkness within and without her only through Thomas Stern. In keeping with the pattern established in the earlier episodes his dark and alien nature is also, though more subtly, rejected.

The encounter with feminine darkness through an ostensibly male figure and the temporary achievement of 'wholeness' through union with that figure is one of the recurrent patterns which Gilbert and Gubar identify as characteristic of women's fiction (1979: 266). Their interpretation of that pattern confirms the suspicion that such figures 'are the product of female fantasies that are much more concerned with power and authority than with romance' (Showalter, 1982 [1978]: 136).[18] In the first three novels of the *Children of Violence* series Martha Quest sought to express her sexuality and to gain access to power, first over her own life, then, in *A Ripple from the Storm*, through political action. In *The Golden Notebook* Lessing abandoned Martha's quest temporarily to explore the frustration of a woman writer who finds the conventions of the novel 'untrue' (Lessing, 1972: 231).[19] That writer is Anna Wulf who has lost the power not only of writing, but also of *being*. Her writing is fragmented into notebooks which cannot form a novelistic whole. Anna herself is shattered into a series of personae; Anna, Elsa, Anna's former self, political activist, author, lover, mother. These personae have no common centre. The integration of the notebooks and that of the (separate) lives which they recount into the 'golden notebook' is achieved only when Anna breaks down 'into' Saul Green. Saul is also a writer, also suffering from writer's block (though on a smaller and shorter scale than Anna), also psychologically unstable. He is Anna's 'non–identical double' (Gilbert and Gubar, 1979: 292).[20] Through their breakdown into each other Anna Wulf and Saul Green constitute an unstable, undifferentiated entity from which each constructs an identity. That they must part at the novel's conclusion again conforms to the pattern identified by Gilbert and Gubar.

Thomas Stern initially functions in *Landlocked* in the same way as Saul Green at the conclusion of *The Golden Notebook, Landlocked* offers considerable insight into the 'conventions of . . . woman-hood' (Showalter, 1982 [1978]: 143) which have ensured the persist-ence of this product of the nineteenth-century literary imagination of women into the twentieth century. The young women who were Martha's comrades in the Zambesian Communist Party in *A Ripple from the Storm* have married and had children in *Landlocked*: 'They were all, already, in their late twenties and early thirties, middle-aged women neurotic with dissatisfaction, just as if they had never made resolutions not to succumb to the colonial small-town atmosphere' (Lessing, 1965: 212). Knowledge and under-standing of the processes by which they reached this condition and of the condition itself have not freed them. Indeed knowledge makes that condition worse without offering any hope of remedy:

> They watched their own deterioration like merciless onlookers. These days all over the world there are people like these, mostly women: the states of mind that once only afflicted people on death-beds or at moments of acute crisis are their permanent condition. Lives that appear to them meaningless, wasted, hang around their necks like decaying carcasses. They are hypnotized into futility by self-observation.
>
> (Lessing, 1965: 212)

Other forms of political futility and paralysis also characterize the novelistic landscape of *Landlocked*. The Zambesian Communist Party has become marginalized and disenchanted in the post-war era of conservatism. Having escaped her 'proper marriage' to Douglas, Martha once again drifts into a marriage she does not desire, this time with the refugee Anton Hesse:

> Already she was feeling under the pressure of the snapping jaws of impatience, the need to move forwards, as if the mar-riage with Anton and what she might become as a result of it were already done and accomplished. It was as if her whole being had concentrated itself into a moment of taking in and absorbing, as if she were swallowing something whole and hurrying on.
>
> (Lessing, 1965: 189–90)

Martha had thought to set her child, Caroline, free from the mother–daughter bond, but Caroline is mothered by Elaine, who has replaced Martha as Douglas's wife, and by Martha's (m)other and another kind of double, May Quest:

> How extraordinary it was that five years before when she had left the child she had said, and believed it, meant it, felt it to be true: one day she'll thank me for setting her free. What on earth had she meant by it? How could she have said it, thought it, felt it? Yet leaving the child, it had been her strongest emotion: I'm setting Caroline free.
>
> (Lessing, 1965: 245)

It is the confrontation with May Quest and the pain of her loss and helplessness in relation to Caroline which threaten disintegration in *Landlocked*: 'Birth is, after all, the ultimate fragmentation the self can undergo, just as "confinement" is, for women, the ultimate pun on imprisonment' (Gilbert and Gubar, 1979: 286).

Martha has escaped her prison and, by never 'relaxing' (Lessing, 1954: 224) with Caroline, has staved off the fragmentation of giving birth. Throughout *Landlocked* the effort of keeping at bay the pain of losing Caroline without even having saved her, freed her, is an extension of that early vigilance against fragmentation in maternity. It is paradoxical, but symptomatic, that Martha perceives her mother and her status as mother as the greatest threats to her identity (Lessing, 1954: 224) and yet the scene in which she denies to Caroline that she is a mother is the scene where Martha comes closest to forfeiting any claim on identity:

> 'Is grand-dad your father?'
> 'Yes, he is.'
> 'Then how can you be my auntie?'
>   Caroline did not sit down, but skipped about the room, and stood on one foot, and clapped her hands back and forth, first behind her, then in front of her – did everything in fact but look at Martha, who sat still and said, nothing. Of course, 'the situation' demanded she should tell some suitable lie. If Mrs Quest had been here the lie would have been forthcoming.
>
> (Lessing, 1965: 245)

That Mr Quest is dying in another room and Mrs Quest absent from this encounter is significant. The old parameters of familial and sexual identity have lapsed. The mother and daughter, Martha and Caroline, are left not only with nothing to say to each other, but without any sense of who they are, particularly in relation to each other.

The relationship between Martha and Thomas Stern is initially posited as a resolution to this quandary of identity. 'A deep forest silence . . . at the bottom of a large garden' (102) becomes the 'centre' (103) of Martha's life. This centre is in marked contrast to the generally arid landscape of *Landlocked* and the 'many-coloured poisonous web of talk' (115) in which the neurotic housewives are trapped. The imagery of the garden and Thomas's occupation as gardener suggest that Lessing is revising the myth of the 'pre-lapsarian garden' (Gilbert and Gubar, 1979: 265).

The specifically sexual nature of Martha and Thomas's Eden also casts an interesting light on Gilbert and Gubar's reading of the 'demon lover' figure in women's fiction (1979: 296). That reading focused on Emily Brontë's Heathcliff[21] and interpreted the childhood unity of Catherine and Heathcliff as an instructive fantasy of female 'wholeness' on Brontë's part. Catherine and her 'whip', Heathcliff,[22] comprise one being, 'a perfect androgyne' (265), 'Catherine-Heathcliff'.

At the end of *Landlocked* Martha imagines she and Thomas once comprised a similar being, 'the combination Thomas, Martha' (Lessing, 1965: 223). The comma is important. While Gilbert and Gubar set their reading of *Wuthering Heights* in a qualified Freudian framework, they also find that

> Like Freud who was driven to grope among such words as *oceanic* when he tried to explain the heaven that lies about us in our infancy, we are obliged to use the paradoxical and metaphorical language of mysticism: phrases like *wholeness, fullness of being* and *androgyny* come inevitably to mind.
>
> (Gilbert and Gubar, 1979: 264)

Equally inevitably there comes to mind the danger of invoking

> the classic conception of bisexuality, which squashed under the emblem of castration fear and along with the fantasy of a 'total' being (though composed of two halves) would do away with the difference experienced as an operation incurring loss, as the mark of dreaded sectility.
>
> (Cixous, 1976: 883–4)

There is a sense in which *The Madwoman in the Attic* and (within the framework of Gilbert and Gubar's reading of it) *Wuthering Heights* identify the advent of awareness of sexual difference as loss. Gilbert and Gubar argue that Catherine's desire for a whip has its origin in penis-envy and describe her relation to Heathcliff in terms of a healing of the wound of castration:

> Heathcliff's presence gives the girl a fullness of being that goes far beyond power in household politics, because as Catherine's whip he is (and she herself recognizes this) an alternative self or double for her, a complementary addition to her being who fleshes out all her lacks the way a bandage might staunch a wound.
>
> (Gilbert and Gubar, 1979: 265)

The closure of this Freudian fantasy is disrupted by linking it to 'power in household politics', but the fantasy of the total being is there none the less. 'This self-effacing, merger-type bisexuality, which would conjure away castration' (Cixous, 1976: 882) is certainly not in keeping with the stormy relationship of Brontë's Catherine and Heathcliff or of Catherine-Heathcliff to itself. It gradually gives way in *Madwoman in the Attic* to 'the *other bisexuality* on which every subject not enclosed in the false theatre of phallocentric representationalism has founded his/her erotic universe' (Cixous, 1976: 882):

> To say Heathcliff is 'female' may at first sound mad or absurd . . . his outward masculinity seems to be definitively demonstrated by his athletic build and military carriage as well as the Byronic sexual charisma he has for ladylike Isabella. And though we saw that Edgar is truly patriarchal despite his apparent effeminacy, there is no real reason why Heathcliff should not simply represent an alternative version of masculinity, the maleness of the younger son, that paradigmatic outsider in partriarchy. To some extent, of course, this is true: Heathcliff clearly is just as male in his Satanic outcast way as Edgar in his angelically established way. But at the same time, on a deeper associative level, Heathcliff is 'female' – on the level where younger sons and bastards and devils unite with women in rebelling against the tyranny of heaven,[23] the level where orphans are female and heirs are male, where flesh is female

and spirit male, earth female, sky male, monsters female, angels male.

(Gilbert and Gubar, 1979: 294)

To the catalogue of outsiders one might add Jews, like Thomas Stern, the paradigmatic dispossessed: 'When you've left one country, then you've left all countries, for ever. I'm a wandering Jew, like my fathers were' (Lessing, 1965: 167). Thomas's invocation of his wandering fathers reminds us that Thomas, like Heathcliff, is 'to some extent' masculine, even if 'at the same time, on a deeper associative level' he is 'female' (Gilbert and Gubar, 1979: 294). These problematics of gender are accentuated in *The Madwoman in the Attic* because the implication of Heathcliff's femaleness is that the relationship through which Cathy staunches the wound of castration is with a *feminine* 'alternative self or double' (265). If Heathcliff is perceived as one who 'fleshes out all her lacks', is not this 'demon lover' (296) then also a mother figure, in Cixous's sense of the mother who 'gives woman to the other woman' (Cixous, 1976: 881). That mother, like Catherine-Heathcliff and 'Thomas, Martha', partakes of the 'other bisexuality' that is 'each one's location in self [*repérage en soi*] of the presence . . . of both sexes, non-exclusion either of the difference or of one sex' (882). All three bear some relation to the fantasy of the Phallic Mother, a fantasy which is linked to the pre-Oedipal stage in which the little girl does not yet 'realize' her disadvantages as castrated little man (Freud, 1981b: vol. 22, 126). The prelapsarian Eden and the 'heaven' that lies about us in our infancy are also fantasies of return to the pre-Oedipal relation to the maternal.

Gilbert and Gubar comment on the significance of the bloody wound inflicted by the Lintons' guard-dog which necessitates Cathy's stay at Thrushcross Grange and her first separation from Heathcliff: 'In a Freudian sense, then, the imagery of this brief but violent episode hints that Catherine has been simultaneously catapulted into adult female sexuality *and* castrated' (1979: 272). The imagery of the Fall which surrounds this exile from the Heights suggests the link between castration and separation from the mother.

What are the implications of all this for *Landlocked*, where separation from her mother is the desired goal of Martha? Throughout the period of her relationship with Thomas, Martha, is on her way elsewhere, 'all the time I was thinking – well, after all, I'm waiting to go to England, so this doesn't really count' (Lessing, 1965: 223). Thomas, as we have seen, becomes progressively more associated with Africa, which she wishes to leave, and with the darkness of the jungle where she once feared she might be lost in her own maternity (1954: 153, 155, 162). In *Landlocked* the paralysis and numbness which had previously characterized Martha's familial and personal life, particularly her relation with her mother, become general. Landlocked Zambesia is shown to have May Quest's potential to induce sleep and death. The lives of the former women activists, described in terms of compulsion and submission to the patterns of previous and despised generations, are indicative of a general political disillusion and the conservative atrophy which has stifled the revolutionary fervour of the war years. The nightmare of repetition fulfils itself and the proximity of this fulfilment frightens and endangers Martha.

Lessing's 'Thomas, Martha' is a sexual entity. Unlike Brontë's 'Catherine-Heathcliff' that entity does not inhabit a social and psychic landscape where the expression of sexuality would in itself be fatal:

> That the historical process does yield moments when that feminist dream of wholeness has real consequences is another point Brontë wishes us to consider, just as she wishes to convey her rueful awareness that, given the prior strength of patriarchal misogyny, those consequences may be painful as well as paradisal.
>
> (Gilbert and Gubar, 1979: 266)

At a different point in the historical process Lessing can develop Brontë's 'dream' to accommodate adult sexuality. It is paradoxical that in *Landlocked* it is also the protagonists' differing involvements in the historical process which become the occasion of their separation. As products of their time, it is difficult for Martha and Thomas to regard their relationship with the visionary and Romantic seriousness of Catherine–Heathcliff:

> How strange it was – marriage and love; one would think the way the newspapers, films, literature, the people who are supposed to express us talk, that we believe marriage, love, to be the desperate, important, deep experiences they say they are. But of course they don't believe any such things. Hardly

anyone believes it. We want them to believe it. Perhaps people
will believe it again.

(Lessing, 1965: 162)

'The feminist dream of wholeness' does not escape the painful
self-observation Martha perceives as typical of her generation.
The important factor in the comparison of *Landlocked* and *Wuthering Heights* is not, however, the difference in intensity and seriousness with which they treat their central couples. It is that the
separation of both couples and the descent into madness and death
of one partner are equally inevitable in both novels. Gilbert and
Gubar comment that Heathcliff's return after Catherine's wedding

> intensifies rather than cures her symptoms. For his return does
> not in any way suggest a healing of the wound of femaleness
> that was inflicted at puberty. Instead, it signals the beginning
> of 'madness', a sort of feverish infection of the wound.
>
> (Gilbert and Gubar, 1979: 279)

The long process of disintegration in the relationship of Thomas
and Martha ends, by contrast, in *his* madness and death. Martha's
inability to recognize the reflection of her 'non-identical double'
on his return resembles Cathy's 'inability to recognize her own
face in the mirror during the mad scene' (282). In Cathy's case,
Gilbert and Gubar comment, 'her fragmentation has now gone
so far beyond the psychic split betokened by her division from
Heathcliff that body and image (or body and soul) have separated'
(283). In Martha's case her non-identical double, Thomas,
becomes lost in a madness which, like Cathy's, 'may really equal
sanity' and which, like hers, ends in death. Just as the 'Thomas,
Martha' bond was more hesitant, with that pause separating the
two terms, so is it more easily displaced. Martha's non-identical
double in *The Four-Gated City* will be Lynda Coleridge. Like
Thomas, Lynda is an outcast who suffers from a madness which
is a kind of truth. With their deaths, Brontë's Cathy and Heathcliff are reunited into/as the Phallic Mother who sustained the
little girl's version of herself as 'handy and free' (Gilbert and
Gubar, 1979: 283). In *Children of Violence* the association of that
'mother who stands up against separation' (Cixous, 1976: 880)
with death is too clear, the sense of death as annihilation too deep
and too dreaded. Instead Lessing abandons the satanic ally of Eve
in favour of the variant of Eve with which Gilbert and Gubar

are most concerned, the madwoman. Lynda Coleridge inhabits the basement not the attic of her husband's home (where Martha becomes housekeeper and ultimately surrogate wife and mother), but the initial similarities to Bertha Mason are striking. These fade as Lynda's madness is gradually perceived to be divinest sense and she becomes prophetic guide to a post-apocalyptic generation.

THE MEDUSA

In 'The laugh of the Medusa' Hélène Cixous attempts to speak from beyond the quest which dominates *Children of Violence*. She uses the image of Medusa as an image of subjectivity based neither on exclusion of difference nor on the fantasy of a total being. Her metaphor for this affirmative feminine subjectivity is motherhood: 'In women there is always more or less of the mother who makes everything alright, who nourishes, and who stands up against separation' (1976: 882). She invokes a relationship with 'the mother' that is the antithesis of Martha Quest's fear and May Quest's loathing. In contrast to Lessing's nightmare of repetition Cixous affirms: 'Begetting a child doesn't mean that the woman or the man must fall ineluctably into patterns or must recharge the circuit of reproduction. If there's a risk there's not an inevitable trap' (890).

Cixous is attempting to break through the 'screening myth' (Campbell, 1974: 152) of the hero and to face the petrifying Medusa directly. She finds she is not petrified, nor restricted 'to a narrow round of uncreative or repetitious duties' (de Beauvoir, 1972: 63, translator's note), but released 'into infinity' (Cixous, 1976: 889), 'the moving, open, transitional space' where she 'dares for the other, wants the other' (893). Reversing the quest of Perseus (and the end of Thomas Stern with whom she has had so much in common), this new female subject goes 'adventuring, without the masculine temerity, into anonymity, which she can merge with without annihilating herself' (888). For 'You have only to look at the Medusa straight on to see her. And she's not deadly. She's beautiful and she's laughing' (885).

Cixous perceives that for the woman the quest to escape the mother is a denial of self. She declares that what has been 'escaped' is not 'a painful encounter . . . with the anguish of feminine fragmentation' (Showalter, 1982 [1978]: 309), but 'the wonder of being several', 'the gift of alterability', 'the erotogeneity of the heterogeneous' (Cixous, 1976: 889) – all those things, in short, which for Cixous constitute the specifically feminine. For Lessing, as for her heroines, the unconscious, 'the dark in us', is the 'scene of a very ancient quest' (Laing, 1967: 112) which culminates in plucking the treasure of identity from the perils of engulfment. For Cixous, *'The Dark Continent is neither dark nor unexplorable'*, not to be integrated any more than the (feminine) 'impossible' subject: 'If she is a whole, it's a whole composed of parts that are wholes, not simply partial objects but a moving, limitlessly changing ensemble, a cosmos tirelessly traversed by Eros, an immense astral space not organized around any one sun that's any more of a star than the others' (889). One implication of Cixous's position is the complete undermining of 'authority' and 'the author'. The text celebrates a positive destructiveness: 'If she's a her-she, it's in order to smash everything, to shatter the framework of institutions, to blow up the law, to break up the "truth" with laughter' (888). This implies an entirely different type of writing, one which Lessing will imagine, perhaps, in the writings of Thomas Stern, but far from any practice of writing she adopts and very far indeed from the injunctions against 'rhetoric' in *The Sentimental Agents in the Volyen Empire*.

Both Cixous and Lessing recognize that the quest myth has implications for their 'identity' and the subjectivity which allows them to write. Cixous occupies the territory of the Medusa, the mother, the monstrous enemy, and transforms it in order to be able to write specifically as a woman; Lessing identifies with the hero, in order to write as something more.

ENGULFMENT AND REPETITION

The quest for identity excludes what the 'hero' most fears. The fear that motivates the quest is of the mother as 'the womb and tomb of the world', but also of the women as 'not-I'. This makes the 'quest' highly problematic for the feminine questing subject. Martha's quest can be seen less as a quest for her 'self' than a quest to escape herself. Lessing's authorial questing may be a similar form of denial.

Lessing's later novels show that she, like Cixous, is engaged in an occupation of and *by* the dark continent of the mother. Lessing's heroines, Lynda and Martha, become the nurturing agents of a new generation, spiritual mothers of a more advanced species. This resurgence of the myth of the eternal mother indicates that repetition is as powerful a force as the drive towards transcendence in Lessing's fiction. Those qualities associated with the mother figure in the early novels become the qualities of the integrated and developed self, the goal of her questing daughter figures, in the later fiction. This is a realization of Martha Quest's nightmare the more ironic in that it is the outcome of Lessing's search for an alternative to such a terrible repetition.

The confusion of the woman in the hall of mirrors which the roles of mother and daughter produce is manifest in Mrs Quest's attempt to nurture in fantasy that self she finds prohibited and denied by reality:

> Mrs. Maynard had arranged for Martha's arrest for 'communist activities'. Martha was in front of judge and jury. Mrs. Quest, chief witness, was testifying that Martha had always been difficult: 'she's as stubborn as a mule, your honour!' But with careful handling, she would become a sensible person. Martha was let off by the judge, on condition that she lived in her mother's house, in her mother's custody.
>
> Mrs. Quest drifted towards sleep. The scent of roses came in through the window, and she smiled. This time they remained in her hand – three crimson roses. The brutal woman, her beautiful mother, remained invisible in her dangerous heaven. The painful girl, Martha, was locked in her bedroom, under orders from court and judge. Mrs. Quest had become her own comforter, her own solace. Having given birth to herself, she cradled Mrs. Quest, a small, frightened girl, who lay in tender arms against a breast covered in the comfort of bright salmon pink, home-knitted wool.
>
> (Lessing, 1965: 85)

With mother and daughter vanquished, Mrs Quest finally finds acceptance and nurture. She must be mother and daughter to herself to exist at all. 'Having given birth to herself' she knows she has a right to exist, but born of another, the other, she has no identity, is denied. In *Memoirs of a Survivor* too the cruel mother can only be transformed by the tender nurture she was denied as well as denying. (This transformation occurs only in the mystical realm and is a necessary prologue to the daughter's initiation into that realm.) In *The Summer Before the Dark* Kate, who in her dreams rescues a stranded seal, rescues herself. She achieves her quest by extending to herself the mothering which, administered to others, deprived her of herself.

Mrs Quest's vindictive dream fantasy is a temporary solace ironically treated in *Landlocked*. After a long detour into speculative fiction Mrs Quest's fantasy recurs as the plot of *The Good Terrorist* (1985b). In that novel, Alice belatedly moves out of her mother's home and establishes a commune, based on ideas with some similarity to those of Martha Quest during her initial involvement with the Zambesian Communist Party. Alice as a type has more in common with Solly Cohen, the hysterical Trotskyite of the party. Her politics, in the context of her own experience and the society which formed her, are portrayed as bigoted, impractical, insane and an excuse, twisted to justify her immoral and selfish acts. Alice's thefts and hypocrisy are subjected to unrelenting moral denunciation in this satirical novel which seems to regard its main protagonist in much the same way as May Quest views her rebellious daughter. Alice becomes unwittingly and yet not innocently involved in murder and destruction. At the end of the novel she is abandoned by Lessing with a contemptuous 'Poor baby!' (1985b: 370) to the combined wrath of the KGB and the British secret service, a fate very like that wished on Martha by her mother in *Landlocked*. In *The Good Terrorist*, Alice's mother has come to deplore the fashionable socialism her daughter has inherited from her. Her marriage has ended. She is exploited by Alice. Her decline into poverty is inevitable. It is Alice's mother who becomes the prime object of the reader's sympathy. She is the main spokesperson for reason and perception, the voice most congruent with that of the author, within the text.

In *The Golden Notebook* and *Landlocked* Lessing grappled with the realistic novel as an unbearably normative engulfment of her 'truths'. When she returns to that form, the authority of the author is subverted, like Martha's identity, by the very attempt to maintain its integrity. Daughter and author define themselves in opposition to the mother. The repressed maternal darkness eventually returns with redoubled force in Lessing's fiction. 'I' and 'not-I' merge in an identity which at the beginning of the quest was seen to be terrifyingly other, to be death itself.

The 'great prize' of 'an "I" who is a *whole* (that of the "character" as well as that of the author), conscious, knowable' (Cixous, 1974: 385), is plucked from the forces of engulfment at the price of identifying with the forces of consciousness and wholeness, language and the mother who holds out against separation – the very forces which initially threatened that engulfment.

CASTRATION OR DECAPITATION?

The return of that which is initially rejected can also be observed in 'The laugh of the Medusa'. In 'Castration or decapitation?' (1981), originally published only one year after 'The laugh of the Medusa', Cixous comments:

> If man operates under the threat of castration, if masculinity is culturally ordered by the castration complex, it might be said that the backlash, the return, on women of this castration anxiety is its displacement as decapitation, execution, of woman, as loss of her head.
>
> (Cixous, 1981: 43)

The Medusa is decapitated by the hero assisted by Athene, goddess of domestic arts (Rose, 1959: 112) and of heroism. Yet in her essay on Medusa, Cixous asserts, 'If there's a risk there's not an inevitable trap' (1976: 890) of the woman 'losing her head' when she becomes a mother. Her dismissal of 'the fear of becoming the accomplice to a sociality' is perilously close to a valorization of an unthinking maternity and a remystified femininity. Cixous takes that risk since she perceives that the only alternative is 'to repress something as simple as the desire for life' (891).

Refusing either to practise that repression or to succumb to mystification, Cixous breaks through the vicious circles of repetition to a vision of 'the child as other, but the other without violence, bypassing loss, struggle' (890–1). Violence, loss, struggle will not be bypassed, however, and Cixous moves again and again from a denial of their power to an engagement with it. It is part of the explicit project of 'The laugh of the Medusa' to 'resist death' (876). Cixous on one level adopts a stance of 'feminine' affirmation that is the negation of all negativity. 'I want all', she declares (891). There is a drive to make the mother all positive and the woman all mother. But the 'feminine imaginary' seeks not one identity but many egos, as Cixous points out in 'The character of character'. In Cixous's case, which is perhaps more straightforward than Lessing's, the identification of Medusa and of self with the 'good mother' is linked to a denial of death and a denial of traditional negatives by translating them into positives. The effect of this is to destabilize not only the polarity of negative and positive or masculine and feminine, but also that of life and death. In this context it is impossible to maintain an 'essentially' good mother figure as the only image of the feminine. Cixous counters and disrupts her own continuum of mother-life-daughter-multiplicity with the image of the 'phallic mother' (889, 892) or 'Grand Mother' (1981: 43). They are phenomena she deplores, but she does not deny their existence of their potency as images.

PERSEUS AS NARCISSUS

All of which poses a certain threat to the identity of the naming, displacing hero. The permutations of the Medusa myth mark the different modes in which the other (the woman, madness) has been restructured as a mirror which functions to reflect sameness. The myth also indicates the extent to which the woman, the maniac, who recognizes and identifies the subject as hero, is no more than a reflection of his own fears and desires. The therapist finds in madness his own reflection. What else could Perseus have seen in Athene's shield? The other is always elsewhere. It is impossible to 'begin from the concept of a unitary whole' (Laing, 1960: 16–18). There is always something else. That is why modern commentators have imitated Perseus' approach to the Medusa. For fear of catching a glimpse of the real Medusa they have pursued her reflection in the shield they have established against their own perception of difference. Having appropriated the power of the gaze they must be careful not to look straight into the light. They must persuade themselves that there is 'nothing' there anyway.[24]

According to Freud, the Medusa's head is a 'symbol of horror', 'the terrifying genitals of the mother' (Freud, 1955: vol. 18, 273–4). Medusa here becomes an agent of the incest taboo. Her head is a trophy of the Virgin Mother. That sanitized version of the terrifying female cannot rid herself of the old horror. The fact that she wears Medusa's head is a symbol of Athene's triumph, but also a sign that that triumph is incomplete. The mother/goddess cannot be completely purged of the monster. Medusa resists Freud's attempt to translate her story into another adventure of Oedipus.

The myth of Medusa exceeds any model which is brought to bear on it. It highlights the anxieties which underpin the narcissism of the mother–son relationship. It marks the fragility of the cultural, sexual and linguistic economy which depends on the feminine as the mirror in which masculine identity can be constructed. It offers a way of talking about the relationship of mother and daughter, a discussion significant in our culture by its absence. In that context a further challenge is posed to the concept of one 'human' norm, one form of identity. The implications of the Medusa story are that the instability of feminine identity is not untypical. No subject can look 'straight' into the mirror. Different modes of seeing and reflecting transect each other, gazes meet. The 'mother' is neither faithful reflection nor comforting mirror. If the guarantor of identity is an unstable mirage all subjects must ask of themselves: 'What space is yours alone? In what frame must you contain yourself? And how to let your face show through, beyond all the masks?' (Irigaray, 1981: 63). Cixous rightly perceives a willingness to see and to hear the Medusa as the way out into a 'moving, open, transitional space' (1976: 893). Medusa dwells 'beyond glorious Ocean in the frontier land towards Night' (Hesiod, 1982: 99). She inhabits a 'universe tensed between the void and infinity' (Kristeva, 1988: 330).

An encounter with the Medusa is an encounter with that which cannot be represented or reflected and will not reflect or represent. In other words it is impossible. This impossible encounter is attempted in the writings of Muriel Spark and Julia Kristeva in particular, but the Medusa haunts women's attempts at self-representation. In *Heroes and Villains* and 'Stabat Mater' an exploration of the maternal is extended into a (Medusan) challenge to the heroic concept of history. Throughout these discussions, celebrations and analyses of the mother and of writing, one can hear the dialogue of what Kristeva calls the 'two major figures of loving discourse . . . within our tradition':

> One works with entities that have been stabilized in the Oedipus complex. . . . The other discovers a wounded, pierced, bleeding Self . . . then proposes its screen of *abjects*, fragile films, neither subjects nor objects, where what is signified is fear, the horror of being *one* for an *other*.
>
> (Kristeva, 1989: 340)

In *Landlocked* and 'The laugh of the Medusa' the conflict between the desire for stability and the horror of being *one* for an *other* (petrification) dissolves into an awareness that the stability of the subject and its engulfment are indistinguishable.

Chapter 2

The mother as language, language as mother

IN-BETWEEN: THE MATERNAL BODY AND WRITING

Contemporary women's writing, whether poetry, theory or fiction, has put maternity into question and, with conscious novelty, into writing. Both Kristeva and Cixous have posited a specific, subversive and empowering connection between writing and the maternal, but it is Cixous who has insisted most on the positive and revolutionary value of that connection.

'*L'écriture feminine*' has been widely documented and discussed.[1] The tenor of much of that commentary has been wary. Cixous's famous exhortations that 'women must write through their bodies' (1976: 886), they must write in mother's milk (881), have become commonplaces. Some commentators (Moi, 1985: 102–6; Showalter, 1986) have feared that this constitutes a reduction of woman to body and women's writing to a maternal babble which denies its own status as cultural construct and sustains the mythology of the 'eternal feminine'. How valid are readings of Cixous as an essentialist writer?

Cixous's linking of the maternal body to writing is certainly crucial to her writing practice and her theory of the specificity of women's writing. 'The laugh of the Medusa' declares that 'woman must write woman. And man, man' (877). Cixous dismisses as ignorance the general critical tendency to 'hesitate to admit or deny outright the possibility of the pertinence of a distinction between feminine and masculine writing' (883). Cixous's early autobiographical novel was entitled *Dedans* (1969). The in-between is her space.[2] 'The laugh of the Medusa' moves between celebration of sexual 'distinction' and rendering that distinction problematical:

> That writing is precisely working (in) the in-between, inspecting the process of the same and of the other without which nothing can live, undoing the work of death – to admit this is first to want the two, as well as both, the ensemble of the one and the other, not fixed in sequences of struggle and expulsion or some other form of death, but infinitely dynamitized by an incessant process of change from one subject to another. A process of different subjects knowing one and other and beginning one another anew only from the living boundaries of the other: a multiple and inexhaustible course with millions of encounters and transformations of the same into the other and into the in-between from which woman takes her forms (and man, in his turn, but that's his other history).
>
> (Cixous, 1976: 883)

Cixous's Derridean influences are rarely more apparent. The movement 'into the in-between' is a textual as well as conceptual feature of Derrida's writings. Witness the following from 'Freud and the scene of writing' (1981: 196–231):

> Force produces meaning (and space) through the power of 'repetition' alone, which inhabits it originarily as its death. This power, that is this lack of power, which opens and limits the labour of force, institutes translatability, makes possible what we call 'language', transforms an absolute idiom into a limit which is always already transgressed: a pure idiom is not language; it becomes so only through repetition; repetition always already divides the point of departure of the first time.
>
> (Derrida, 1981: 213)

Citing Derrida here seems an effective way of counteracting the commonly held assumption that an underlying biological essentialism prevails in Cixous's writing and particularly in her most widely read text, 'The laugh of the Medusa'. The transformation of 'an absolute idiom into a limit which is always already transgressed' is not generally perceived to be the central textual practice of 'The laugh of the Medusa'. Yet one can observe that transformation in progress, most dynamically, through the text's process of repetition, a process too often read as simple reiteration. An example of this practice of transgressive repetition is the exploration of the breakdown of 'sexual opposition' (Cixous, 1976: 883). Cixous first states that 'sexual opposition, which has always worked for man's profit to the point of reducing writing, too, to his laws, is only a historico-cultural limit'. She launches an immediate challenge to that limit: 'There is, there will be more and more rapidly pervasive now, a fiction that produces irreducible effects of femininity.' This challenge is ambivalent, transgressive of 'sexual opposition', it pushes back the limit which denotes writing as masculine territory. Yet it is to some extent defined in terms of the sexual opposition it opposes – feminine/ masculine.

'The laugh of the Medusa' goes on to pose a second challenge to sexual and other forms of opposition. This is the exhortation to write 'in-between' (883) cited above. This challenge is posed first as an attack on those who refuse to acknowledge 'the pertinence of a distinction between feminine and masculine writing'. Only when the importance of the distinction is established can the process of traversing and exploding its terms begin. The incessant movement back and forth between opposition and exchange is achieved through repetition. This repetition will always introduce a variant, slight or startling, which will retrospectively destabilize the opposition opposed and set a prospective limit on the process of exchange and multiplicity so that the two are never quite distinct, never quite amalgamated within a generic 'both'.

The connection with Derrida's work is not made explicit, but there is an implicit engagement with the problems posed for a liberation ideology based on the celebration of feminine difference by the efficacy of the textual and conceptual strategies of a male theorist in the destabilization of the sexual opposition which 'has always worked for man's profit'. Like Irigaray who, despite the obvious engagement with and influence of Lacanian psychoanalysis in *Speculum of the Other Woman*, declines to name Jacques Lacan in that text, Cixous does not pay due deference (though there is a footnoted reference to Derrida).[3] As with Irigaray, there is an appropriation of what is useful as well as an acknowledgement that there is a definite limit to the usefulness of the writings of men, however they may participate in feminine writing practice.[4] 'The laugh of the Medusa' once again engages in a pattern of varied repetition, movement back and forth and onwards between a variety of positions, acknowledgement of the value of 'literature' as traditionally defined,[5] a redefinition of literature, an appropriation of its subversive potential to the 'feminine' and a repudiation of 'masculinist' writing which sometimes encompasses almost all that is defined as literature, sometimes is quite specific:

> Nearly the entire history of writing is confounded with the history of reason of which it is at once the effect, the support, and one of the privileged alibis. It has been one with the phallocentric tradition. It is indeed that same self-admiring, self-stimulating, self-congratulatory phallocentrism.
>   With some exceptions . . .
>
> (Cixous, 1976: 879)

Those who are outraged by Cixous's 'woman must write woman. And man, man' (877) must put it in the context of her acknowledgement of those exceptions, male writers in whose texts 'the poet slips something by, for a brief span, of woman'. 'If it weren't for them, I wouldn't be writing (I, woman, escapee).' This ambivalence is part of the process by which Cixous ceaselessly establishes exclusive alternatives, opposites, only in order to shatter them into multiple possibilities, and issues imperatives in the here and now only in order to distract from them with reminiscence, dream, prophecy and divergence.

Cixous may acknowledge the inscription of femininity in Genet, but it is not the mere inscription of femininity that will bring about a 'staggering alteration in power relations' (882):

> It is by writing, from and toward women, and by taking up the challenge of speech which has been governed by the phallus, that women will confirm women in a place other than that which is reserved in and by the symbolic, that is, in a place other than silence. Women should break out of the snare of silence.
>
> (Cixous, 1976: 881)

It can only be by their own writing, speaking, acting, by taking up the challenge themselves, that women 'will produce far more radical effects of political and social change than some might like to think' (880). The necessity of women's agency in writing and history appears contrary to the 'incessant process of exchange from one subject to another' (881). In 'The laugh of the Medusa' those contradictions become another opposition to be exploded

(and engaged). 'As subject for history woman always occurs simultaneously in several places' (880). The unceasing demand for
'the two as well as both' (881) ensures that contradiction is the
logic of 'The laugh of the Medusa' and logic is superseded in the
text by the proliferation of desire. It is a text that slithers out of
the grasp of any interpretation which seeks to stabilize and define
it. 'They riveted us between two horrifying myths: between the
Medusa and the abyss' (883). 'The laugh of the Medusa' seizes
the territory in-between as the territory of women. Even in baldly
stating the transfixed dilemma of woman in relation to culture's
mythic 'Woman', Cixous confuses its terms: Medusa lived on the
verge of the abyss, 'in the frontier land towards Night' (Hesiod,
1982: 99). The emphasis on being riveted between and on
'between' as a place of stasis and paralysis is put into question
and itself puts into question the earlier emphasis on 'in-between'
(883) as fluidity and ceaseless (ex)change.

Cixous's Medusa is a creature in-between. She is the mythological expression of the symbolic inter-dict on the feminine *and* of
the power of the feminine to break through inter-diction and
exert its force: 'the more sternly she is cut down, the more
frightening will her Gorgoneum be' (Campbell, 1974: 153): 'When
the "repressed" of their culture and their society returns, it's an
explosive, *utterly destructive* staggering return, with a force never
yet unleashed and equal to the most forbidding of suppressions'
(Cixous, 1976: 884). Cixous (re)possesses the terrifying power
projected on to the feminine, returning the gaze of the other with
all the power of difference in her Medusa's head and rejoining
that head with a body which writes – 'More body, hence more
writing' (886).

It should not be unexpected then that the body of that writing
is the site of a traversal of the in-between of language itself. The
implications of some of Cixous's linguistic play are effectively
lost in translation, a factor that has been important in the Anglo-
American reception of her work. In her own reading of Clarice
Lispector, Cixous warns that 'Because a text is printed, one often
forgets that it is mobile. It is in movement. One should always
bring back the movement of the text' (1990: 100). It is arguable
whether *Reading with Clarice Lispector* succeeds in that 'capacity
for improvisation' (4), the 'transgressive' reading practice which
Cixous identifies as feminine.[6] Its assertion that 'a text says something very different from what it is supposed to say or thinks it

says' (101) is nevertheless worth recalling in reading 'The laugh of the Medusa'. Cixous can use the structure of the French language to destabilize opposites where they are most vulnerable, in language itself, and can destabilize that linguistic structure by (literally) playing with the (sexual) opposition basic to it. So, for example, the apparently straightforward identification of woman with the 'dark continent' (877–8) in 'The laugh of the Medusa' is complicated by moving between masculine and feminine:

> *On peut leur apprendre, dès qu'elles commencent à parler, en même temps que leur nom, que leur région est noire: parce que tu es Afrique, tu es noire. Ton continent est noir. Le noir est dangereux. Dans le noir tu ne vois rien, tu as peur. Ne bouge pas car tu risques de tomber. Surtout ne va pas dans la forêt. Et l'horreur du noir, nous l'avons intériorisée.*
>
> (Cixous, 1976 [1975]: 41)

Two complex movements are accomplished here. On the more obvious level, Cixous moves from talking about women in the third person, *elles*, to the second person, *tu*. The one who addresses women here thus ironically identifies herself with the authorities who induce in women fear of their own darkness. In the final sentence above, however, the writer becomes part of the commonality of women: '*l'horreur du noir, nous l'avons intériorisée*'. Internalization is precisely what makes it so easy to mimic and participate in the voice of our own enemies.

Concurrent with this there is a movement between masculine and feminine where Cixous exploits the different genders of nouns in the French language. Women are first identified as a feminine '*région*' (nf). Their feminine region is contrasted with their masculine '*nom*' (nm). While woman is addressed in the second person and that person becomes individual, '*tu*', you yourself the reader, she is described in terms of feminine nouns and adjectives: '*Tu es Afrique, tu es noire.*' Then something changes. Woman no longer *is* a continent, but possesses one, '*Ton continent est noir*', and that continent which she possesses is, grammatically at least, masculine. The darkness and the continent of the woman are now described in masculine terms: '*Le noir est dangereux*'. Abstracted, no longer an attribute of the woman, the darkness becomes, by the logic of the French language, masculine. Moreover, the object of the writer's analysis is now defined as this masculine entity.

Cixous gradually detaches the attribute of 'darkness' from women and identifies it as an alien, masculine construct before returning herself to the first person plural of womanhood to share the horror of the dark. '*Et l'horreur du noir, nous l'avons intériorisée.*' The texture of Cixous's prose and her linguistic play serve several functions in this passage. The analogy of colonial and sexual oppression is established and disrupted. It is not simply a matter of identifying as a woman with the colonized territory of the 'dark continent'. One is also made aware that '*le noir*' is a construction and projection of an alien consciousness. The sexual categories are disturbed. Cixous does not, as she is sometimes accused of doing, simply re-present traditional 'femininity' in a positive and revolutionary light. In the process of identifying with the Freudian metaphor of woman as dark continent and teasing out the status of the dark continent itself as a metaphor for the (analytical) colonizer's relation to the colonized (feminine), Cixous problematizes both metaphors. The traditional feminine, '*Afrique*', '*noire*', becomes masculine, '*ton continent*', '*le noir*'. Freud's lecture on femininity notoriously banishes women from the ranks of the analysts to form the object of analysis: 'Those of you who are women . . . you are yourselves the problem' (Freud, 1955: vol. 18, 144). Cixous presents Freud's dark continent as a masculine construct which is the object of analysis by a commonalty of writer and readers which is feminine.

This complex movement backwards and forwards, in-between masculine and feminine, subject and object, constitutes the texture of Cixous's writing. It is unfortunate that this rich texture has been left out of so many accounts of Cixous's work. The accusation of essentialism is not sustainable against texts which are consistent only in their inconsistency, their disruption of traditional and conventional categories and their unravelling of the linguistic bases of opposition, certainty and gender. It is a risky strategy and for Cixous the risk of misreading and misrepresentation has been realized. It is a risk which is inevitable to the feminine practice of writing she proposes and a risk which scares others from such a writing practice.

'The laugh of the Medusa' actualizes the fearless writing practice it anticipates for women. It is for this reason, I think, that women who have hesitated to endorse its perceived essentialism or to risk identification with 'the feminine' have nevertheless found its recklessness exhilarating and have sometimes even heeded its exhortation to 'write her self. . . . Write your self' (1976: 880). Despite the penalties, recklessness as well as controversy happily persists in Cixous's writing:

> How terrible it is that we spend precious months of our existence trying to give 'proofs', falling into the trap of critical interpellation, allowing ourselves to be led before the tribunal where we are told: give us proof, explain to us what feminine writing or sexual difference is. And if we were more courageous than I am, we would say: a flute for your proof, I am alive.
>
> (Sellers, 1988: 20)

'The laugh of the Medusa' allows itself to be led before the tribunal, and it answers the tribunal on its own terms, not by the rules of evidence. It does not dispense entirely with explanation, but its answer to the question, what are 'feminine writing and sexual difference', is in every warp and weave of itself as text, 'I am alive'.

LANGUAGE AS ENGULFMENT

The tone of Doris Lessing's exposition of the relation between language and the feminine could not be more different. Yet there are substantial similarities between her perception of the role of the maternal in language and Cixous's perception of that role, though Lessing's evaluation of it differs dramatically from Cixous's enjoyment of it.

Lessing, in an introduction to a collection of her *African Stories* (1964), has compared two early stories, 'The pig' and 'The trinket box':

> I see them as two forks of a road. The second – intense, careful, self-conscious, mannered – could have led to a style of writing usually described as 'feminine'. The style of *The Pig* is straight, broad, direct; is much less beguiling, but is the highway to a kind of writing that has the freedom to develop as it likes.
>
> (Lessing, 1964: 9)

Even at this early stage there is a direct connection made between writing, particularly writing that is or expresses the 'feminine', and beguilement (an enchantment like that practised by the wicked mother). A quest is initiated for a style of writing which is free, direct and *not* feminine.

Language is identified with the mother in her most petrifying aspect. In *Martha Quest*:

> Mrs Quest's voice murmured like the spells of a witch, 'You must be tired, darling; don't overtire yourself, dear.' And when these remarks were directed at Martha, she felt herself claimed by the nightmare . . . and, in fact, at the word 'tired' she felt herself tired and had to shake herself.
>
> (Lessing, 1952: 31)

For Lessing, as the reference to 'The trinket box' shows, 'literary' language is invested with this power of evil enchantment. Later she will accuse it of engulfing truth in 'lying nostalgia', a false order or disorder. In *Martha Quest* poetry is the agent of paralysis and languor, of sleep, death and the mother. It occurs to Martha:

> That the phrase 'Martha is a great reader' was being used by herself exactly as her mother used it, and with as little reason. For what was she reading? She read the same books over and over again, in between intervals of distracted daydreaming, in a trance of recognition, and in always the same place, under the big tree that was her refuge, through which the heat pumped like a narcotic. She read poetry, not for the sense of the words, but for the melodies which confirmed the rhythm of the moving grasses and the swaying of the leaves over her head, or that ideal landscape of white cities and noble people which lay over the actual vistas of harsh grass and stunted trees like a golden mirage.
>
> (Lessing, 1952: 35)

The murmur of Lessing's prose becomes momentarily as hypnotic as Mrs Quest's insidious spells. But Martha 'went through the house searching for something different' (35), and Lessing, for similar reasons, eventually does likewise. It is ironic that Martha should find, in her pursuit of more useful reading, a work by H. G. Wells.[7]

Over the period 1952 to 1969 Doris Lessing produced six novels, as well as a considerable amount of shorter fiction, non-fiction and drama. Of these six novels all but *The Golden Notebook* form a novel sequence, *Children of Violence*. This begins as the epitome of late twentieth-century realism and ends with a startling departure into the realms of prophecy and speculative fiction. The first novel in the series, *Martha Quest*, narrates the induction into adulthood of an imaginative young girl in the repressive colonial society of Zambesia. That induction is a matter of loss; loss of potential, of autonomy, of hope. Intregrated with Martha's story is that of a world apparently inexorably moving towards the outbreak of war. At the end of the novel Martha enters a conventional marriage with a mediocre young man named Douglas, just as the Second World War breaks out. *A Proper Marriage* tells the story of that marriage. Martha's stifling existence as a suburban housewife is symptomatic of the stagnation and corruption of Zambesia. Her escape from the 'comfortable concentration camp' (Friedan, 1963: 266) is described in *A Ripple from the Storm*. This third novel in the *Children of Violence* series is not unaware of the ironies involved in its portrayal of the possibility of change, influx of strangers and general disruption of colonialism and colonial and domestic stagnation which the war brings to Martha and Zambesia. Martha leaves her husband and her daughter, Caroline, with the hope that she is 'setting Caroline free' (Lessing, 1965: 245). Her involvement in the Zambesian Communist Party and the internal dynamics of that party are the central concerns of the novel.

Landlocked (1965) is the fourth part of *Children of Violence*. It marks a return to that series after the writing of *The Golden Notebook* (1962 [1972]), the major formal experiment which marked Lessing's dissatisfaction with the novel form in general and realism in particular. *Landlocked* is in many respects a return to the formal constraints and conventions of the earlier *Children of Violence* novels. It constitutes a pause before the radical break with realism which comes in *The Four-Gated City* (1969).

Despite its formal conventions, *Landlocked* is as engaged as *The Golden Notebook* with the unmanageable forces of madness, language, the maternal and the problematic nature of feminine identity. That engagement is in many ways more thorough and more problematic in this 'conventional' novel than in the novels that precede and follow it. *The Four-Gated City* makes a logical jump from the cold war to a fragile and depopulated post-nuclear world. *Briefing for a Descent into Hell* (1971) ponders the possible identity of Charles Watkins, professor, patient in a psychiatric ward, messenger from the gods, and asks what identity is possible when social identity has broken down. *The Summer Before the*

Dark (1973) registers the haunting presence of imminent apocalypse. Kate Brown, middle-aged housewife with no children at home any more, an absent, uninterested husband and nothing whatsoever to do, seeks her identity in a barren dream landscape where she must rescue a seal which may be herself or the possibility of global survival or both.

Canopus in Argos: Archives (1979–83) is the second series in Lessing's novelistic career. Like *Children of Violence* it comprises five novels, *Re: Colonized Planet 5, Shikasta* (1979) eschews narrative form completely and is presented as series of reports and case studies on Shikasta, a planet identifiable with Earth, presented by their agent to the relevant authorities in the cosmic empire of Canopus. *The Marriages Between Zones Three, Four and Five* (1980) concerns the Zones around Shikasta, Zones which constitute different levels of being, which levels are problematically both political and spiritual. *The Sirian Experiments* (1981) concerns the misguided experiments conducted on Shikasta by the Sirian Empire, a less enlightened rival of Canopus. It is presented as the memoir of an exiled female administrator whose co-operation with Canopus has incurred the wrath of the Sirian Empire she serves. *The Making of the Representative for Planet 8* (1982) is, with *The Marriages Between Zones Three, Four and Five*, among the most lyrical of the *Canopus in Argos* novels. It concerns the fate of the dying Planet Eight and the release of its spirit in the form of the 'representative', the collective identity of the planet's inhabitants. The last of the *Canopus in Argos* novels, *The Sentimental Agents in the Volyen Empire* (1983), is like *Shikasta* largely recounted from the perspective of a Canopean agent. It concerns the 'rhetorical disease' which sweeps through the Volyen Empire and its satellite states. This disease is nothing less than the linguistic obfuscation of pure thought until it becomes mere sentiment.

Liberated into the realm of speculation and prophecy by her quest. Lessing leaves behind, at least temporarily, the problem of language's inadequacy to her purposes and its complicity with what 'is usually described as "feminine" '. Language's duplicity will none the less continue to undermine the concept of an integrated and unalienated 'character' and of any 'I' that is whole, conscious and knowable. It will remain the agent of 'death' and of the narcotic immanence with which it was identified in *Martha Quest*. Lessing may be far less positive about it, but for her as for Cixous, poetic language is Medusan.

SPLITS AND CONFUSION: SCHIZOPHRENESE

Laing, in *The Divided Self*, (1960) proposes that the schizophrenic resists understanding and equates it with a threat to his autonomy – particularly in the form of engulfment, a threat uneasily identified with the mother. The schizophrenic's incomprehensibility is not merely a product of resistance to understanding, however, but endemic to his/her condition:

> Even when the patient is striving to tell us in as clear and straightforward a way as he knows how, the nature of his anxieties and his experiences, structured as they are in a radically different way from ours, the speech content is necessarily difficult to follow.
>
> (Laing, 1960: 175)

Laing appears to have contracted the linguistic perplexity of his patients. It is not surprising that the techniques of 'schizophrenese', like the distinction between sanity and madness, force him to resort to description by negation and qualification:

> Moreover, the formal elements of speech are in themselves ordered in unusual ways, and these formal peculiarities seem, at least to some extent, to be the reflection in language of the alternative ordering of his experience, with splits in it where we take coherence for granted, and the running together (confusion) of elements that we keep apart.
>
> (Laing, 1960: 175)

The basis of Laing's concept of healing is a 'person to person' relation between psychiatrist and patient: in Anna Wulf's terms they each name the other in an acceptable way (Lessing, 1972: 468). To establish such a relation it is necessary that the physician 'recognizes the patient's total being and accepts it' (Laing, 1960: 178) and will allow himself to perceive and 'articulate what the other's world is' (24). The therapeutic value of this is described by a recovered schizophrenic, who comments on her psychiatrist: 'Meeting you made me feel like a traveller who's been lost in a land where no-one speaks his language. . . . Then, suddenly, he meets a stranger who can speak English' (quoted in Laing, 1960: 178). This mutual recognition is 'the main agent in uniting the patient, in allowing the pieces to come together and cohere' (178).

Yet the medium through which recognition and reintegration are reached, the shared language, is itself 'alienated'.

What the psychiatrist committed to 'existential phenomenology' (24) confronts is an experience conveyed in terms of 'splits' and 'confusion', displacement and condensation, metaphor and metonymy. Comparing schizophrenese as described by Laing and the 'id ambiguously uttered' as described by Cixous (1976: 889), we find the common expressive technique of an 'alternative ordering of experience'. Naming is compromised, yet the only hopeless cases Laing concedes are those patients who can no longer speak. Here Laing himself seems to have reached the point where 'the shadow of his mother fell across his inner self as well as his outer self' (Laing, 1960: 110).

When Laing rejects 'repression, denial, splitting, projection, introjection' as 'forms of destructive action on experience', he is rejecting language and everything that makes language possible. When Lessing does likewise, she finds herself embracing the mother who stands up against separation, the mother who was initially experienced as repression, denial, splitting and the nightmare of repetition.

In the texts of Lessing and Cixous we are dealing with motherhood as a cultural and linguistic matrix (mother in language and culture, culture and language as mother) as well as biological motherhood. The dilemma of Laing, of his patient David, of Martha or Anna or any 'author', the heroic dilemma, is to produce (write, act) without being reproduced (inscribed in a pre-existing system or structure). The dilemma of the Medusa, not only Cixous, but also again Lessing, is to produce (write) *and* reproduce – we are back to 'and, and, and', which multiplying affirmation is threatened by an inveterately homogenizing discourse with translation to 'not either or'. 'The mother, too, is a metaphor', Cixous admonishes, warning herself most of all. Yet as her own text evinces, it is difficult to maintain the struggle by the mother without capitulating to essentialism and to reproduction of existing cultural mores. A similar capture appears to be the fate of the hero. Lessing is implicated in both endeavours. Indeed, the emerging pattern of her fiction appears to be that the hero loses by his or her defeat of the Medusa and assumes the identity of and so perhaps the different 'quest' of precisely those monstrous forces he or she has defeated.

THOMAS'S TESTAMENT

Landlocked gives a remarkable example of the techniques of schizophrenese and of the shadow the mother casts on textual production. A bundle of papers, written by Thomas Stern during his last months in the Zambesia valley, is delivered to Martha after his death. Names – 'manuscript' (Lessing, 1965: 280), 'document' (279), 'papers' (276), 'testament' (279) – abound for these writings: literature, novel, art are not among them. Ant-eaten and almost obliterated by rain, Thomas's writings seem almost inseparable from nature. From that closeness comes incoherence, not the clarity and order which in *The Sentimental Agents in the Volyen Empire* and even in *The Golden Notebook* are associated with the (hoped for) breakdown of the distance between sign and referent. This 'natural' text is disorderly, confusing: 'The pages were not numbered, and apparently had never been put in order. How was Martha or anybody to know what Thomas had meant?'(276). This is a text 'with splits in it where we take coherence for granted and the running together (confusion) of elements that we keep apart' (Laing, 1960: 175). It is a double text that becomes plural and is entirely open-ended. The voices of Thomas's fragmentary selves interrupt, comment on and disrupt each other. It is a text from 'the frontier land towards Night' (Hesiod, 1982: 99), from some territory in-between madness and death which might, perhaps, be the place of 'truth':

> How much had been destroyed or lost? Also, there were notes, comments, scribbled over and across and on the margins of the original text, in red pencil. These, hard to decipher, were in themselves a different story, or at least, made of the original a different story.
>
> (Lessing, 1965: 276)

This is reminiscent of Catherine Earnshaw's scribbling of alternative names in the margin of the family Bible. Lessing's description of Thomas's testament corresponds to Cixous's description of a feminine writing practice: Thomas has 'let it articulate a profusion of meanings that run through it in every direction' (Cixous, 1976: 883). It too makes 'the old single-grooved mother tongue reverberate with more than one language':

> A paragraph about life in Sochazen was followed by poetry, in Polish. Translated, it turned out to be a folk song. Then,

how his mother cooked potatoes. Then, across this, in red pencil: If these people could be persuaded to grow potatoes – but what use if the salt has lost its savour? A great many Jewish jokes, or rather Yiddish.

(Lessing, 1965: 277)

The death of Thomas Stern is not enough to banish this focus of disruption from Lessing's work. At the end of *Landlocked*, Martha 'could not make herself throw it away. When it was the only thing left in the empty flat, after she had finished packing to go to England, she threw it into her suitcase and took it with her' (280). If Martha never tells us to what Thomas's 'testament' testifies, it is because this anti-text is the last remnant of the indefinable in *Children of Violence*. Thomas is pared down by the rigour of Lessing's plot to a kind of mad taper, beckoning the way to violence and annihilation. Thomas, the 'character', is annihilated, yet the writings persist. Lessing makes recurrent references to them in *The Four-Gated City*. His manuscript is rewritten by Mark Coleridge (Lessing, 1969: 474–5). This revision, this uneasiness, is an acknowledgement that the immolation of irrationality at the shrine of transcendence has not been complete.

The madness, sexuality and difference projected on to Thomas and the negation of self and fear and loathing of the female projected on to May Quest are overcome as the figures on to which they are projected are banished and reduced and reinterpreted. The medium of this triumph and the substance of these projections cannot be banished. It is not the creature or subordinate of the author. Language remains as the irreducible core of darkness within.

Lessing's advocacy of a transparent, 'straight, broad and direct' (Lessing, 1964: 9), language is no more or less than a desire to tame this darkness too, to reduce language to the faithful mirror of a reality of her own creation. Her yearning for a more tractable medium produces paradoxical expositions, rather than resolutions, of the problem. Thomas's testament is simultaneously an attempt to portray a style of writing adequate to terrible truths and also a disruption of any endeavour to postulate truths. It is a destruction as much as a use of language, 'the wonder' but also the pain 'of being several' (Cixous, 1976: 887).

SOUNDS EXPRESSING A CONDITION

The next description of a 'break down into' a more accurate language comes in *Briefing for a Descent into Hell*. Charlie, in his madness, seems to find a mode of expressing his new knowledge through, or perhaps despite, language. When he is 'not himself' (1971: 197),

> Sometimes it seemed as if the sound, and not the meaning of a word or syllable in a sentence gave birth to the next sentence or word. When this happened it gave the impression of super-ficiality, of being scatty or demented. But we have perhaps to think of the relation of a sound with its meaning. Of course poets do this all the time . . . how a verbal current may match an inner reality, sounds expressing a condition?
>
> (Lessing, 1971: 200)

This description of Charlie's speech is contained in a letter sent to his psychiatrist by Rosemary Baines, another of the female mystics that so proliferate in Lessing's later fiction. An absolute relation between sound and meaning is hinted at in her letter, something beyond words which would validate words anew.

The description of Charlie's speech is curiously ambiguous. This indirect attempt to render meaning absolute conjures up 'the contrary force to "meaning" ' (Kristeva, 1986: 17–18), the narcotic sensuousness of language rejected in *Martha Quest*. Charlie's linguistic excesses are strongly reminiscent of the operation of the semiotic as described by Kristeva. The semiotic is the trace of 'the actual organization, or disposition, within the body, of instinctual drives . . . as they affect language and its practice' – 'the sound . . . gave birth to the next sentence or word.' Charlie's ramblings are explicitly linked to poetry and a very emphatic connection is made in *Martha Quest* between poetry and maternal immanence. The semiotic is rooted in the pre-Oedipal relation to the mother. The 'origin' to which Charlie's discourse relates is none other than the dreaded maternal body.

THE NAMING GAME

Lessing's development as a novelist, her move from realism to speculative fiction, follows the pattern of the 'game' played by Anna Wulf in *The Golden Notebook*:

First I created the room I sat in, object by object, 'naming'
everything, bed, chair, curtains till it was whole in my mind,
then move out of the room, creating the house, then out of
the house slowly creating the street, then rise into the air . . .
then slowly, slowly, I would create the world, continent by
continent, ocean by ocean (but the point of 'the game' was to
create this vastness while holding the bedroom, the house, the
street in their littleness in my mind at the same time) until the
point was reached when I moved out into space, and watched
the world, a sunlit ball in the sky, turning and rolling beneath
me . . . with the stars around me, and the little earth turning
underneath me. I'd try to imagine at the same time, a drop of
water swarming with life, or a green leaf. Sometimes I could
reach what I wanted, a simultaneous knowledge of vastness
and smallness. Or I would concentrate on a single creature . . .
and try to create, to 'name' the being of the flower, the moth,
the fish, slowly creating around it the forest, or the seapool,
or the space of blowing night air that tilted my wings. And
then, out suddenly from the smallness into space.

(Lessing, 1972: 531)

Anna Wulf's game is one of reassurance, recovery of her self and
her world from the 'laws of dissolution' (231). It is the game of
identity: it orders and above all it names. *The Golden Notebook*
recognizes that naming *is* 'creation'.

It is an uneasy and partial recognition. 'First I created the room
I sat in, object by object, "naming" everything' (531). Naming
is the game, yet naming appears in parenthesis throughout the
passage describing how the game is played. Words are contaminated so they must be distanced from the voice of the author
surrogate, Anna. 'Naming', that volatile process, must only par-
enthetically be the means towards creation, unity, wholeness.
Under the pressure of unifying the vastness and the littleness, the
game itself retreats into parenthesis: 'The point of "the game"
was to create this vastness while holding the bedroom, the house,
the street in their littleness in my mind at the same time' (531).
The quotation marks conceal under the guise of an external
authority the slender claim of this fragile self to harness the
multiplicity of 'everything' into one thing of its own creation.

The price paid and the means to reach the point 'when I moved
out into space, and watched the world, a sunlit ball in the sky,

turning and rolling beneath me . . . with the stars around me, and the little earth turning underneath me' are revealed under this pressure. To reassure herself, Anna 'would concentrate on a single creature . . . and try to create, to "name" ' (531). To name is to create and so 'creation' is compromised, prone to 'lying nostalgia' (231). It can no longer be distinguished from 'writing'. The golden notebook becomes no more than the sum of the other notebooks. Their chaos is not transcended. They simply fall 'into a pattern', and 'That', as Anna has pointed out, 'is why all this is untrue' (231).

ALIENATION AND COGNITION

The introduction of a cosmic perspective proves for Lessing as for Anna no escape from, but an intensification of, the problem of 'naming'. The 'space' fiction postulates a unifying wisdom which, like the Canopean agents, can encounter confusion and rejection, but which remains above corruption, absolute and disembodied. The author's 'omniscience', her 'vision', unifies a text as fragmentary as *Shikasta* or a series of highly disparate novels like the *Canopus in Argos* series. Yet this vision remains unspecified, inviolate from the corruptions of language and novelistic convention.

The cost of such defence against engulfment is high, as Laing is acutely aware in relation to his patients. The life of the 'real', withdrawn self becomes radically impoverished. Its ineffectiveness in the external world counters its omnipotence in the world of its own creation. By the end of *The Making of the Representative for Planet 8* everything is lost to the collective hymn of the 'Representative': the 'reality' is extracted from the once colourful planet, now an icy white stone.

The distinguishing characteristic of speculative fiction is its use of alternation of cognition and alienation.[8] 'Creating the vastness' (alienation) while holding on to the familiar, the nameable (cognition), speculative fiction is another variant on Anna Wulf's game. 'Alienation' as a term for a literary technique derives from Brecht's theories of drama (1973). It describes a theatrical technique which actively seeks to prevent identification with characters and situations, inviting instead analysis and criticism. In science fiction this comes to operate as an exotic or unfamiliar element which allows the familiar (cognitive) to be presented in a new light and so made available to questioning.

It is through the process of identification that a reader can, perhaps, be manipulated by the author provided that the author is prepared to limit his or her scope to that with which the reader can readily identify. In denying access to this identification a text invites and produces a type of reading which is an uncontrollable element, a threat to any authorial 'intent' since 'alienation' insists on critical interaction with and free interpretation of the text.

Canopus in Argos is occasionally uneasy with the textual openness implicit in the speculative genre. This is indicated by the sporadic movement into allegory and by the imbalance in favour of cognition in some of the novels in the series. *The Marriages Between Zones Three, Four and Five* is the most obvious example of this: the allegory and the human situations which provide the cognitive factor prove mutually exclusive. A schematic allegory of spiritual progress emerges in the description of the Zones and their interaction. This interaction is sparked by the marriage of Al·Ith, queen of the super-civilized but smug Zone Three, and Ben-Ata, king of the warlike and repressive Zone Four. A linear progress from the barbarism of Zone Five to the ethereal spirituality of Zone Two emerges as the true path from which all the Zones have erred and to which Al·Ith must lead a return.

Lessing describes with considerable sympathy (reminiscent of the early descriptions of Martha's relationship with Thomas in *Landlocked*) the growing trust and affection which develop between Al·Ith and Ben-Ata after their forced marriage. The development of a romantic attachment between two representatives of radically different cultures which thus prove complementary is scarcely the most original of plots. Carter employs it as mythological paradigm in *Heroes and Villains*. The traditional reading sympathies of the reader are invoked. When the traditional happy ending evaporates under the demands of spiritual growth, it is not altogether likely that these sympathies are undermined. Throughout the novel the use of such very traditional material and such pervasive stereotypes concentrates attention on the protagonists and invokes the conventional 'meanings' of such a narrative. The cosmic forces, into whose service Lessing attempts to press the elements of a folk-tale, will undoubtedly be of secondary interest to the reader. Lessing herself occasionally seems to be enjoying her story-telling too much to pause for spiritual contemplation.

The transition is jarring and the discordance puts both the reader's learned reading responses and the 'message' of Lessing's allegory into question. Even in this new genre the 'lying nostalgia' of the conventions of fiction produces false patterns, enmeshing the author's 'real' meaning in pre-existing forms. The attempt to confront and oppose such patterns, like the attempt to confront and oppose the mother who threatens engulfment, seems to reaffirm their power. Like language, fiction undermines the 'game' of unity and authority. When Lessing speaks of the past, as in most of the *Children of Violence* series, she pronounces on the actual; when she speaks of the future, her 'reports' are transparently hypotheses. Like the schizophrenic she creates a world, or in this case a cosmos, for the purpose of maintaining her omniscience in it. The price paid for the authority of the author is that she must operate in a sphere where her general comments are not general, but specific to her own creation. Her fiction becomes indisputably self-reflexive and authorial omniscience is reduced to a fiction.

The Sentimental Agents in the Volyen Empire is at the farthest reach of Lessing's fantasy and simultaneously the closest to domestic British politics for quite a long time. In this novel 'Rhetoric' is satirized as a disease, the delights of natural beauty are spurned as ensnaring deceptions and there is a call for a clear and concise language reminiscent of that which so pleased Lessing in 'The Pig'. In this novel such a use of language is postulated as the only means towards the resolution of political chaos and as the medium of universal harmony. A transparent language in such a novel would clarify only a fiction, a displacement and translation of 'reality'.

The novel is presented as a series of reports by Klorathy, an agent and diplomat of the Canopean Empire. The report format is presumably an attempt to evade the distortions of narrative patterns and novelistic form. Klorathy acknowledges that he himself succumbs occasionally to the Rhetorical plague rampant on Volyen and its colonized planets. Hence within the novel's own framework he is an unreliable narrator. Klorathy is a kind of bureaucratic angel with precedents in all the *Canopus in Argos* novels. Through his battle with the rhetorical disease the interrogation of authority and omniscience neglected since *Landlocked* again forces itself to the centre of Lessing's fiction. Introducing occasional reports by other Canopean agents allows Lessing to maintain some distance from Klorathy's faintly tainted perspective, however, and when she returns to realism in *The Good Terrorist* (1985b) she assumes a tone of extreme authorial certainty. Fabulation was introduced to counter the distortions of language and novelistic convention. Then satire, plain and salutary, is introduced to do what fabulation had failed to do.

WOMEN AND MADNESS

We may find in Laing a key to the paradoxical process by which Lessing attempts to maintain authority as writing agent. Laing repudiates psychological practice which denies that the patient is a 'person', a 'totality', and reduces him or her to a series of mechanisms. The only basis for therapy is a 'person to person' relation between therapist and patient, he argues: 'This book begins and ends with the person' (Laing, 1967: 26). He has perceived the implications of his colleagues' approach: positing the patient as an amalgam of functions, it is difficult for the physician to maintain his concept of himself as something more, something whole.

The maintenance of a concept of selfhood, an 'I', is the stake for which Laing's game is played. This is most obvious when the psychiatrist confronts the 'horrible', 'dilapidated hebephrenic':

> An 'I' has not ceased to exist, but it is without substance, it is disembodied, it lacks the quality of realness and it has no identity, it has no 'me' to go with it. It may seem a contradiction in terms to say that the 'I' lacks identity but this seems to be so. At any rate, without such a last shred or scrap of self, an 'I' therapy of any kind would be impossible. There seems insufficient reason to believe that there is not such a last shred in any patient who can still speak, or at least execute some integrated movements.
>
> (Laing, 1960: 186)

In the theory as in the most advanced stage of defence against engulfment or petrification 'the "true" self becomes a mere vanishing point' (182).

Laing's work can be read as an attempt to uphold the 'real self' against engulfment by insanity and the disintegrative effects of

naming. He quotes Jung who argued that the schizophrenic ceases
to be a schizophrenic when he meets someone who understands
him. The implication of this is that the therapist is no longer
forced to confront madness, but is met by recognition. While
considering the patient as a person, Laing insists the patient must
return the compliment. Patient and therapist recognize each other
and so endow each other with an identity. This recognition is
mutual but unequal. Shoshana Felman has pointed out in 'Women
and madness: the critical phallacy' (1975) that:

> The woman is 'madness' to the extent that she is Other, *different*
> from man.[9] But 'madness' is the absence of 'womanhood' to
> the extent that 'womanhood' is what resembles the Masculine
> equivalent, in the polar division of sexual roles. If so the woman
> is 'madness' since the woman is *difference*; but 'madness' is
> 'non-woman' since madness is the *lack of resemblance*. What the
> narcissistic economy of the Masculine universal equivalent tries
> to eliminate, under the label 'madness' is nothing other than
> *feminine difference*.
>
> (Felman, 1975: 8)

Women patients figure disproportionately in *Sanity, Madness and
the Family* (1970). There and elsewhere, Laing consistently evades
the issues of gender and of the mother – daughter relationship.
The persistent recurrence of these factors, despite the denial of
their importance, indicates how crucial and how feared is the role
of the feminine in Laing's work. The denial of madness as otherness implicit in Laing's formulation of 'recognition' is an inevitable corollary of the denial of sexual difference. The attempt to
invert madness is an attempt to eliminate the feminine.

Felman analyses a tale which has considerable relevance for an
understanding of the male therapist's desire (Laing's desire) for
'recognition' from his predominantly female patients. Balzac's
novella 'Adieu' is recounted from the perspective of Pierre, who
has lost his mistress, Stephanie, in the course of the Napoleonic
wars. When he does find her again, she is mad and will not
speak, except to utter 'Adieu'. She does not recognize him.

Stephanie has completely abandoned her socially defined role.
She refuses to signify or to reflect the male protagonist. Her
words are out of context; which is to say that she sunders signifier
from signified.[10]

Pierre's response is identical to Laing's. He seeks to re-establish recognition and communication. He succeeds by re-creating the scene of their parting – restoring her words to their proper context, closing the embarrassing gap between signifier and signified. He is finally recognized, but the woman dies at the moment her 'reason' is restored. The masculine self must be asserted even at the expense of the annihilation of the other.

Is a similar move executed in Lessing's fiction? Lessing's experiment with form and her abandonment of realism in favour of speculative fiction attempt to maintain a stance of authority and to evade the engulfment threatened by her own sex, by the dominant culture and even by the practice of her art. Within Lessing's own terms that endeavour has failed. The attempt to produce independently and 'originally' has resulted in reproduction of culturally determined modes of understanding and patterns of identity which opposition appears to refresh, rather than undermine. This reproduction is a function of Lessing's attempt to maintain authorial 'intent' as the determining factor of her fiction and her insistence, epitomized in the 'game', on the centrality of the self and on the necessity and positive value of a concept of identity which proves to be an agent of conformity.

In this context Lessing's formal experiments can be seen as her battle to find a form of fiction which will fulfil her need for 'an identification circuit' (Cixous, 1974: 385). The extent to which the fictional genres and forms and ways of using language she employs prove intractable to this purpose is the extent to which to which they prove inimical to unity, sanity, transcendence and the elimination of difference.

In the three novels *The Golden Notebook*, *Landlocked* and *The Four-Gated City*, the intentions of the author become progressively more implicated in the cultural matrix against which those intentions were initially defined. That opposition always carried within it the dread of assimilation, rather like Martha Quest's resolve not to end up like her mother. The dread, which in Laingian terminology has been identified as the fear of engulfment, proves justified as Lessing's fiction begins to exhibit in itself the determinism it has so often exposed. As this process continues, fiction's subversion of a radically compromised authorial 'intent' is not only a form of engulfment, but an evasion of engulfment.

As the solid and substantial stuff of realism ceases to be the stuff of Lessing's fiction, the solidity of 'names' evaporates. Lessing's fictional cosmos is as fanciful and insubstantial as the invisible sustenance with which Canopus nurtures its empire. Naming, fickle and contaminated as it is, now carries the burden of self-sustaining persuasiveness. The comfortable familiar recedes. The referential aspirations of Lessing's fiction expand to attempt a rendering of the ineffable. The fiction must and does move further from the 'straight, broad and direct' (Lessing, 1964: 9). It comes to depend on the narcotic:

> melodies which confirmed the rhythm of the moving grasses and the swaying of the leaves over her head, or that ideal landscape of white cities and noble people which lay over the actual vistas of harsh grass and stunted trees like a golden mirage.
>
> (Lessing, 1952: 35)

The lyricism rejected in *Martha Quest* becomes the pervasive tone of *The Marriages Between Zones Three, Four and Five* and even of *The Making of the Representative for Planet 8*. Perhaps this is why *The Sentimental Agents in the Volyen Empire* (which follows them) is so very uneasy with language and employs such a dislocated form of narrative. In *Landlocked* when Lessing described Martha living harmoniously she resorts to precisely the sort of literary language she rejects in *Martha Quest* and the preface to *African Stories:*

> From this centre she now lived . . . a loft of aromatic wood from whose crooked window could be seen only sky and the boughs of trees, above a brick floor hissing sweetly from the slow drippings and wellings from a hundred growing plants, in a shed whose wooden walls grew from lawns where the swinging arc of a water-sprayer flung rainbows all day long, although, being January, it rained most afternoons.
>
> (Lessing, 1965: 103)

Lessing's predicament is that she is as self-conscious a writer of self-reflective fiction as is inevitable to the age in which she lives, yet she resists the underlying paradoxes to which her fiction must again and again return. Language evades every authorial strategy and remains the last and inviolable residue of darkness, the territory of the mother which not only cannot be occupied, but which undermines the negative view of mother by its own attraction and necessity. In Lessing's fiction, as in 'The laugh of the Medusa', the inevitable cycle of petrification and engulfment emerges as a truth as incomplete as any other.

HOW IS IT POSSIBLE TO WRITE AS A WOMAN?

Lessing moves from frustration at language's inability to describe how things are in *The Golden Notebook* to frustration at its inability to prescribe how things should be in *The Sentimental Agents in the Volyen Empire*. Cixous acknowledges that 'Woman has always functioned "within" the discourse of man, a signifier which has always referred back to the opposite signifier which annihilates its specific energy and diminishes or stifles its different sounds' (Cixous, 1976: 887). She none the less declares that 'it is not to be feared that language conceals an invisible adversary'. Yet the new woman writer must know that 'it is time for her to dislocate this "within" . . . to make it hers . . . to invent for herself a language to get inside of'.

Both writers in their very different ways confront the question 'How is it possible to write as a woman?'. This is a different problem for each of them. Lessing grapples with the verb as the impossibility: Cixous declares the subject, so tenuously a subject – as a woman, a subject in place of, as simile for, a woman – indeed impossible. So Cixous also transfers her attention to the verb. She adopts a subjectivity which is not subjectivity as a means to an immediate relation to language. This offers the opportunity to participate in language's processes from the inside and allows an insight into those processes. Cixous herself cannot maintain the dizzying perspective which ensues with any great consistency. Lessing reverses Cixous's position in relation to the verb, to writing above all. This is the impetus to her paralysing consistency. It has the advantage of pushing her towards an extreme as illuminating and as bewilderingly close to the darkness as any available to Cixous.

For Lessing it is the possibility that the subject is situated in the verb that must be held off as the ultimate chaos. The possibility that the 'author' is only a writer, within writing only a function of writing, is what would make writing as creation impossible. Situating the verb in the subject, reducing it to a function of the subject, Lessing contracts the question 'How is it possible to write as a woman?' to 'How can I write?'. This paradoxically makes the woman that the 'I' now represents disappear. It must always imply a further question, 'How *should* I write?'. The 'author' must, in aspiring to authority, also defer to authority, seeking to create a standard outside herself which will validate her self and legitimize her writing. In refusing to submit the subject to doubt and to question, Lessing finds herself surrendering the subject. She is no longer 'a woman', still less a particular woman, but is objectified. She becomes the 'master' of language and so submits to those very processes of language against which *Canopus in Argos* will entrench a fantasy of the objective subject transcendent.

A backlash of imagery unnerves 'The laugh of the Medusa', shattering its assertions and inducing the very multiplicity and heterogeneity to which Cixous aspired. The stance of the author in Lessing's fiction may become assimilated to the forces against which it had identified itself. Yet the great threat which permeates *The Golden Notebook*, the threat that the intent of the author is not the ultimate determining factor of any novel, persists to become the saving grace of subsequent novels. The fictionality of fiction and the instability of language resist an intent which would reduce them to mere instruments of a transcendent truth.

Every development in Lessing's fiction which appears to be a further engulfment of difference and specificity in a unifying vision is also evidence of the impossibility of rendering any identification circuit absolute. In 'The laugh of the Medusa' the extravagance of metaphor and assertion destabilize identity, and authority is rejected in a 'tarantella' (Cixous and Clément, 1986: 19–22) of logical contradiction and linguistic play. 'Holding on' (Lessing, 1972: 531) and disintegration prove inextricable processes. Assertions of truth become expositions of its impossibility and attempts to assert or reject femininity in writing produce both contrary and indistinguishable results. 'And the one doesn't stir without the other' (Irigaray, 1981: 67).

Chapter 3

History and women's time

Landlocked and 'The laugh of the Medusa' foregrounded the relationship between maternity and language and their treatment of that relationship poses one question very clearly. What is the relationship between maternity, language and the feminine subject's access to history? Does participation in language and history necessarily involve a repudiation of maternity? Or is the case that the celebration of a positive relationship to the maternal is necessary if women are to transform language and change history?

These questions are addressed in *Heroes and Villains* (1969) by Angela Carter and in the lyrical and philosophical essay 'Stabat Mater' by Julia Kristeva.[1] Both of these texts reimagine myths; Kristeva interrogates the myth of the Virgin Mother, Carter rewrites the myth of the hero. In interrogating myth, both analyse and attempt to revise the parameters and definition of history. It is, paradoxically, through their interrogation of the significance of maternity for feminine subjectivity that both texts engage with history (and historicity).[2]

Two strands of thought have emerged in feminism with regard to maternity. One concentrates on maternity as exile from history, the other on the maternal as a powerful disruption of the linear history from which women have been excluded. These appear to be incompatible positions, yet neither can ever be fully extricated from the other, as we will see. In general, Carter is more concerned with the perils and snares in which maternity confines femininity and Kristeva with maternity's challenging and subversive aspects. Yet each of these positions is presented with reservations and qualifications. Maternity is not amenable to any one reading and the recurrent disruptive factor in any formulation of its significance is the recognition that the mother is always also a daughter. In other words, the discussion of the relation of the maternal and history returns us to the mother–daughter relationship.

Kristeva, like Cixous, explicitly addresses the question of language's function as mother and the mother's function in language. Unlike Cixous, however, she assumes neither that language holds no hidden enemies for the 'feminine' speaking subject nor that those aspects of language and literary practice closest to the 'maternal body' are unambiguously affirmative. On the contrary she posits a close relationship between the maternal, the poetic and death (or more specifically, the 'death drives'). Kristeva's recognition of the dangers implicit in the breakdown of the symbolic order is possibly closer to Lessing than Cixous. In *About Chinese Women* the dilemma crucial to the development of Lessing's fiction is succinctly stated:

> A woman has nothing to laugh about when the symbolic order collapses. She can take pleasure in it, if by identifying with the mother, the vaginal body, she imagines she is the sublime, repressed forces which return through the fissures of the order. But she can just as easily die from this upheaval . . . if she has been deprived of a successful maternal identification and has found in the symbolic paternal order her one superficial, belated and easily severed link with life.
>
> (Kristeva, 1986: 150)

Kristeva appreciates how fragile the border is between 'the id ambiguously uttered' (Cixous, 1976: 889) and the bewildered and fragmented utterances of the psychotic, unable to 'get messages out' (Lessing, 1965: 280). Lessing draws back from that border. At the end of *Landlocked* Martha throws Thomas Stern's testament to the insights and tortured possibilities of that dangerous psychic territory into a suitcase. The *Children of Violence* series progresses to a refusal of such insights as well as a banishment of the spectre of madness. Kristeva's project in texts as diverse as *The Revolution in Poetic Language*, *About Chinese Women* and 'Stabat Mater' has consistently been to explore and to map out precisely this region of borders and boundaries, testing its limitations and its liberating excesses and exploring its significance for women as subject to and subjects of discourse.

Angela Carter's use of the genres of science fiction and fantasy, her willingness to experiment with form and her reinvention of myth give her also a certain amount of common ground with Lessing. Unlike Lessing, however, she does not appear to have written anything which could be mistaken for realism. Her first novel, *The Magic Toyshop* (1967), is the nearest she has come to writing traditional realism, but its use of fairy-tale motifs, fantasy and dreams ensures its exclusion from the ranks of the conventional or the realistic. Carter's use of traditional myths and images is closer to Cixous's iconoclasm than Lessing's revisions. Her appropriation of Freudian imagery and mythology operates on a quite different level from Lessing's use of Laing and is very much in harmony with the work of Cixous and Irigaray.

THE THETIC AND THE ANACHRONIC

For Kristeva, language itself is a liminal area, a territory defined by the disputes and fleeting alliances between the symbolic, which generates meaning, and the semiotic, which resists meaning and generates pleasure. Kristeva formulated the concepts of semiotic, symbolic and thetic in *The Revolution in Poetic Language* (1984), which was her doctoral thesis and first major publication and which introduced the most influential ideas developed in her major work. Separation, lack and castration and so the possibility of language are designated by the 'thetic boundary'. The thetic is the rupture which both constitutes the symbolic (language, the law) and designates the semiotic (the 'drives', poetry) as the resurgence of that which the symbolic denies. It is not simply that the symbolic creates the semiotic by opposition or repression nor that the semiotic is the 'precondition' of the symbolic. The semiotic is identified with the pre-Oedipal relation to the mother while the thetic which makes the symbolic possible is regarded precisely as the interruption of that relation. Yet neither the semiotic nor the symbolic is a 'stage', any more than the thetic rupture is an event. When introducing the concepts of the semiotic and the symbolic, Kristeva emphasized that they were inextricable:

> The two trends just mentioned designate *two modalities* of what is, for us, the same signifying process. We shall call the first 'the semiotic' and the second 'the symbolic'. These two modalities are inseparable within the *signifying process* that constitutes language, and the dialectic between them determines the type of discourse (narrative, metalanguage, theory, poetry,

etc.) involved; in other words, so-called 'natural' language, allows the different modes of articulation of the semiotic and symbolic. . . . Because the subject is always *both* semiotic *and* symbolic, no signifying system he produces can be either 'exclusively' semiotic or 'exclusively' symbolic, and is instead necessarily marked by an indebtedness to both.

(Kristeva, 1984: 23–4)

Both semiotic and symbolic might be better described in terms of space than time. *The Revolution in Poetic Language* short-circuits any attempt to assign semiotic or symbolic a temporal location: 'Theory can "situate" such processes and relations diachronically within the process of the constitution of the subject precisely because *they function synchronically within the signifying process of the subject himself*' (96).

Entry into linear temporality is made possible only by accession to the symbolic order and so it is impossible to situate the thetic *in* time. It is paradoxically a *place* in time: it is also where the subject takes its place as subject to history (here access to history and to the symbolic order are regarded as inextricable). As the condition of history (for the subject), it is also prehistorical, in the same way as it is presymbolic: which is to say that the thetic precedes symbolic and historical order only after the institution of that order. The thetic marks the limit of time, the place where time intersects with something else. In other words, the thetic is anachronic.

Anachronism has already been appropriated as a form of critical practice in an essay by Richard Rand, 'Ozone: an essay on Keats' (1987). Rand anachronistically uses ozone as a metaphor for Keats's poetic strategies. Rand's use of anachronism is somewhat different from the anachronic practice which will be identified here as a narrative strategy of speculative fiction, specifically Lessing's *The Marriages Between Zones Three, Four and Five* (the third volume of *Canopus in Argos*) and Carter's *Heroes and Villains*. The 'chronic' elements of anachronism are not allowed free play in Rand's essay on Keats. Rand cites the two definitions of 'anachronism' offered by Webster's Dictionary: 'an error in chronology, especially: a chronological misplacing of persons, events, objects, or customs in regard to each other', or 'a person or a thing that is chronologically out of place, especially: one that belongs to a former time and is incongruous if found in the present'.[3] Rand ignores the metaphorical 'incongruity' of these definitions. Anachronism is time out of 'place'. A 'chronological misplacing' is more than a contradiction in terms, it is a description of time in terms of space made inevitable by the transgression of the linear principle of history, the transgression which constitutes anachronism. Further, 'a person or a thing that is chronologically out of *place*' disrupts the present and presence and so the entire concept of 'history' as a linear sequence of self-contained moments.

Anachronism suggests 'Cronos' as well as 'chronos': it is a preconditon of history as well as history, an indiscriminate darkness as well as the fine discriminations which bring time to light by counting it. That which misplaces time then is 'anachronic', anarchic, but signified through the order it transgresses, holding together the categories of space and time and yet destroying them. Since the anachronic does not oppose but disrupts time, it cannot be said to be defined as its negative. Nor does it have an 'identity' of its own.

The thetic is consistently described in spatial rather than temporal terms in Kristeva's writings. 'The thetic phase' is 'the place of the Other', 'a threshold between two heterogeneous realms' (1984: 48), 'a traversable boundary' (51). Thus despite its association with the Lacanian mirror stage, it is less a stage than an anachronic recurrence, a place to which subjectivity must constantly return to define itself and a place where subjectivity loses itself.

Within such a spatial framework (or space-time dimension) there is no finality, no final separation or triumph of either symbolic or semiotic. The nature of the subject becomes a question of (possible) positions rather than one of definition or lack of it.

The transversal of time by this spatial dimension recurs throughout Kristeva's writing and is in many ways its most interesting feature. It need hardly be noted that while language as speech is inscribed in time, and writing is inscribed in space, meaning is anachronically produced. This is true in speech where the spoken word means in relation to an infinite chain of signification and so occupies a position in relation to a simultaneous multiplicity of possibilities which cannot be simultaneously realized in time. It is also true in writing where chronological order intersects with spatial ordering (position on the page) and where the reading process introduces another anachronic element (since the reading subject intervenes in both orders to produce the text). There are contradictions between the thetic and the anachronic, however. Kristeva is quite explicit that practice is impossible without the thetic and that a text 'in order to hold together as text' requires 'a completion [*finition*], a structuration, a kind of totalization of semiotic motility. This completion consti-tutes a synthesis that requires the thesis of language in order to come about, and the semiotic pulverizes it only to make a new device' (51). The thetic must then tend towards stability and is in this respect conservative. But the thetic, precisely because it is the positing of symbolic and semiotic is clearly distinct 'from a castration imposed once and for all, perpetuating the well-ordered signifier and positing as sacred and unalterable within the enclos-ure of the Other' (51). It is a rupture and contains within it a tendency towards self-rupture and in this respect, the thetic can be a site of subversion and change. It is 'a traversable boundary':

> though absolutely necessary, the thetic is not exclusive: the semiotic constantly tears it open. . . . This is particularly evi-dent in poetic language since, for there to be a transgression of the symbolic, there must be an irruption of the drives in the universal signifying order, that of 'natural' language, which binds together the social unit.
>
> (62)

Poetic practice depends on the possibility that the positing of the thetic can be very forceful, yet very unstable. The anachronic comes into play in the instability of the thetic.

Anachronic and thetic are interconnected and inhabit the same threshold – of language, of subjectivity, of history – but they are distinct and to some extent in conflict. The anachronic is predicated on the instability of the thetic, but unlike the thetic it tends inevi-tably towards disruption. It is not a phase or even a position, but a force, aligned with the semiotic and so, also, with the death drives.

WOMEN'S TIME

What are the implications of this spatialized time for a discussion of women's relation to history? Are either semiotic disruption of the symbolic or anachronic disruption of history available or desirable instruments in the attempt to renegotiate the socio-symbolic contract? For there is a danger of reinstituting woman's exile from the arena of time and change to a quasi-mystical realm that looks suspiciously like the eternal feminine.

The semiotic as vestige of the relation to the maternal body is also the vestige of a period when the primary relations were spatial not temporal and the subject did not yet exist. In the 1979 essay 'Women's time' (1986: 187–213), Kristeva describes maternity and in particular pregnancy as operating in a different time, outside linear temporality. Since this different 'time' is described as 'cyclical' and 'monumental' it becomes apparent that it is more space than time, perhaps a conjunction of the two. 'Women's time' is, it seems, anachronic – it also keeps pace with the New Physics where there is neither space nor time, only space/time (Hawking, 1988: 15–35). Attempts to describe this women's space/time vary as hypotheses of its relation to the semiotic and to writing vary, but it can be said that at its best it is a margin of subversion. At its worst it may be an enclosure.

FANTASY, SPECULATIVE FICTION AND SUBVERSION

Angela Carter's fiction and theory stress the danger of enclosure more often than they celebrate marginality. None the less, they exploit marginal positions and subversive strategies quite as much as Kristeva's writings and, like them, they test limits. Novels such as *The Magic Toyshop* (1967) and *Love* (1971) blur the edges of realism, dissolving the rigours of plot and characterization in phantasmagorical productions attributed to the disturbed and disturbing psyches of their protagonists. In some respects these novels have much in common with *The Four-Gated City*. Like Lessing's novel they operate on the basis of a radical disruption of expectations, though they burst out of the conventions of the novel of plausibility into fantasy, not science fiction: 'Fantasy tells of limits, and it is particularly revealing in pointing out the edges of the real' (Bessière, 1974: 62). It is as interrogations of the 'real' and as play in the field of limits that Carter's fantasy and Kristeva's theory will be seen to have most in common.

Such play is automatically an exploration of the (im)possibilities of language. Fantasy, by its very ability to make non-sense its sense and impossibility its reality, radically undermines the refer-ential claims of language. It is the genre of 'thingless names' (Beckett, 1959; Jackson, 1971: 38). As self-reflexive linguistic arti-

fice, fantasy has much in common with the science fiction mode
employed by Lessing. Use of the term 'speculative' as opposed
to 'science' fiction illuminates the difference between the two
modes, however.[4] The interaction of cognition and alienation
which characterizes science fiction constitutes a speculative mode:
it elaborates an hypothesis from given premises. In other words
speculative fiction asks, 'What if . . .?' Its relation to perceived
'reality' is one of interrogation. Fantasy's relation to reality, however, is one of negation. 'Fantasy embodies a "negative subjunctivity" – that is, fantasy is fantasy because it contravenes the real
and violates it' (Russ, 1973: 52). 'Negative subjunctivity' can
contradict the real, but it cannot escape it. 'The actual world is
constantly present in fantasy, by negation.' The negativity of
fantasy has certain traits in common with the Kristevan concept
of negativity as rejection, described as 'the fourth "term" of the
dialectic' (Kristeva, 1984: 109–13), the dynamic of change and of
the (e)mergence and collapse of the subject, the symbolic and
language.[5] In this context 'negative subjunctivity' can be seen as
allied to the death drives[6] and so as participating in the semiotic
and concentrating its recurrent upheaval against the symbolic.

Such access and allies would appear to privilege fantasy as a
genre of subversion. There is a danger nonetheless, that fantasy's
'subversion' may be illusory if reality is contravened only in order
to be reinstituted. If a simple opposition between fantasy and
reality is established then the fantasy is not even escapist,[7] but
reactionary. It becomes no more than a fit of freakishness which
reinstitutes the norms on which it depends to define it by opposition.[8]

Speculative fiction guards against such a relation by the device
of alienation, by providing a futuristic or quasi-scientific context
in which the unexpected rules. The presence of familiar elements
gives plausibility to the 'What if . . . ?' and gives the reader a
framework of references to work with. The cognitive elements
are also there to be made strange, however, and the interaction
of familiar and alien is, in truly speculative fiction, a mutual
putting-into-question. The 'authorization' of future possibility as
an equal rival and sustained interruption of present 'reality' is a
strategy best described as anachronic.

Three of Carter's novels can be described as speculative fiction:
Heroes and Villains (1969), *The Infernal Desire Machines of Doctor
Hoffman* (1972) and *The Passion of New Eve* (1977). These novels

are situated in another border area, that between science fiction and fantasy. *Heroes and Villains* is set in a post-nuclear future, but the protagonists are mythic and the action is identified with the dreams of the 'heroine', Marianne (Carter, 1969: 137). In *The Infernal Desire Machines of Doctor Hoffman* advanced technology harnesses erotic energy to make the fantasies of individuals manifest as effective reality. *The Passion of New Eve* is set in a near-future, disintegrating America. This context is used to debunk the myth of maternal omniscience as well as masculinist arrogance and to explore bisexuality. A conjunction of interrogation and negation is achieved: in effect, these novels ask, what if reality was *not* so, was not what our most deeply held myths, beliefs and schemes say it is? The rigorous alienation of speculative fiction joins forces with fantasy and functions, like Doctor Hoffman's machines, to release the repressed. The particular disturbing force of Carter's work derives from this combination.

In *Heroes and Villains* the myths of the hero, the (tribal) mother and the phantasms of Freud's family romance form both the fantasy elements and the cognitive components of a science fiction romance. They may be unreal, but they are familiar. The main protagonist, Marianne, is a 'Professor's' daughter. The society of the Professors has evolved from the elite groups who were allocated refuge in the bunkers during a long-past nuclear war. Those who have survived outside the bunkers and the villages which replace them are divided into two groups: the Mutants, whose origin is obvious, and the Barbarians, who have escaped the worst effects of radiation and live a nomadic existence raiding the Professors' villages. As a child Marianne witnesses a raid on her village by the Barbarians and sees one of them kill her brother. After the death of her father she helps a Barbarian raider, Jewel, to escape and leaves with him herself to become eventually a Barbarian leader. The relationship of Jewel and Marianne is antagonistic as well as sexual. In the tradition of romance, Jewel turns out to be the Barbarian who killed her brother. In the tradition of the myth of the hero, Marianne is recognized by Jewel as a kind of doom upon him. Jewel's mentor and the tribe's witch-doctor is a renegade Professor, Donally, who manipulates the superstition of Jewel and the tribe. Donally attempts to integrate Marianne into the tribe by marrying her to Jewel. The uneasy alliance of Marianne and Jewel overthrows Donally's power in the tribe when Marianne becomes pregnant. Donally revenges himself by engineering Jewel's death, but Marianne survives and seems poised to combine both their roles at the novel's end.

MONUMENTAL TIME

The plot has much in common with that of Lessing's *The Marriages Between Zones Three, Four and Five,* though the opposing cultures in Carter's novel are not seen as ordered stages in the path of spiritual progress, but are engaged in a desperate dialectic, each anathema and necessary to the other. The repressive, settled and industrious society of the 'Professors' very gradually succumbs to the scavenging 'Barbarians', whose living will disappear with the enemies whose produce they raid. They kill and need each other. It is interesting that Lessing's allegory transforms historical stages into topographical areas and so endows them with spiritual significance. Carter, in contrast, projects the 'two nations' of the present into a post-apocalyptic death struggle and moves from an exploration of the economic to the symbolic basis of social relations. *The Marriages Between Zones Three, Four and Five* moves towards a restoration of dialectical struggle as the principle of life, but also endorses a dubious spiritual and political hierarchy. 'Primitive,' tribal Zone Five is portrayed as furthest from the light. It is also closest to contemporary 'under-developed' societies. Zone Three, the highest stage of social organization portrayed in the novel, may be said to embody the aspirations of an enlightened, social democratic, probably Scandinavian, republic.

The endorsement of such a hierarchy is weakened by the substitution of topography for temporality. The marriage of a Marxist concept of history to the traditional 'path' of spiritual progress in this novel paradoxically precipitates the collapse of history into geography and the disintegration of progress into flux. The 'dialectic of enlightenment' (Horkheimer and Adorno, 1973) erodes the boundaries that are the only points of reference in the attempt to approach 'truth'.

Travel occurs between the Zones, not only forwards, from Zones Five to Four and Four to Three, but backwards also. The first and most important journey in the novel is Al-Ith's journey back to Zone Four from the more advanced Zone Three. Only after such regression (for she does develop some of the characteristics of Zone Four's inhabitants) can she progress to the borders of Zone Two. Further, as Virginia Tiger has pointed out, the oppressed women of Zone Four are a major cataclysmic force in the novel (Tiger, 1987). They break down all the categories, moving backwards and forwards between Zones and violating the proper pace and mode of progress. Their visit to Zone Three is premature though Dabeeb, who is their representative voice in the novel, insists: 'That it was their place and their right to go, since it was they who had kept the old knowledge alive for so long' (Lessing, 1980: 219). This journey is inappropriate, however, and disconcerts the people of both Zones Three and Four: 'Their coming at all was sensed to be ill-judged. Much worse damage had been done by them than by the officious and doltish soldiers who had come to fetch Al-Ith at the beginning. . . . All of us questioned the marriage again, and felt undermined: some were even wondering about the Providers – if they had made a mistake or were careless in allowing themselves to be wrongly interpreted. Such thoughts were new with us, and an uneasy troubling current was set at work throughout the Zone' (231). Lessing repudiates the women's insistence on translating their new-found spiritual freedom into action. Dabeeb, earlier so rebellious, must acknowledge: 'I don't know how it happened that I was so sure we should all come – but I do see now . . . what got into me? And I have done harm, yes, we can all see that' (231). These unruly women are none the less the ones who have 'kept the old knowledge alive for so long', through their songs, which, as they force the inhabitants of Zone Three to realize, 'are not only known in the watery realms "down there" – just as theirs are to us – but are also told and sung in the sandy camps and around the desert fires of Zone Five' (245). Once again the feminine and the poetic appear in Lessing's fiction as a dangerous alliance and once again these elements persist and insist on their power. We can see the semiotic in dynamic action in such a novel. The very inclusion of the tale of the women's disruptive journey is testament to the impossibility of any final victory for symbolic power. The feminine, poetic and unruly, cannot be banished. It is perhaps inevitable that the other great threat in the novel to the 'Providers" schemes to restore spiritual striving and a new order to the Zones is Murti, who replaces Al-Ith as ruler of Zone Three and who resembles nothing more than the fairy-tale jealous stepsister.

Under pressure from these feminine elements and the songs with which they are associated, the programmatic structure of the Zones' relation to each other breaks down. That structure had itself translated an historical continuum into spatial 'Zones'; when the boundaries between these are themselves transgressed and each Zone becomes less distinct from the others, there are no reliable co-ordinates, spatial, temporal, or even spiritual, remaining. The chants and songs which the women bring from Zone to Zone blur the distinction between progression and regression. Zone Six, described in *Shikasta*, stretches into infinity behind this narrative and Zones One and Two are beyond imagining. The limitless space/time which is the novel's landscape will not allow beginnings and ends to be identified.

It must be remembered that the novel 'sequence', *Canopus in Argos*, is nothing of the sort. No chronology can be established which relates all the texts in a temporal sequence (some obviously deal with simultaneous situations, but this relation is not constant).[9] *Canopus in Argos* possesses no form or structure which makes it inevitable or necessary to read any one before or after another.

What Kristeva calls 'monumental' time, 'all encompassing and infinite like imaginary space' (1986: 191), confounds linear time in *The Marriages Between Zones Three, Four and Five* and precipitates the disintegration of both *telos* and origin.

CYCLICAL TIME

Conventional temporality fares no better in *Heroes and Villains*. Marianne tells Jewel he is an anachronism: ' "What's an anachronism," he said darkly. "Teach me what an anachronism is." "A pun in time," she replied cunningly, so that he would not understand her' (Carter, 1969: 56). The sorcerer-priest Donally comments, 'Time is going backwards and coiling up; who let the spring go, I wonder, so that history would back on itself?' (93).

Cyclical time takes over here. That is precisely what renders the novel so problematic. Cyclical time can be associated with stultifying 'immanence' (de Beauvoir, 1972: 94) or with the danger of petrification, as it is in *Children of Violence*. It could be described as the space to which women are banished when they are exiled from history. Kristeva describes it spectacularly differently, reclaiming it as a space dizzying in its vastness rather than as 'confinement or restriction to a narrow round of uncreative or repetitious duties' (de Beauvoir, 1972: 63). In 'Women's time':

There are cycles, gestation, the eternal recurrence of a biological
rhythm which conforms to that of nature and imposes a temporality whose stereotyping may shock, but whose regularity and
unison with what is experienced as extra-subjective time, cosmic
time, occasion vertiginous visions and unnameable *jouissance*.[10]

(Kristeva, 1986: 191)

Vertigo often precipitates a fall and the logic of this 'time' in *Heroes
and Villains* is the eternal recurrence of a vicious circle, a shocking,
stereotyping victory of maternity over the woman as protagonist,
as thinker, as producer of her own story. Carter's text directly
addresses the issue which disrupts any comfortable conclusions in
the work of Cixous and Lessing and which sometimes threatens
to overwhelm that of Kristeva: 'I think therefore I am, but if I
take time off from thinking, what then?' (Carter, 1969: 98). This
question is posed by Donally, the sinister architect of the symbolic
in *Heroes and Villains*. He repeatedly scrawls epigrams, ciphers and
questions on the crumbling walls of the shelters where Marianne
takes refuge with the Barbarians. The question of the self's fate
without consciousness or when consciousness is no longer in control is his greatest challenge to this girl who 'keeps on utilizing
her perceptions until the very end' (81). It is also, of course, the
greatest challenge which the concept of a decentred self poses for
feminism. Women have sought independence, autonomy, historical and political agency, all of those things which have traditionally
defined 'human' subjectivity. That definition has collapsed under
the onslaught of contemporary critical theory, perhaps primarily
under the onslaught of feminism's claims that women will no
longer guarantee the subject's autonomy and agency, but will
instead exercise it. If the self is no more than a fragile illusion,
sustained by a dualism inimical to women, prey to unconscious
drives and produced by language, what is left to resist hegemony
and seek change? Towards the end of *Heroes and Villains*, Marianne,
pregnant, trapped, finds 'she was not able to think' (149) and 'then'
the age-old pattern recurs. Jewel dies, becomes a hero and so fulfils
the destiny which Donally insisted would be his, that of the new
Arthur, 'the Messiah of the Yahoos'. Marianne survives, becomes
a mother and the Tiger Lady' (150), 'Eve at the end of the world'
(124). Through Marianne and her child will be completed the
process begun by Donally and, reluctantly, Jewel. The novel ends
poised for the transformation of the tribe from a loose family

grouping to a structured society. If a woman takes time off from thinking, it seems, she is in danger of becoming a mother goddess.

FEMALE FANTASIES CONCERNED WITH POWER

In *This Sex Which is Not One*, Luce Irigaray warns that inherent in 'the race for power', inextricably linked to the attempt of 'the female imaginary' to 'represent itself', is the danger 'yet again', of 'a privileging of the maternal over the feminine' (1985b: 30). In *Heroes and Villains* there are recurrent textual signals that the feminine protagonist's claim on subjectivity is fragile. Her sexuality is projected on to a masculine figure, a demon lover. Marianne, significantly when both Jewel and her own situation are most beyond her control and comprehension, calls him 'the furious invention of my virgin nights' (Carter, 1969: 137). In this novel, as in *Landlocked*, it is the male protagonist who is closest to the libido – Jewel is more than reminiscent of Thomas Stern. This recurrent association of the masculine and the libidinal raises severe problems for the subversive alliance between the feminine and the unconscious postulated by Cixous, Kristeva and Irigaray (obviously, the nature and meaning of that alliance is treated very differently by each of these three). Marianne, who considers herself 'the only rational woman left in the whole world' (Carter, 1969: 55), is oriented towards ego – and, in view of her reverence for the memory of her Professor father, super-ego. Jewel, as a projection of egoistic fantasy and return of the repressed, is more complex. In reading *Landlocked* in terms of Gilbert and Gubar's analysis of the 'demon lover' figure in women's fiction and in my own reading of *Landlocked* it was assumed that the female protagonist would be identified with ego. The male 'character' that fulfils the function of non-identical double then becomes by turn alter-ego and projection of the dissociated id. This pattern in women's fiction would initially appear to confirm Freud's description of the libido in masculine terms:

There is only one libido, which serves both the masculine and feminine sexual function. To it itself we cannot assign any sex: if following the conventional equation of activity and masculinity, we are inclined to describe it as masculine we must not forget that it also covers trends with a passive aim. Nevertheless the juxtaposition 'feminine libido' is without justification. Furthermore it is our impression that more constraint has been applied to the libido when it is pressed into the service of the feminine function, and that – to speak teleologically – Nature takes less careful account of its [the function's] demands than in the case of masculinity. And the reason for this may be – thinking once again teleologically – in the fact that the accomplishment of the aim of biology has been entrusted to the aggressiveness of men and has been made to some extent independent of women's consent.

(Freud, 1981b: vol. 22, 131)

As Laura Mulvey points out, Freud shifts here from 'the use of active/masculine as *metaphor* for the function of libido to an invocation of Nature and biology that appears to leave the metaphoric usage behind' (1990: 26). This doom at the hand of biology and the denial of woman's autonomy is the substance of Martha Quest's nightmare. Freud's denial of 'feminine libido' is, however, at odds with the *telos* of that denial: 'Woman would be the basis, the inscriptional space for the representatives of the masculine unconscious' (Irigaray, 1985a: 111). The problem for Freud is that in the light of his assertion that 'sexual life is dominated by the polarity of masculine and feminine . . . the notion suggests itself of considering the relation of the libido to its antithesis' (Freud 1981: vol. 22, 131), but such a relation is unthinkable: 'the feminine cannot be conceptualized as different, but rather only as *opposition* (passivity) in an antinomic sense or as *similarity* (the phallic phase)' (Mulvey 1990: 26). So following the 'conventional equation of masculinity and activity' Freud is 'inclined' to describe the libido as masculine. The unconscious, however, is inclined to be projected on to the feminine. The refusal to juxtapose the 'feminine' and the 'libido' (Freud, 1981b: vol. 22, 131) opens up a disjunction between libido and unconscious where the feminine disrupts the 'conventional equation of activity and masculinity'. The projection of the libido on to male figures in *Wuthering Heights*, *Landlocked* and *Heroes and Villains* would indicate on one level that the unconscious is always projected on to the 'opposite' sex and, as the extract from Freud above epitomizes, woman is always the opposite sex. In the confrontation between the maternal and the feminine speaking, acting subject she is even the opposite of herself as protagonist, Perseus *and* Medusa. Jewel, Thomas Stern and Heathcliff are projections of libido, which need not be assigned a sex since only one is thinkable. They are also, however, the inscriptional space for the unconscious, thus fulfilling a function which Irigaray identifies as feminine. These demon lover figures thus confound the differentiation between masculine and feminine. This is the key to the ambivalence which Gilbert and Gubar detect in Brontë's Heathcliff and to the figure of Jewel in *Heroes and Villains*.

The fact that both of these ambiguously male figures are outsiders and foreigners and both wanderers is crucial.

> In the fascinated rejection that the foreigner arouses in us, there is a share of uncanny strangeness in the sense of the depersonalization that Freud discovered in it, and which takes up again our infantile desires and fear of the other – the other of death, the other of woman, the other of uncontrollable desire. The foreigner is within us, and when we flee from our struggle against the foreigner, we are fighting the unconscious, that 'improper' facet of our impossible 'own and proper'.
>
> (Kristeva, 1991: 19)

Thomas Stern, the wandering Jew, Jewel, the itinerant Barbarian, are already *'unheimlich'* and homeless. As foreigners, others, they are already feminized.

THE ORIGIN OF CASTRATION

Carter rewrites the Heathcliff 'demon lover' motif in *Heroes and Villains*.[11] It is possible to compare the rape scene in *Heroes and Villains* with the scene in *Wuthering Heights* where Catherine is savaged by the Lintons' guard-dog. Gilbert and Gubar interpret the latter as simultaneously marking Catherine's entry into adult female sexuality' *and* castration (1979: 272). In *Wuthering Heights* this incident brings about Catherine's separation from Heathcliff. In *Heroes and Villains* Marianne and Jewel play out what might be a parody or grotesque inversion of the violent love scene of Brontë's protagonists, later in *Wuthering Heights*, which precipitates Catherine's death. Commenting on the wound inflicted by Skulker on Catherine, Gilbert and Gubar observe:

> Obviously such bleeding has sexual connotations, especially when it occurs in a pubescent girl. Crippling injuries to the feet are equally resonant, moreover, almost always signifying symbolic castration, as in the stories of Oedipus, Achilles and

the Fisher King. Additionally, it need hardly be noted that Skulker's equipment for aggression – his huge purple tongue and pendant lips, for instance – sounds extraordinarily phallic. In a Freudian sense then, the imagery of this brief but violent episode hints that Catherine has been simultaneously catapulted into adult female sexuality and castrated.

(Gilbert and Gubar, 1979: 272)

The otherwise gratuitously bloody defloration of Marianne is equally suggestive. In *Heroes and Villains* the 'totemic animal' (Gilbert and Gubar, 1979: 272) which rapes/castrates her and the other self of the heroine are one. Marianne makes this explicit. There is an ironic resonance of the Fall in her comparison of Jewel's attack on her with an earlier incident where she was bitten by a snake: 'It hurt far worse than the snake-bite because it was intentional' (Carter, 1969: 55). Like Brontë, Carter is engaged in rewriting the myth of the Fall. The 'snake', Jewel, has had Adam and Eve tattooed on his back by Donally:

> He took a fortnight and I was delirious most of the time but the needles didn't poison my blood because Mrs Greene looked after them. Though green in fact is the worst, green hurts most of all. You'll notice what a lot of green there is in the picture.
>
> (Carter, 1969: 86)

The relation of the feminine to the maternal once again forms a backdrop to the 'Fall' into castration. The outrageous conceit at the heart of Freud's denial of 'feminine libido' (1981b: vol. 22, 131) is its proposal that women are irrelevant to 'the aim of biology'. Childbirth is dissociated from the maternal body as well as the mother's will and is made an attribute of an abstract 'Nature'. The description of conception and childbirth in terms of *telos* again displaces reproduction from the realm of the physical into a quasi-metaphysical project of the 'idea', Nature. The possibility of a feminine libidinal economy (Sellers, 1988) is eliminated under the same sign that banishes the maternal body, the sign of castration:

> This 'castration' that Freud accounts for in terms of 'nature', 'anatomy', could equally well be interpreted as that prohibition that enjoins woman – at least in this history – from ever imagining, fancying, re-presenting, symbolizing, etc. (and none of these words is adequate as all are borrowed from a discourse which aids and abets that prohibition) her own relation to

beginning. The 'fact of castration' has to be understood as a definitive prohibition against establishing one's own economy of the desire for origin. Hence the hole, the lack, the fault, the 'castration' that greets the little girl as she enters as a subject into representative systems.

(Irigaray, 1985a: 83)

If a Lacanian perspective is superimposed on this Freudian framework another related pattern emerges. Marianne, in effect, is a subject striving to cohere, she 'thinks', she 'is'. Jewel sees in her 'the map of a country in which I only exist by virtue of the extravagance of my metaphors' (Carter, 1969: 120). *Heroes and Villains* 'brings into play' (Irigaray, 1985b: 30) the female imaginary, that is, it explores from a feminine perspective, 'the imaginary relation, that between the ego and its images' (Lacan, 1977: ix). That process generates an intoxicating subversion by negation (fantasy) and interrogation (science or speculative fiction) of myth, history, sexuality, language and the novel. Yet its guerrilla tactics demonstrate the aptness of Carter's comment on de Sade's sexual guerrilla, Juliette: 'Juliette, secularized as she is, is in the service of the goddess too, even if of the goddess in her demonic aspect, the goddess as antithesis' (1979: 111). The logic of the narrative is that if the feminine subject 'takes time off from thinking' (1969: 98), 'then', there occurs precisely that return to the privilege of the maternal over the feminine which Irigaray fears. It culminates in the collapse of sexuality into reproduction, an equation which Carter posits as the most insidious enemy of women. The female imaginary would appear to self-destruct.

MATERNITY AND HISTORY

There is no way out of time.

(Carter, 1979: 110)

In *The Sadeian Woman* (1979) Carter presents the notion of 'women's time' rather differently from Kristeva's exhilarating rewrite of woman's relation to history. Carter's formulation of the mother–daughter relationship appears close to that implicit in the early novels of the *Children of Violence* series 'the daughter may achieve autonomy only through destroying the mother, who represents her own reproductive function, also, who is both her own mother and the potential mother within herself'

(124). Carter is commenting on de Sade's *Philosophy in the Bedroom* (1965a). Irigaray, in 'And the one doesn't stir without the other', comments that 'mother and daughter live as each one the other's image' (125). The indistinct identities and interplay of voices between mother and daughter are also recognized in *The Sadeian Woman*:

> If the daughter is a mocking memory to the mother – 'As I am so you once were' – then the mother is a horrid warning to her daughter. 'As I am, so you will be.' Mother seeks to ensure the continuance of her own repression, and her hypocritical solicitude for the younger woman's moral, that is, sexual welfare masks a desire to reduce her daughter to the same state of contingent passivity she herself inhabits.
>
> (Carter, 1979: 124)

Carter's 'Exercise in cultural history' goes further than Irigaray's 'Forgive me, Mother, I prefer a woman to you' (Irigaray, 1981: 67). It simultaneously postulates the radical separation of 'mother' and 'woman' and the explosive possibility of their combination.

Carter celebrates a radical and final disruption of 'the nightmare of repetition'. The medium of this revolution is quite simple. Carter is one of the few writers under discussion to ask specifically *why* maternity is now available for discussion as myth, for interrogation, acceptance, or rejection:

> Techniques of contraception and surgically safe abortion have given women the choice to be sexually active yet intentionally infertile for more of their lives than was possible at any time in history until now.
>
> (Carter, 1979: 107)

It could be said that both the theory and practice of women's writing in the late twentieth century are in the process of inscribing and must be inscribed in that transformation. The cultural lag between the advent of the dislocation of sexuality and reproduction and 'the several millennia in which this fact was not self-evident at all, since it was continually obscured by enforced pregnancies' and 'endless or at best lengthy series of childbirths and miscarriages' (Pratt, 1972: 488) appears to be closing in *The Sadeian Woman*:

> The goddess is dead.

And, with the imaginary construct of the goddess, dies the notion of eternity, whose place on earth was her womb. If the goddess is dead, there is nowhere for eternity to hide. The last resort of homecoming is denied us. We are confronted with mortality, as if for the first time.

There is no way out of time. We must learn to live in this world . . . because it is the only world that we will ever know.

I think that is why so many people find the idea of the emancipation of women frightening. It represents the final secularization of mankind.

(Carter, 1979: 110)

But is this not rejection of the mother and with her much that constitutes the specifically feminine, rejection (as with Lessing) of self as woman?

The Sadeian Woman acknowledges that this may be the price of the sexual and intellectual terrorism necessary 'to pare a good deal of the fraudulent magic from the idea of women' (109). The discussion of *Philosophy in the Bedroom* identifies the point at which de Sade retreats from the erotic relation of mother and daughter as the point at which his aim of 'perpetual immoral subversion of the established order' (132) is betrayed: 'He is on the point of becoming a revolutionary pornographer; but he, finally, lacks the courage. He reverts, now, to being a simple pornographer' (132). That the maternal function is compatible with pleasure is too dangerous an admission, even for the most inveterate iconoclast. 'Mother' 'cannot be corrupted into the experience of sexual pleasure and so set free. She is locked forever in the fortress of her flesh, a sleeping beauty whose lapse of being is absolute and eternal' (128). An explanation for the inevitability of such lapses is given in *The Sadeian Woman*. Eugenie, in her attack on her mother, 'attacks only that part of herself, her reproductive function, she can afford to lose' (131). That loss is the price of autonomy, independence. However:

The violation of the mother is no more than a performance, a show; it demonstrates and creates Eugenie's autonomy, but also the limits of her autonomy, for her freedom is well policed by the faceless authority beyond the nursery, outside the mirror,[12] the father who knows all, sees all and permits almost everything, except absolute freedom.

(Carter, 1979: 131)

If mother is the threat of confinement(s), repression, repetition, exile, father is the guarantor of autonomy, action and independence to act – within 'history', which he defines.

BREAKING UP (HIS)STORY

A recurrent conflict emerges in the writings of Carter and Kristeva between resistance to history as the agent of determinism and desire for access to history as the arena of change. Each asks if to enter history is to become the slave of history:

> Women are caught . . . in a very real contradiction. . . . As long as women remain silent, they will be outside the historical process. But if they begin to speak and write *as men do*, they will enter history subdued and alienated; it is a history that, logically speaking, their speech should disrupt.
>
> (Gauthier, 1981: 163)

'Woman's time', the cycles of gestation and the mo(nu)ments of eternity, is, for Kristeva, the place of just such a disruption. Carter calls it 'the great, good place' (1979: 108) – that is, nowhere:

> The theory of maternal superiority is one of the most damaging of all consolatory fictions and women themselves cannot leave it alone, although it springs from the timeless, placeless, fantasy land of archetypes where all the embodiments of biological supremacy live.
>
> (Carter, 1979: 106)

The Sadeian Woman is very much at odds here with Cixous's description of the all-affirming mother, who 'will never be lacking' (Cixous, 1976: 893) The myth of 'Mother'

> puts those women who wholeheartedly subscribe to it in voluntary exile from the historic world, this world, in its historic time that is counted out minute by minute, in which no event exists for itself but is determined by an interlocking web of circumstances, where actions achieve effects and my fertility is governed by my diet, the age at which I reached puberty, my bodily juices, my decisions.
>
> (Carter, 1979: 106)

Kristeva, in 'Women's time' and *The Revolution in Poetic Language*, puts the notion of exile from history in a new light. It is not simply absence from the temporal continuum of causation and so activity, but also access to another 'sphere', another space, which can disrupt, traverse and transgress history. Carter speaks of sexual terrorism as a mode of purging the old mystifications which have exiled women to eternity; that is, to maternity:

> The womb . . . is a fleshly link between past and future, the physical location of an everlasting present tense that can usefully serve as a symbol of eternity, a concept which has always presented some difficulties in visualization.
>
> (Carter, 1979: 108)

Kristeva posits the maternal as a border from which textual terrorism can be launched. The question remains whether access to history, because it requires the assumption of subjectivity, also requires subjection. If this is so, the option for women in relation to writing and to history is simply between two forms of exile, from articulation and action or from themselves.

So there is the 'Tiger Lady', the Goddess, or Juliette the guerrilla, and while Carter scorns the former, she distrusts the latter, 'but' wonders how she can be done without:

> With apologies to Apollinaire, I do not think I want Juliette to renew my world; but, her work of destruction complete, she will, with her own death, have removed a repressive and authoritarian superstructure that has prevented a good deal of the work of renewal.
>
> (Carter, 1979: 111)

Kristeva commented in *About Chinese Women* that 'A woman has nothing to laugh about when the symbolic order collapses' (1986: 150). *Heroes and Villains*, like 'The laugh of the Medusa' and some of Lessing's experiments with speculative fiction, explores the danger that such collapse merely initiates renewal. Goddess and guerrilla, the two forms of exile, present another form of the Medusan impasse which was explored in the texts of Lessing and Cixous: 'For Juliette, secularized as she is, is in the service of the goddess too, even if of the goddess in her demonic aspect, the goddess as antithesis' (Carter, 1979: 111). Eternal goddess, dying and (possibly) reviving god/hero; these are the elements to which the narrative structure of *Heroes and Villains* consistently alludes. Marianne finds the tribe's 'sign' against the evil eye is the sign of the cross, Jewel is to be the 'Messiah of the Yahoos', or the new Arthur (124). These 'archetypes' and their myth are subjected to the alienating interrogation of a post-nuclear setting, however. In such a setting any renewal is inevitably warped, the concept of eternal continuity has become ironic. Carter engages in that mythologizing of myth which Barthes advocates as the most effective method of revealing the signifying structure which myth must conceal if it is to operate as purveyor of universal unchangeability (Barthes, 1972). Indeed, one of Donally's aphorisms neatly summarizes much of Barthes's argument, 'MISTRUST APPEARANCES; THEY NEVER CONCEAL ANYTHING' (Carter, 1969: 60). Donally's imperative is typical of this novel's 'negations'. The mythologist is also the literary and sexual terrorist: 'Juliette, as Theodor Adorno and Max Horkheimer say, embodies "intellectual pleasure in regression" [history wound back on itself]. She attacks civilization with its own weapons. She exercises rigorously rational thought; she creates systems; she exhibits an iron self-control' (148). There is much of the Marianne of *Heroes and Villains* in this, particularly Marianne as artist/dreamer, whose 'furious invention' this is. She never completes her work of destruction, however, and the renewal promised in the conclusion may be the establishment, not the removal, of 'a repressive and authoritarian superstructure' (111).

UNDOING THE SACRIFICIAL CONTRACT

Heroes and Villains de(con)structs the socio-symbolic contract, not least by availing itself of the myth of sacrifice so crucial to it. Jewel, as Messiah, Arthur, hero, is the blood sacrifice demanded by the Mother Goddess and the socio-symbolic contract. In *Revolution in Poetic Language* Kristeva comments on the view of classical anthropology and sociology which characterizes sacrifice as both violent and regulatory; 'by focussing violence on a victim', sacrifice 'displaces it on to the symbolic order *at the very moment* at which this order is being founded' (1984: 75). The founding sacrifice is an act of exclusion which is forced to recognize, express and release those forces it will sacrifice and exclude. When history winds back on itself, as it does in *Heroes and Villains*, the founding sacrifice is exposed and the repressed returns. The sacrifice is not defined by the death of a hero, nor even by the sublimation of anarchic id, according to Kristeva:

For sacrifice designates, precisely, the watershed on the basis of
which the social and symbolic are instituted: the thetic that
confines violence to a single place, making it a signifier . . . it
indicates that all order is based on representation: what is violent
is the irruption of the symbol, killing substance to make it
signify.

(Kristeva, 1984: 75)

The thetic is 'the threshold of language', the break where subjectivity is instituted, the point at which identity is posited on separation, specifically a separation of object from subject (Kristeva,
1986: 98–100). With its institution of identity *and* difference, the
thetic *is* the founding sacrifice and the watershed where what is
sacrificed erupts and is incorporated into the socio-symbolic
order. So 'Marianne' is engulfed in the role of Tiger Lady (Carter,
1969: 150), queen. Jewel, who exists only by virtue of the extravagance of his metaphors, dies and so attains to a form of 'reality'.
Curiously humanized by his death wish, Jewel neglects his image
of magnificent ferocity and Marianne, glimpsing him in a mirror,
is disconcerted, disappointed, 'dream and reality merged with
such violence she laughed hysterically' (146). The (re)institution
of the symbolic is marked by the death of the self-consciously
and apparently metaphorical, the death of Jewel, the 'sign of the
idea of a hero' (72). Representation will henceforth be concealed
and concealing, but the novel attempts to lay bare the structure
of that deceit and its complicity with power – 'I'll be the Tiger
Lady and rule them with a rod of iron' (150). Winding history
back on itself *Heroes and Villains* attempts to undo the Gordian
knot of civilization.

MEDUSA AND THE SPHINX

It is once again productive to read *Heroes and Villains* in the
context of *Wuthering Heights* and to re-examine the function of
the Thomas Stern character in *Landlocked* in conjunction with
Carter's use of a relatively similar figure in *Heroes and Villains*.
Jewel, like Brontë's Heathcliff, is associated with the lost brother
of the feminine protagonist. Where Heathcliff takes the place of
the dead brother of the Earnshaws and supplants Hindley, Jewel
has killed Marianne's brother while Marianne watched from a
window (5–6). The scene on their wedding night, in which Jewel

and Marianne recognize and remember each other, is one where identity becomes fluid and the principle of substitution and displacement becomes central: 'Her heart sank and she recognized him, though he had completely changed. "You were much younger, then," she said. "And looked more like Precious than yourself" ' (79). In suggesting the interchangeability of Jewel and his brother Precious, Marianne suggests the interchangeability of Jewel and her own brother.

Another substitution or displacement is also suggested. As a child watching the fight between her brother and Jewel, Marianne 'saw them staring at one another, both oddly startled as if this was the last thing they expected to happen, this embrace to the kill' (5). As a woman she reassures Jewel, 'I am only in your bed by accident, anyway' (80), but he is convinced that she will be 'the death of me' (79, 80).

That they recognize each other as the protagonists in the earlier scene of Marianne's brother's death is significant. It aligns their story with the incest motif in Brontë and with the incest-by-mistake Oedipal scenario. 'Who'd have thought I ever could recognize you' (79), Jewel wonders.

In an essay on 'The scope of anthropology', Lévi-Strauss relates a story of the Iroquois and Algonquin North American Indians. Sexual advances are made to a young girl by a man whom she believes to be her brother. She accuses the brother who proves his innocence by presenting his double to her and killing him before her eyes. This murder is also a death sentence on himself since he believes his destiny and that of his double are inextricable (Lévi-Strauss, 1977: vol. 2, 2–24). Marianne sees Jewel kill her brother before her eyes and in her eyes Jewel sees his death sentence. The resemblances to Lévi-Strauss's tale are resonant. On Donally's bookshelves Marianne observes the works of 'Lévi-Strauss . . . marked by fire and flood' (Carter, 1969: 62). In the Algonquin-Iroquois tale the murdered man's mother is a powerful sorceress who will want vengeance for her son's death if she discovers it. The girl and her brother can mislead her only by marrying each other, since 'the old woman would not suspect the hoax' (Lévi-Strauss, 1977: vol. 2, 21). Lévi-Strauss identifies parallels with the Oedipus legend:[13] 'The precautions taken to avoid incest make incest in fact inevitable. In both cases a sensational turn of events results from the fact that the characters originally introduced as distinct are identified with each other'

(21). In both instances there is also a link between incest and a riddle. Riddles are rare in the tales of the Algonquin it seems, but they do have a myth 'where owls (or the ancestors of owls) ask a riddle which the hero must answer on pain of death' (22). The victim's mother was associated with owls in the incest story and in the hoax played on her the incest is itself a kind of riddle. Donally's scrawled epigrams, specifically the crucial

> I think therefore I am, but if I take time off from thinking what then?
>
> (Carter, 1969: 98)

are riddles to Marianne on a conceptual level, riddles to Jewel because he cannot read. Jewel presents himself to Marianne in their recognition scene as a text to be read, another kind of riddle: 'You can read, read me' (79). The riddle element is provided in *Wuthering Heights* by Lockwood's dream of the 'seven times seventy-seventh sin' and by Catherine's scrawls in the margins of the Bible, her alternative names, 'Catherine Earnshaw, Catherine Heathcliff, Catherine Linton': 'Like the solved riddle incest brings together terms meant to remain separate. The son is joined with the mother, the brother with the sister *in the same way* as the answer succeeds against all odds in rejoining its question' (Lévi-Strauss, 1977 vol. 2, 23). Lévi-Strauss identifies the Grail legend with that of Oedipus and of the Algonquin girl and her brother's double. Percival's inability to ask the right question is the obverse of the inability to give the right answer (to a riddle). Both display a similar 'lack of reciprocity', 'Percival thus appears as an inverted Oedipus.' In this context one can recall Martha's quest and the riddle of Thomas Stern's testament (Lessing, 1965: 279). Martha proceeds with her quest when Mark Coleridge has rewritten that testament in *The Four-Gated City*. In *Landlocked*, however, the riddle remains unsolved: 'How was Martha, or anybody, to know what Thomas had meant?' (Lessing, 1965: 276). Landlocked Zambesia remains a wasteland awaiting salvation:

> Martha shut her eyes and listened – water, water falling, water. Somewhere was water, was rescue, was the sea. In this nightmare she was caught in, in which they were all caught, they must remember that outside, somewhere else, was light, was the sound of water breaking on rocks. Somewhere lay shores where waves ran in all day with a jostling rush like horses

racing . . . Somewhere, outside this tall plateau where sudden hot rain, skies of brass, dry scents, dry wastes of grass imprisoned its creatures in a watchful tension like sleeplessness, somewhere hundreds of miles away, the ground fell, it slid to the sea.

(Lessing, 1965: 244)

'If there were only water amongst the rock . . .' (Eliot, 1961: 64).[14] This kind of imagery for the paralysis of colonial southern Africa is not new to Lessing's work: her first novel was entitled *The Grass is Singing*.[15]

Though there is a relationship between *Landlocked, Heroes and Villains* and *Wuthering Heights*, it is paradoxically Martha's inability to solve the riddle that enables her to progress in her quest in *Children of Violence*. The incest motif is also least pronounced in *Landlocked*, though Thomas Stern is linked with Martha's father who 'lay whimpering in his cage of decaying, smelling flesh' (Lessing, 1965: 244) while Thomas was 'going crazy in that village' (280). The letter telling Martha that Thomas has died arrives on the night of Mr Quest's death and each man dies 'futilely, away from his own people, and among strangers' (254). The lesser impact of the incest motif in Lessing's use of the 'demon lover' pattern is concomitant with *Children of Violence*'s relative unwillingness to approach 'the watershed on which the social and symbolic are instituted' (Kristeva, 1984: 31). Lessing is less eager to undo history.

Gilbert and Gubar describe *Wuthering Heights* as a myth of origins: 'myth-making in the functional sense of problem-solving' (1979: 256). They read the novel as a revision from a 'feminist' perspective of *Paradise Lost* and the book of Genesis. In its attempt to wind history back on itself (Carter, 1969: 93) *Heroes and Villains* is equally concerned with origins and particularly with unravelling myths of origin. The incest/riddle motif is crucial to this:

We know what function is fulfilled by the incest prohibition in primitive societies. By casting, so to speak, the sisters and daughters out of the consanguine group, and by assigning to them husbands coming from other groups, the prohibition creates bonds of alliance between these natural groups, the first ones which can be called social, the incest prohibition is thus the basis of human society: in a sense it *is* the society.

(Lévi-Strauss, 1977: vol. 2, 19)

The foreignness of the demon lover figures in *Heroes and Villains*, *Landlocked* and *Wuthering Heights* indicates that the horror of incest is allied to a horror of uncontrolled exogamy. The sisters and daughters' are *assigned* husbands from 'other' but clearly identified and allied 'groups'. Once again *'unheimliche'* female sexuality and the foreigner are identified. Lévi-Strauss does not pursue this inevitable counterpart to the incest prohibition. That prohibition is his 'myth of how culture came about' (Gilbert and Gubar, 1979: 257) and like Freud he sets about 'naturalizing' it (1981b: vol. 22, 131; see above). Lévi-Strauss does so by emptying the signifier 'woman' – and all other signifiers – of substance. They become units of exchange:[16]

> To the two possibilities which could capture his imagination – a summer or a winter equally eternal, the former licentious to the point of corruption [incest], the latter to the point of sterility [impotence] – man must resign himself to preferring the equilibrium and periodicity of seasonal rhythm. In the natural order, the latter fulfils the same function as the exchange of women in marriage and the exchange of words in conversation do in society, provided that they are both practised with the frank intention of communicating: in other words, without ruse or perversity, and above all without hidden motives.
>
> (Lévi-Strauss, 1977: vol 2, 24)

The equation of natural processes and social processes is mediated through women [17] and words. Man re(as)signs to himself a natural periodicity from which the periodicity and fertility of the woman's body will now be a deviation, atemporal, 'woman's time'. The transparency of the signifiers exchanged between men is vital, so in a move analogous to Freud's elimination of the maternal body under the sign of abstract 'Nature', the substance of woman is annihilated. Indeed that annihilation, that 'casting out', is the 'Nature' of society itself. Cast out and assigned husbands from other groups (Lévi-Strauss, 1977: vol. 2, 19) – this describes the situation not only of Marianne, but of Catherine Earnshaw after her marriage to Linton:

> Supposing at twelve years old, I had been wrenched from the Heights . . . and my all in all, as Heathcliff was at that time, and been converted at a stroke into Mrs Linton, the lady of

Thrushcross Grange, and the wife of a stranger: an exile and an outcast, thenceforth, from what had been my world.

(Brontë, 1965 [1847]: 163)

In *Heroes and Villains* Carter executes a kind of revenge upon anthropology. 'Consider your researches into the *moeurs* of savage tribes completed,' Donally tells Marianne (Carter, 1969: 132) ' "Not yet," she temporized. "They're not completed yet." ' Marianne is the anthropologist in the text, her alienation guarantees her the role:

In ethnographic experience the observer apprehends himself as his own instrument of observation. Clearly he must learn to know himself to obtain, from a *self* who reveals himself as *another* to the *I* who uses him, an evaluation which will become an integral part of the observation of other selves.

(Lévi-Strauss, 1977: vol. 2, 36)

During her wedding, 'an ordeal by imagery' (Carter, 1969: 81), Marianne adopts just such a double role of observer and instrument of observation:

There were gold braid and feathers in Jewel's hair and very long earrings of carved silver in his ears. Darkness was made explicit in the altered contours of his face. He was like a work of art, as if created, not begotten, a fantastic dandy of the void whose true nature had been entirely subsumed to the alien and terrible beauty of a rhetorical gesture. His appearance was abstracted from his body and he was wilfully reduced to sign language. He had become the sign of the idea of a hero: and she herself had been forced to impersonate the sign of a memory of a bride. But though she knew quite well she herself was only impersonating the sign, she could not tell whether Jewel was impersonating that other sign or had, indeed, become it.

(Carter, 1969: 72)

The 'frank exchange' (Lévi-Strauss, 1977: vol. 2, 24) of women and signs is brought to an abrupt standstill here. A woman who observes and understands her own function as sign and is conscious that her role as unit of exchange is an impersonation, disturbs the basis of society itself. She exposes its 'ruses', its 'hidden motives', and denaturalizes it. Here at the marriage ceremony which is intended to integrate the woman into the tribe,

'Swallow you up and incorporate you' (Carter, 1969: 56), Carter disrupts the logic of sacrifice which kills 'substance to make it signify' (Kristeva, 1984: 31). The sacrificial nature of this wedding is observed by Marianne: 'I thought he [Donally] was going to kill me, cut me up, fry me and distribute me in ritual gobbets to the tribe' (76).[18] The conventional signifier, 'the sign of a memory of a bride' (72), assumes the function of observing subject. Marianne never relinquishes the power of the gaze, a Medusa-like power which is associated with Jewel's fear that she will be the death of him: 'Who'ld have thought I ever could recognize you, unless what I thought was true, that this child who looked so severe would be the death of me' (79). Later he will observe, 'She converted me into something else by seeing me' (122).

Since the anthropologist/observer of the wedding ritual is feminine, the factor which Lévi-Strauss suppresses in his formulation of social exchange is foregrounded. Despite his preceding discussion of matrilinear societies, he suppresses the possibility that men, like women, may be units of exchange. In *Heroes and Villains*, however, Jewel too is a 'sign' and is if anything more alienated by this function that Marianne, who is at least conscious of an observing self not implicated in the process of social integration and exchange: 'Though she knew quite well she herself was only impersonating this sign, she could not tell whether Jewel was impersonating this sign or had, indeed, become it' (72). This suspicion that Jewel can be completely absorbed into his function as signifier of the 'idea of a hero' is well founded. He tells Donally:

> 'When I painted my face and so on, I became the frightening thing myself and ceased altogether to be anything but the thing I was, an implement for killing people.'
> 'And she watched you.'
> 'She converted me into something else by seeing me.'
> (Carter, 1969: 122)

Marianne's power to convert Jewel into something else by seeing him may, of course, suggest that Jewel has adopted the 'feminine' role in relation to Marianne's 'masculine' gaze, her ego-orientated subjectivity. This would be in keeping with the function of the 'demon lover' as inscription of the feminine unconscious: in his association with that feminine unconscious, Jewel is a feminine figure. The scenario is more complex than mere inversion of sexual roles, however.

In Carter's as in Brontë's revisionary myth of origin, the 'sign of the idea of a hero' performs a dual function as brother/lover and other self. The transgression of the incest taboo is not explicit in either *Heroes and Villains* or *Wuthering Heights*, but the approach to it through the demon lovers, Jewel and Heathcliff, is necessary if either novel is to 'wind history back on itself' (Carter, 1969: 93) and subvert the myth of origin which condemns the feminine subject to castration and perpetual 'exile': 'The "fact of castration" has to be understood as a definitive prohibition against establishing one's own [as a woman] economy of the desire for origin' (Irigaray, 1985a: 83). Both *Wuthering Heights* and *Heroes and Villains* transgress this prohibition. They ask, from a feminine perspective, 'how culture came about' (Gilbert and Gubar, 1979: 257). Both novels 'without refusing or sidestepping the socio-symbolic order' (Kristeva, 1986: 200) are 'trying to explore the constitution and functioning of this contract, starting less from the knowledge about it (anthropology, psychoanalysis, linguistics) than from the very personal affect experienced when facing it as subject and as a woman'. The congruence of this exploration and the forms it takes in Gilbert and Gubar's reading of *Wuthering Heights*, in *Landlocked* and *Heroes and Villains* would certainly seem to support Kristeva's statement that:

> The new generation of women[19] is showing that its major social concern has become the socio-symbolic contract as a sacrificial contract. If anthropologists and psychologists, for at least a century, have not stopped insisting on this in their attention to 'savage thought', wars, the discourse of dreams or writers, women are today affirming – and we consequently face a mass phenomenon – that they are forced to experience this contract against their will. Based on this, they are attempting a revolt which they see as a resurrection but which society as a whole understands as murder. This attempt can lead us to a not less and sometimes more deadly violence. Or to a cultural innovation. Probably both at once. But that is precisely what the stakes are, and they are of epochal significance.
>
> (Kristeva, 1986: 200)

In *Heroes and Villains*, *Landlocked* and *Wuthering Heights* the foreignness of the demon lover figures is linked to the maternal body and to the search for origin. In other words these women's stories of origin present the mother's womb as itself *unheimlich*. Not only is homecoming impossible, it is no longer possible to postulate home or origin as the premiss for an 'us' or an exclusion of the other. Nothing is stranger than where we come from. Interrogation of her own relation to origin by a female protagonist subverts the metaphors and ideology of social, ethnic and national belonging. This is the consequence of 'the final secularization of mankind'. This is the source of the pervasive sense of loss in modernism and postmodernism,[20] of their characteristic alienation.

The new and fragile basis it offers for the social contract may yet mark the point at which western culture ceases to mourn the illusion of one's 'own and proper' place and acknowledges 'the difference within us in its most bewildering state and presents it as the ultimate condition of our being *with* others' (Kristeva, 1991: 192).

THE DISCOURSE OF INEQUALITY: ROUSSEAU AND ENGELS

The extensive use of 'speculative' or fantastic narrative modes by contemporary women writers can be seen as a function of the 'revolt' against the socio-symbolic sacrifice of women. Alienation from the logic of sacrifice is a direct function of the speculative mode employed in *Heroes and Villains*. That alienation is accomplished most effectively when Carter exposes the two most prevalent western prototypes of utopia to the harsh light of the post-nuclear age. A society of philosophers turns out to be barbaric, rooted in exclusion and evasion. Such a society is literally a besieged bunker. The Barbarians themselves are 'too sophisticated' (Carter, 1969: 120), ignoble, disease-ridden, still savage. Just as these societies themselves wage their unwinnable war of attrition against each other, so *Heroes and Villains* pits the fantasies of Plato and Rousseau against each other and wages war on the concept of a 'Golden Age', either past or future.

The interrogation of Rousseau's *Discourse on the Origin of Inequality* and *The Social Contract* (1973) in *Heroes and Villains* is central to the novel's analysis of the socio-symbolic contract.[21] 'With the patriarchal family we enter the field of written history', commented Engels (1972: 122). Undoing the former, *Heroes and Villains* unravels the latter.

A lyrical adulation of 'savage', primal man from Rousseau's *Discourse on the Origin of Inequality* is quoted in *Heroes and Villains*, ironically attributed to Marianne. On the eve of her wedding, she romanticizes Jewel's brother, Precious. To her, he looked 'Just as if he had come from the hands of original nature, an animal weaker than some and less agile than others, but, taking him all round the most advantageously organized of any' (Carter, 1969: 65; Rousseau, 1973: 53). This is the fantasy of the 'Professor girl', however, who sees in Precious both 'pure essence of man in his most innocent state' (Carter, 1969: 65) and, paradoxically, a creature 'more nearly related to the river than to herself'. This fantasy of 'essential man' is disturbed when she discovers that his eyes are closed: 'Perhaps he was dreaming; but she could not conceive what dreams the Barbarians dreamed, unless she herself was playing a part in one of them' (Carter, 1969: 65). Rousseau, it seems, would be similarly perplexed. For to talk of the Barbarians in terms of the *Discourse on the Origin of Inequality* is to talk of them as already poised on the threshold of civilization. 'Straight from the hands of original nature' they are already out of those hands and heading towards a 'limit-point' (Althusser, 1972: 118) where Rousseau will institute a contract, a willed act of social cohesion. As 'origin' this contract will become the point on to which, in space or in time, what precedes or follows it will be mapped:

> The history of systems of signs includes logical evolutions related to different levels of structuration . . . these systems do not coincide either in their logical structure or in their historical affiliations. They are as if diffracted upon a temporal dimension, from whose density synchrony draws its consistency; and for lack of which it would dissolve into a tenuous and impalpable essence, a ghost of reality.
>
> (Lévi-Strauss, 1977: vol. 2, 17)

Rousseau's insistent postulation of origins is predicated on the construction of time as a succession of such moments of perfect synchrony. That, after all, is 'history' and those who would reshape it must of necessity change its co-ordinates.

CHOOSING ALIENATION

The Social Contract and the *Discourse on the Origin of Inequality* are thus engaged in establishing (political) priorities and Carter's ironic quote indicates that *Heroes and Villains* is engaged in changing those priorities. For Rousseau, as for feminism, any question of identity is also a question(ing) of power: 'It would be better, before examining the act by which a people gives itself to a king, to examine that by which a people is a people; for this act, being necessarily prior to the other, is the true foundation of society' (Rousseau, 1973: 190). The 'act' must be presupposed or subjection to a monarch could only be replaced by subjection to circumstance, a return to 'barbarism'. So the will to act must be created. Not only the will to act, however, but the will 'to act in concert' (191), the act by which a people is a people – the will to power and the positing of an identity:

> The problem is to find a form of association which will defend and protect with the whole common force the person and goods of each associate, and in which each, while uniting himself with all, may still obey himself alone, and remain as free as before. This is the fundamental problem to which the Social Contract provides the solution.
>
> (Rousseau, 1973: 191)

Rousseau is almost as frank as Marianne here in his acknowledgement that his contract is a fiction produced to fulfil a need. Paradoxically, for this admirer of man in a state of nature, there can be nothing natural about the foundation of society. 'The social order' must 'be founded on conventions' (182). Indeed it is only 'conventionally' that the solution to Rousseau's problem above can be imagined. As Louis Althusser has pointed out (1972: 113–60), to rescue man from *subjection* to 'total alienation', Rousseau offers him the *choice* of total alienation. The clauses of the social contract 'may be reduced to one – the total alienation of each associate, together with all his rights, to the whole community' (Rousseau, 1973: 191). Rousseau, it must be pointed out, qualifies this resolution – summarized by Althusser as 'Total alienation is the solution to the state of total alienation' (1972: 127). It is immediately preceded by the prospect of the contract's dissolution: 'On the violation of the social contract, each regains his original rights and resumes his natural liberties, while losing the conventional liberty in favour of which he renounced it' (Rousseau, 1973: 182). We begin to see the function of origin and nature in *The Social Contract*, as the guarantee of 'the choice' of contractual obligation and 'conventional liberty'. It is necessary for man to be 'born free' (181), in order that he may choose his own chains.

LOSING COMMUNALITY

A similar movement can be observed in *The Origin of the Family, Private Property and the State*. Engels's engagement with the dynamics of change does not preclude and perhaps imposes all the more forcibly the necessity of fixing points of 'origin' on which may be diffracted conflicting sign and other systems to create an image of uniform progress, a 'dialectical average' (Althusser, 1972: 127). The title of his attempt to change the co-ordinates of 'written history' could be read as an ironic subtitle to *Heroes and Villains*, which, projecting these origins into the future, transforms time as past events into time as possible futures.

Engels is fond enough of speculation about the future. His theories of the distant past and future of relations between the sexes are the crisis points of his argument. Like *The Discourse on the Origin of Inequality*, his *Origin of the Family, Private Property and the State* creates an image of a golden age of unthinking bliss, which, unlike Rousseau, Engels characterizes as complete communality. Both obviously share an inability to escape the influence of the book of Genesis, and a curious partiality to the concept of the 'happy Fall', perhaps because it gives each the chance to play saviour. For both, losing paradise is the necessary price of access to consciousness, the tree of knowledge. Both promise a *conscious* return to the Eden that preceded consciousness. In Rousseau's case this will be return to liberty; in Engels to communality.

Engels puts sexual relations at the heart of his myth of fall and salvation. Rousseau also establishes private property, root of 'so many horrors and misfortunes' (1973: 84), and the family in one sentence (87). Engels, however, pays much more attention to the division of labour between the sexes and to the institution of monogamy and overthrow of 'mother right' as 'the world historical defeat of the female sex' (Engels, 1972: 120). His explanation of the 'origin' of that institution, however, may be a product of the assumptions of his era, but it also foreshadows his difficulty in imagining any radical changes in women's relation to the forces of production or reproduction. Engels's fantasy here owes much to Rousseau:

> The more the traditional sexual relations[22] lost the naive, primitive character of forest life, owing to the development of economic conditions with consequent undermining of the old communism and growing density of population, the more oppressive and humiliating must the women have felt them to be, and the greater their longing for the right of chastity, of temporary or permanent marriage with one man only as a way of release. This advance could not have originated with the men if only because it has never occurred to men to renounce the pleasures of actual group marriage.
>
> Only when the women had brought the transition to pairing marriage were the men able to introduce strict monogamy – though indeed only for women.
>
> (Engels, 1972: 117)

This is not merely a quaint example of Engels's Victorianism. If he is to attribute to women a progressive role in 'history', he must attribute to them a decisive role in their own degradation. Engels is again and more insidiously returning to Judaeo–Christian myth. Men are allowed to retain 'the naive, primitive character of forest life' in their sexual relations: they will never 'renounce the *pleasures* of actual group marriage'. It is the women who fall from the grace of naivety and create the concept of sexuality as 'oppressive and humiliating'. Thus feminine 'chastity' here comes to precede the conditions that created it, the shift towards patrilinear inheritance, a change which Engels can elsewhere analyse with considerable clarity.

The production of such myths of feminine essence is not confined to Engels's speculations on the past. When the capitalist system is overthrown and women are integrated into public labour and freed from 'anxiety about the "consequences" ' of engaging in sexual activity, (139) will not women then regain the naive pleasures of sexuality unfettered by repressive economic conditions? The question troubles Engels and he poses it as a question, a problem not unrelated to that posed by Rousseau and similarly resolved. For liberation from the conditions that created and sustained the form of sexual relations which he describes as both alienating and oppressive to women, will be achieved by a different *form* of the same relation: 'Monogamy, instead of collapsing, at last becomes a reality – also for men.' Engels's insistence that the transformation of private property into social property will not result in an upsurge of unconstrained female desire, but in monogamy for both sexes, *freely* entered into by both parties, is parallel to Rousseau's attempt to render total alienation into its opposite by the same means, the concept of 'free' choice. 'With the patriarchal family, we enter the field of written history.' Engels is trying to save the 'advances' of civilization by turning the alienation which makes 'history' possible into yet another version of Rousseau's contract.

Since both make clear that language is a key attribute of civilization, the institution of language (as the instrument of history) is obviously also at stake. The 'limit-points' of civilization and barbarism posited by *Discourse on the Origin of Inequality* and *The Origin of the Family, Private Property and the State* mask the thetic and Engels rightly identifies *both* the acquisition of language and the overthrow of mother right with the 'threshold' of civilization. So we return to the problematic nature of the 'socio-symbolic contract' for the feminine subject.

Both Althusser, in relation to *The Social Contract*, and Engels, in relation to bourgeois marriage, make the point that a contract between unequal partners is, in its own terms, no contract, but the imposition of force (Althusser, 1972: 128ff.; Engels, 1972: 142–3). Althusser goes on to point out that the contract which Rousseau describes as that between two aspects of the same whole is in fact between one party which exists prior to the contract, the individuals who will 'alienate' themselves to the community, and another which 'is itself the *product* of the contract' (Althusser, 1972: 129), that very community.

Engels's ideal monogamy is similarly contracted between the actual and that potential which the contract actualizes.[23] The coming revolution must obviously be described in the future tense; it *will* eliminate the issue of inheritance, it *will* transform 'private housekeeping into social industry' (Engels, 1972: 139): 'The position of men *will* be very much altered. But that of women, all women, *undergoes* significant change'. The slither into the continuous present persists throughout a eulogy to sexual love, free from 'the anxiety about bequeathing and inheriting', which culminates in 'a girl . . . giving herself completely to the

man she loves'. This disturbance of tense and its use in naturalizing thetic disruptions of his myth of origin constitutes an eruption
of anachronic elements in Engels's text. This eruption is followed
by questions about the future, vexing and alarming questions:
'Will that [the transformation of sexual relations] not suffice to
bring about the gradual growth of unconstrained sexual inter-
course?' (139). Engels's negative reply is not simply an attempt
to refute any association of communism and promiscuity. What
is at stake, as we have seen, is the precondition of history.
Assuming man to be social, as Rousseau does not, Engels understands that there must be introduced some basic relation which
is not 'natural', which is conventional and contractual, before
civilization, the Law of the Father, can be instituted. Engels calls
this relation monogamy, a relation which, in terms of his own
theories of the 'origin' of societies, constitutes a 'form' of primary
alienation. He describes the lower stage of barbarism thus: 'The
division of labour is purely primitive, between the sexes only.'
'The first great *social*[24] division of labour', we later learn, is
between pastoral and hunting tribes. Once again the social differences between the sexes are naturalized.

If *The Origin of the Family, Private Property and the State* fails to
account for sexuality and reproduction in its attempt to redefine
the 'origins' of society, it is because it too, like Rousseau's *The
Social Contract*, must hold something in reserve. In *Speculum of the
Other Woman* Luce Irigaray comments that 'Woman' constitutes

A reserve supply of negativity . . . in a partly fictional progress
toward the mastery of power. . . . Off-stage, off-side, beyond
representation, beyond selfhood. A power in reserve for the
dialectical operations to come.

(Irigaray, 1985a: 22)

In order to legitimate the new co-ordinates of history, Engels
must also write the impossibility of prehistory. Women and sexuality must be exiled from history in order to represent what
history is *not*. Like Lévi-Strauss and Freud, Engels naturalizes a
'primary' alienation of women. Once again we have come to 'the
watershed on the basis of which the social and symbolic are
instituted' (Kristeva, 1984: 75). 'A certain practice accompanies'
the 'sacrifice', however:

Through, with and despite the positing of sacrifice, this practice

deploys the expenditure/unthinking [*dépense*] of semiotic violence, breaks through the symbolic border, and tends to dis-
solve the logical order, which is, in short, the outer limit
founding the human and social. This practice is the representation which generally precedes sacrifice.

(Kristeva, 1984: 75)

Rousseau's contract dissolves in linguistic subtlety, anachronic
disruptions upset Engels's neat assignment of origins.

The Origin of the Family, Private Property and the State and *The
Social Contract* are 'interested' in converting process into contract,
that is, in establishing the primacy of the Law and the Law of
the Father. In banishing, to the asocial or prehistorical, elements
which would threaten that primacy, however, each text bears
traces of that which it denies. Althusser has illuminated the
manner in which Rousseau changes things by changing names:

> The people can only be said to 'contract with itself' by a *play
> on words*, on this occasion on the word that designates RP1[25]
> as the 'people', a term only strictly applicable to the RP2, the
> community (the object of the contract being to think the act
> by which 'a people is a people').

(Althusser, 1972: 131)

The similarity of the process in Engels is remarkable. Stripping
away all the other 'conventions' which might constitute society,
The Origin of the Family, Private Property and the State inverts the
terms of the one convention it naturalizes and desocializes. It
describes what is only potential, women as equal partners in the
marital contract, as actual, just as Rousseau describes the community yet to be formed as prior and party to his contract. The
actual capacity of (at least some) men to make such a 'free'
contract becomes by contrast speculative, yet to be achieved, 'the
position of men *will* be very much changed'. That which is
already assumed by the contract becomes conditional; that which
is only actualized *through* the contract is, by the change of tense,
made to appear to precede the contract.

And what is the result of this new sexual relation, liberated
from bourgeois anxiety? A 'girl' giving herself completely to the
man she loves' (Engels, 1972: 139). So Engels like Rousseau has
by changing names turned total alienation into total freedom:

Rousseau, aware of this discrepancy, cannot but *mask* it with the very terms he uses when he has to note it: in fact he negates this Discrepancy either by designating the RP1 by the name of the RP2 (the people), or the RP2 by the name of the RP1 (the individual). Rousseau is lucid, but he can do no other. He cannot renounce this Discrepancy, which is the very solution, in the shape of the procedure which inscribes this discrepancy, not in the solution but in the conditions of the solution. That is why when Rousseau directly encounters this Discrepancy, he deals with it by denegation.

(Althusser, 1972: 131)

Althusser concludes, 'Denegation is repression', but it is also repression at its weakest, when the repressed returns too forcefully to be deflected and repression must resort to inversion or denial:

Among the Shawnees, Miamis and Delawares the custom has grown up of giving the children a gentile name of their father's gens in order to transfer them into it, thus enabling them to inherit from him.

'Man's innate casuistry. To change things by changing their names! And to find loopholes for violating tradition while maintaining tradition, when direct interest supplied sufficient impulse.'

(Engels, 1972: 120 note, quoting Marx)

Engels's project may have certain similarities to that of the Shawnees and their neighbours, but his innate casuistry is to maintain tradition while appearing to violate it. At the point where language and history institute each other, that which they exclude erupts, it returns with all the power of the repressed:

By *reproducing signifiers* . . . the subject crosses the border of the symbolic and reaches the semiotic chora, which is on the other side of the social frontier. The re-enacting of the signifying path taken from the symbolic unfolds the symbolic itself and – through the border that sacrifice is about to or has already presented on stage – opens it up to the motility where all meaning is erased.

(Kristeva, 1984: 79)

The border of the semiotic becomes the shore of an amniotic

ocean in *Heroes and Villains*.[26] The dissolution of Anna Wulf's game of naming, the play for identity, takes place:

> Before them and around them were all the wonders of the seashore, to which Marianne could scarcely put a single name, though everything had once been scrupulously named. The fans, fronds, ribbons, wreaths, garlands and lashes of weed had once been divided into their separate families, wracks, tangles, dulses, etc. . . . The spiny skinned family of echinoderms, which include the brittle stars, feather stars, the sea cucumbers with their mouth fringe of wispy gills and the sea lilies which have ten feathery arms waving in the water. The Jellyfish. And innumerable other names.
>
> Losing their names, these things underwent a process of uncreation and reverted to chaos, existing only to themselves in an unstructured world where they were not formally acknowledged, becoming an ever-widening margin of undifferentiated and nameless matter surrounding the outposts of man, who no longer made himself familiar with these things or rendered them authentic in his experience by the gift of naming.
>
> (Carter, 1969: 136–7)

We have come to the margin, the shore of language.

It is not surprising that semiotic violence 'breaks through' in the final stages of *Heroes and Villains*, but it can also be traced in *The Social Contract* and *The Origin of the Family, Private Property and the State*. Neither Rousseau nor Engels, in their approach to the founding sacrifice, can avoid the encounter with the end of language, though they, unlike Carter, attempt to conceal and contain this irruption of the semiotic and of violence. The substance of language and of women keeps interrupting the logic of sacrifice.

In *The Discourse on the Origin of Inequality* and *The Origin of the Family, Private Property and the State* as in *Heroes and Villains*, the establishment of the symbolic structure is accompanied by the irruption of all that order represses. Rousseau and Engels are involved not only in suppressing the discrepancies in their own arguments, but in masking the medium of that suppression, the 'play on words'. Since each depends on the prehistorical, the prelinguistic, to guarantee his 'contracts', such a deceit unmasks itself. This must offer some hope for the redefinition of history through the celebration and exploration of what history excludes.

Despite its reservations and fears, *Heroes and Villains* engages in just such a celebration and exploration. Far from concealing the thetic and sacrifice, this novel insists upon it and relishes the contradictions which make the thetic the mark of both the triumph of the symbolic *and* of the anachronic instability inherent in this stabilizing phase. Maternity may be a trap, but Marianne will not be 'got rid of' (Carter, 1969: 150) 'as easily as that'. She will be 'the Tiger Lady', we recall, 'and rule them with a rod of iron'. The substitution of matriarchy is no more than an inversion, according to Irigaray, but this potential matriarch is no earth mother. She is closer to 'the goddess in her antithesis' – Juliette becomes Durand. Thus her potential reign of terror is an image of an anti-society.

The potentialities of Marianne's tribe are left as ambiguous as the probable sex of Marianne's baby and are relevant only in their ambiguity. The sacrifice occurs and recurs. Marianne is raped, is married, Jewel dies; all three incidents accompanied by blood. Rape and marriage make some 'progress' towards integrating Marianne into Donally's power structure. The rape results in what Jewel describes as 'a necessary wound', the 'castration' perhaps which marks the feminine subject's accession to the symbolic order. Jewel's death, which induces her to indulge in 'sympathetic magic' (149), appears to complete the process. More than ironically, however, all other potential leaders *except* Marianne have died or been banished in the attempt to 'integrate' her.

Some residue of resistance to the 'contract' persists even in texts which positively re-endorse it. Rousseau cannot banish logical discrepancy and 'particular interest'. The spectre of 'feminine promiscuity' haunts the monogamous slumbers with which Engels attempts to close the discussion of the family. Rousseau sees the return to barbarism, or rather pre-civilization, as inevitable and even necessary. The quote from Morgan with which Engels concludes his chapter, 'The family', leaves open the possibility of a radical disruption of the relations of production and reproduction: 'Should the monogamian family in the distant future fail to answer the requirements of society . . . it is impossible to predict the nature of its successor' (Engels, 1972: 146). It must be asked whether Marianne's ferocity at the end of *Heroes and Villains*, her rejection of the sacrifice, is just such a reservation: that is, the element of reserve within the parties which is necessary to render the contract valid. She calls herself the Tiger Lady: it

is Donally's name, but she, with Jewel, drove Donally away. She
has betrayed the allegiances of her natural father, betrayed her
intellectual father, Donally, and betrayed her husband, Jewel, at
the first opportunity. Yet she is scarcely formed for guilt and
expresses no regrets for these betrayals.

The novel's conclusion points to the danger that the removal
of the maternal guarantee and the subversion of the socio-
symbolic order reduces sociality to blood-ties and the panic-
stricken repudiation of the other which makes tribal warfare not
only inevitable but constitutive of the tribe. *Heroes and Villains*
asks if, in overthrowing a totalizing ideology based on sameness,
one may not unleash a totalitarian violence which cannot accept
the otherness it can no longer evade. Marianne will be the greatest
loser if this occurs: her assimilation to the 'eternal feminine' would
form the linchpin of the frightening new order.

If there are dangers, there are also possibilities implicit in the
novel's ending. Marianne has understood she is a stranger to
herself. She knows who she is and is not when she stops thinking.
As 'Eve at the end of the world' (Carter, 1969: 124) she has tasted
knowledge.

Among the ever shifting names in *Heroes and Villains*, however,
Marianne is also called 'a little Lilith' (ibid.), Lilith who absolutely
refused to be party to the contract and whom the Law of the
Father turned into a most Medusa-like monster instead.

Lilith with a little knowledge would be a dangerous woman
indeed.

Chapter 4

(Un)Like Subjects

LOOKING BACK THROUGH OUR MOTHERS

In *Heroes and Villains* the prospect of infinite nameless things drew attention to names in themselves. In *The Social Contract* and *The Origin of the Family, Private Property and the State*, the intractable materiality of language insisted upon itself at the very point at which that materiality was concealed and denied by a sleight of philosophical hand. The specific gendering of this move in Engels's text is indicative of a 'crisis' which emerged in the nineteenth century and continues at the end of the twentieth. Engels can no longer assume the function of the feminine as mediator between nature and culture: he must *tell* us that there is a distinction between the sexual and the social (Engels, 1972: 139). He does move some way towards socializing the sexual in *The Origin of the Family, Private Property and the State*. In chronicling the 'world historical defeat of the female sex' he at least acknowledges that the female sex has a history. What is at stake for Engels, more acutely than for Rousseau, is a recuperation, a recolonization of the prehistorical territory of Woman as the other of history in the service of a new history:

> The period from 1800 to 1848 produced as many women writers as had the entire eighteenth century; and the 'women of '48,' the 'socialists of 1880,' and so on began a tradition of feminism in France concerned primarily with the problem of how to provide women with the status of subjects in history.
> Can it be that this new phase in women's discursive activity in the nineteenth century bears no relationship to the localization by philosophers of the second major epistemological break in the history of the West? That is, could it be that the

'two major transitions in Western thought' might be directly
linked to the subject of woman? Could not, for example, the
great Utopian theories of the nineteenth century be a kind of
ultimate effort to do without *the* Other?

(Jardine, 1985: 96–7)

The extent of the challenge posed by the discursivity of women
is indicated by Alice Jardine's proposal in *Gynesis* (1985) that
it is possible to 'perceive "feminism" not simply as being the
"symptom" or "result" of a contemporary crisis in legitimation
and meaning, but indeed as providing the *internal coherence* of
history itself' (97). There is a connection between this reimagining
of history and Showalter's incorporation of contemporary criticism into 'women's time' (Showalter, 1984: 42; see Introduction).
Like Showalter, Jardine is concerned with the implications for
women of the emergence of poststructuralist and deconstruc-
tionist theory as a response to a 'crisis in figurability', which is
above all a crisis in figuring women. Both women theorists
ponder whether the concern to articulate the 'other' may not also
be an attempt to pre-empt her articulation of her (other) self.
Unlike Showalter's work, Jardine's definition of history through
its relation to its 'other' is very much in keeping with the discourses of crisis and loss (of legitimacy) which she analyses. She
goes further than the male writers she discusses, however, in
redefining the terms in which that 'loss' is understood. The new
space which is created by Jardine's reconfiguration of woman and
modernity is one where history is defined by its interruption, an
interruption by the voice of what it designates as its silent and
formless opposite.[1]

BEARING THE WORD

Words do not speak, while women do; as producers of signs,
women can never be reduced to the status of symbols or tokens.

(Lévi-Strauss, 1977: vol. 2, 61)

Margaret Homans has characterized nineteenth-century women's
writing in terms of the conflict between woman, who bears meaning in and of herself as symbol within masculine discourse, and
writer, who bears the word quite differently. *Bearing the Word*
(1986) is centrally concerned with George Eliot and with the

burden of the Victorian ideology of womanhood in her work. Homans examines the modes in which the socio-symbolic role of the feminine subject in transmitting 'the word' of a (masculine) other is subverted by the woman writer even where (most emphatically where) the woman writer appears to submit to and reinforce that feminine role within her fiction. Commenting on Eliot's 'reading' of Wordsworth in *The Mill on the Floss*, Homans notes:

> When Eliot's heroines are torn between the imaginary world of Wordsworth and the practical world of the older brothers, they thematize the tension between Eliot's desire to listen silently to or repeat Wordsworth and her desire to show that what she reads in his authoritative texts was originally her own. To have the heroine enter fully into the world of imagination would be to concur that there are no truths beyond Wordsworth's, while to have her wholly allied with the brother would be, for Eliot, to deny altogether the values she shares with Wordsworth. Defending herself from the powerful male authority by inventing (or trusting) another, Eliot finds a way to be at once original and deferential.
>
> (Homans, 1986: 138)

This reading of Eliot helps to explain her position of authority within the literary canon; she affirms patriarchal authority even while she appropriates it. Central to Homans's reading of Eliot, however, is the insight that the woman writer/reader turns the brothers' 'instructions' (120) into something else by repeating them. Homans notes that Wordsworth's 'Tintern Abbey' and 'Nutting' are framed by a relationship between brother and sister defined by his role as speaker and hers as listener *and* embodiment of his discourse: 'he speaks, and for her to hear his words is, implicitly, to enact them' (120). Eliot sets up similar scenes in which the brother instructs and the sister listens/enacts. The literalizations of male texts by female protagonists are, however, drastic misreadings of those texts. Maggie Tulliver's literalization of Thomas à Kempis turns renunciation into assertion and

> To repeat Wordsworth literally would in any case be a contradiction in terms. Eliot exploits this contradiction fully: to pay proper homage to Wordsworth would be to have him speak through her as Maggie lets Thomas à Kempis speak through her; but to do so is necessarily to get Wordsworth wrong . . .

the more literal the repetition, the more divergent from, and subversive of, Wordsworth's aims, for to read Wordsworth literally in a female context is to become a realist.

(Homans, 1986: 138)

Homans points to a scene in *Middlemarch* where Dorothea seems poised on the brink of a visionary and Romantic transcendence, experiencing an internalization of outer 'forms' and 'the replacement of outer by inner light' (147):

> she did not really see the streak of sunlight on the floor more than she saw the statues: she was inwardly seeing the light of years to come in her own home and over the English fields and elms and hedge-bordered highroads; and feeling that the way in which they might be filled with joyful devotedness was not so clear to her as it had been.

(Eliot, 1973 [1871–2]: 185)

Dorothea turns away from this ironic and desolate inner light and her glimpse of it is framed by Will Ladislaw's steady gaze upon her. Eliot is correcting Will's perception that Dorothea is looking (outward) at the streak of light. Her preference for this natural object over the statues in the Vatican has a symbolic significance for Will which is sustainable only as long as her highly unromantic inner vision remains inarticulate. Eliot, in this meeting between Dorothea and Will, establishes a complex confrontation between realism and Romanticism:

> When Dorothea is, like Wordsworth at his highest moments of inward vision, blind to sunlight and to statues, her inner seeing of an inner light reveals to her ironically only the grimmest of realistic pictures. . . . It is that inward vision itself, and its inevitable fulfillment, against which she is in most need of defenses.

(Homans, 1986: 148)

The defence to which she turns is of course Will Ladislaw, who obligingly defines Dorothea in terms of an outer light which casts less desolate shadows than the light she sees within herself. Dorothea ceases to be 'Milton's daughter' only in order to bear another meaning. The brief episode in which she is the source of her own light and meaning is portentous of the enormous sense of loss which Alice Jardine identifies as the keynote of contemporary discourses concerned with 'legitimation':

> Loss of legitimation, loss of authority, loss of seduction, loss of genius – *loss*. I thread my way quickly through the narratives of these few somewhat randomly chosen theoretical fictions to emphasize only a small corner of the contemporary network that articulates this loss by speaking of woman – and women.
> (Jardine, 1985: 68)

The centrality of sexual relations to Engels's recuperation of (the 'legitimacy' of) the social contract is explicable in these terms and can be identified with the rebellious Will Ladislaw's appropriation of Dorothea (who as Milton's daughter and Casaubon's wife was the symbol of conservative and paternal power) to legitimate his own, new modes of knowledge and of seeing.

Eliot is quite as acutely aware as Engels of the stakes in this game of power and knowledge. During the short period when Dorothea originates rather than bears meaning, the foundation of western civilization and culture is uprooted. 'The field of written history' (Engels, 1972: 122) is strewn with debris. Rome, which has so often symbolized the triumphant continuity of western civilization, becomes the scene of the wreck of that civilization, a place of 'stupendous fragmentariness', of 'gigantic broken revelations', of 'ruins and basilicas', a 'vast wreck of ambitious ideals' (175–6).[2] 'A woman has nothing to laugh about when the symbolic order collapses' (Kristeva, 1986: 150) and it is not altogether surprising that Dorothea seeks refuge in what appears to be a new order.

Kristeva allows the possibility that a strong maternal identification may shield the daughter from the collapse of paternal legitimation. Homans sees Dorothea's turning away from her inner light towards 'the meeting eyes of love' (chapter 20) as a turning towards 'an imagined past . . . a reversion to innocence and to a metaphoric childhood' (Homans, 1986: 148) and notes that Eliot frequently describes Dorothea and Will as children when they are together or thinking of each other. In this context it is possible to read Will, a kind of imaginary brother, as well as Tom Tulliver and even Wordsworth, as fulfilling the role of non–identical double in Eliot's texts. They are very different from Thomas Stern and Jewel, however, and the beloved and impossible brothers of Eliot's heroines are often closer to Brontë's Hindley than Heathcliff. They represent paternal and patriarchal authority, but they also represent the reduction of that authority to the more manageable proportions of a sibling rival. Homans comments that the male poet, Wordsworth, has available to him an empowering relationship with nature as mother which is unavailable to Eliot as a woman writer. It is also true, however, that Eliot uses Wordsworth's texts to mediate the relationship of her own texts to a maternal nature which threatens 'stultifying immanence', death or literalization to the female figures in those texts. In this sense the brother figures in Eliot's writing fulfil the same function as the demon lovers in Brontë's and Carter's novels: they facilitate the postulation of a feminine relation to origin.

In *Middlemarch* Dorothea engages in the attempt to establish such a relationship, but does not succeed in it. Will also fails, however, in *his* attempt to exploit *his* own relation to origin. He will never be a Wordsworth, any more than Casaubon could have been a Milton. If Dorothea might be perceived as recuperating some of her relationship to the long-dead mother through her imaginative return to childhood with Will, it is difficult to avoid the conclusion that *Middlemarch* is more centrally concerned with the loss of 'legitimate' fathers. Eliot is in some ways as eager as Engels to seek a consolation for that loss. *Middlemarch*'s replacement of Dorothea's marriage to Casaubon by her marriage to Will is a variant of the reinstitution of those sexual relations initially presented as a form of oppression as a form of freedom in *The Origin of the Family, Private Property and the State*.

Eliot's sacrifice of Dorothea to the socio-symbolic contract is grudging, but perception of its inevitability is one of the primary features which distinguishes nineteenth- from twentieth-century women's fiction. According to Kristeva's schema in 'Women's time', Eliot's writing would correspond to the first generation of feminism which 'aspired to gain a place in linear time as the time of project and history' (Kristeva, 1986: 193). The divergence of *Wuthering Heights* from this project indicates that Kristeva is quite right to be uneasy with any chronological mapping of these generations. Moreover Eliot is herself uneasy and dissatisfied with 'the time of project and history'. In the images of Roman desolation there is not only a critique of Rome and the history it represents. There is also a much more urgent expression of the collapse of that history than either Rousseau or even Engels will admit. In the closing comments on the dissipation of Dorothea's potential,

Middlemarch does not trouble too much to conceal the nature of the sacrifice on which the monument of western culture and history is founded.

DAUGHTER OF THE FATHER? OR DAUGHTER OF THE MOTHER?

Carter, in her most recent novel, *Wise Children*, explores another possibility, one which has strong affinities with Eliot's strategic use of Wordsworth. The novel focuses on the fictionality of paternity ' "Father" is a hypothesis, while "mother" is a fact', comments Dora Chance, the illegitimate narrator of her theatrical family's history (Carter, 1991: 223). (Almost all the characters in the novel are the subjects of disputed paternity.) The myth of maternity is simultaneously undermined, however, by focusing on the *practice* of mothering. Dora's assertion that 'mother' is a fact distinct from the social and familial fictions that constitute paternity is undermined by its context. She is answering the query: 'Has it ever occurred to you that your mother might not be your mother?' (223). Dora and her twin sister, Nora, understand themselves to have been raised by their dead mother's former employer. The possibility that this adoptive 'Grandma' was their natural mother is dismissed: 'Grandma was fifty if she was a day when we came along and she'd have been proud as a peacock, she'd never have made up some cock and bull story about a chambermaid to explain us away, why should she?' (223). None the less the question cannot be banished. Dora earlier asserted that 'a mother is always a mother since a mother is a biological fact, but a father is a moveable feast' (216). Eventually she finds herself thinking, 'If only our mother could have been there to see. But which mother? . . . That's a problem' (226). Maternity too moves out of the realm of biological certainty: 'Mother is as mother does' (223).

This concern with biological origin and the questions of identity it raises is, for Carter as for Lessing, inextricable from the problem of literary authority for the woman writer. In *Wise Children*, Carter plays legitimate and traditional authority, in the form of Shakespeare, off against illegitimate and modernist literary authority, in the form of Joyce. The biological father of Dora and Nora Chance is Melchior Hazard, the last in a dynasty of Shakespearian actors. Melchior abandons his daughters, refusing to acknowledge kinship outside the law. He has and is an illusion of grandeur. His brief invasion of Hollywood becomes a parody of empire: 'acquiring control of the major public dreaming facility in the whole world. Shakespeare's revenge for the War of Independence. Once Melchior was in charge of the fabulous machine, he would bestride the globe' (Carter, 1991: 148). Melchior's ambitions are mere dreams of empire, however, nostalgic fantasies where history is replayed as spectacle and tragedy as musical comedy. (Melchior and his twin Peregrine have a great success with a show entitled *What! You Will!* in which Melchior stars as 'the eponymous William Shakespeare' [89]). In the Hazard family's attachment to Shakespeare and the public's attachment to the Hazards, Carter satirizes 'British patriotic and national identities, as they appear mediated through the cultural reproduction of Shakespearian drama' (Holderness, 1991: 75). The phenomenon partakes fully of that 'nostalgia, a craving, unappeasable hunger for what is irretrievably lost', that Graham Holderness has identified as the source of a peculiarly British form of postmodern and post-colonial 'patriotism' centred on key cultural icons, most notably Shakespeare. It is not surprising then that Carter seeks to demystify traditional and patriarchal authority through the Shakespearian figure of Melchior. According to Holderness, the cultural mediation of nationalism into 'patriotism' makes it possible to evade such disappointing realities as the loss of empire and of economic and military eminence:

> That loss may be regarded also as neither complete nor inconsolable, since the utterances of a 'patriotric poet' such as William Shakespeare (or Noël Coward)[3] can transcend the absence and negation of history, and suffuse the soul with – not exactly a new fulfilment, but at least a new longing, a new mixing of memory and desire.
>
> (Holderness, 1991: 75)

At the end of *Wise Children*, Melchior's vast longings are seen as the pathetic attempts of a neglected child to recapture his relation with his father:

> Here was the source of all that regal, tragic fancy dress – the purple robe, the rings, the pendant. . . . The son put on the lost father's clothes . . . hadn't he, as if the child had not been

the father of the man, in his case, but, during his whole long
life, the man had waited to become the father of himself.
(Carter, 1991: 224)

Melchior's kingdom is always already lost. Of all the Shakespearian roles he plays, he is most closely associated with Lear. He has
two 'wicked daughters' (193)[4] and though Dora proclaims herself
'a touch long in the tooth for Cordelia' (226) she does briefly play
that role to Melchior near the novel's end.

The only colony to figure directly in the novel is North America,
partly because it has superseded the power of the 'parent' country
and inverted the relation of centre to margin. America is the always
already lost colony in the mythography of the novel. Melchior
aspires to the grandeur of his pioneering father, Ranulph, but even
in Ranulph's heroic age – which corresponded with that of the
British Empire – America was a post-colonial threat to stability
and order. It was there that the impoverished Ranulph finally lost
the ability to distinguish between external reality and the internal
reality of his fantasy. 'By then, Old Ranulph couldn't tell the
difference between Shakespeare and living' (21), and during a run
of *Othello*, killed his wife, her lover and himself. It is in Hollywood, during the exhausting filming of *A Midsummer Night's
Dream*,[5] that Dora, wiser than her father, realizes that the cultural
icons he venerates are commodities, as indeed Melchior, Nora and
Dora herself are commodities in the cultural market-place:

We were both product *and* process, simultaneously, and it very
near broke us. And what did all our hard work add up to? Just
another Saturday night at the pictures! Your one shilling and
ninepenn'orth. Your helping of dark. What an equation. Our
sweated labour = your bit of fun.
'Like tarts,' said Nora, with prim distaste.
(Carter, 1991: 142)

When she finds Shakespeare on a bank-note Dora recognizes that
the culture on which the earlier generation of Hazards had sought
to capitalize has 'turned into actual currency' (191). It is not only
the daughters, but also the fathers who are units of exchange.
Melchior too is the 'sign of the idea of a hero' (Carter, 1969:
72). He is presented throughout the novel as an accumulation of
theatrical gestures: 'Smile in public, cry in public, live in public,
die in public' (1991: 205).

The same air of artificiality characterizes his twin brother Peregrine, but while Melchior plays at life, seeking to turn illusion into reality, Peregrine plays tricks, turning reality into a realm of magic and illusion. Dora apologizes, but cannot avoid 'describing him in the language of the pulp romance' (30). Peregrine, a wanderer as his name suggests, is largely associated with first North and then South America. (The two boys were separated after their parents' death.) If his brother seeks to regain lost territories and make them his own, Peregrine seeks exile: 'He reached his boredom threshold and was gone' (143). Melchior is a Shakespearian hero: Peregrine's name identifies him with a minor character in Jonson and an outsider at that. He is a teller of tales, as well as a conjuror: 'He gave us all histories, we could choose which ones we wanted – but they kept on changing, so' (31). His Joycean connections surface gradually. He addresses Nora and Dora as 'floradora', linking the singing and dancing sisters with Joyce's 'Sirens' (Joyce, 1986 [1922]: 210–39). His name, which has such an excess of connections and meanings, is also that of two of the compilers of the *Annals of the Four Masters*, 'the Gaelic book which is most frequently mentioned' in *Finnegans Wake* (Atherton, 1974: 89). Peregrine's most striking Joycean feature, however, is his resurrection on the occasion of his brother's (and his own) hundredth birthday: ' "Thunder and lightning!" sang our Peregrine. "Did yez think I was dead?" ' (Carter, 1991: 206). Peregrine acts as father to the daughters his brother won't acknowledge and is Melchior's double and opposite. In contrast to his brother's obsession with their father, Peregrine 'was his mother's boy' (18). He is Dora's complement and ally, non-identical double to her as well as to Melchior. Peregrine is closer to the demon lover than Heathcliff, Jewel, or Thomas Stern, since he is the only one who returns from the dead.[6] The incest and quest motifs are comically fused when Dora seduces Peregrine on her seventy-fifth and his hundredth birthday. This is the ultimate degree of carnival[7] – and the ultimate compliment to Joycean vitality. Not only does Peregrine rise from the dead, but he brings with him Tiffany (a member of the illegitimate extended family 'invented' (35) by Grandma) who was believed to have drowned herself, and new life in the form of the twin children of Dora's half-brother, Gareth.

Wise Children does more than displace traditional by modernist literary authority, though such a displacement occurs. Melchior, who cannot compete with his brother's Lazarus act, is finally 'upstaged' (207) and 'with his crown still on, though much askew' (228), he presides over the closing carnival less as the ghost of imperial majesty than as lord of misrule. Both Melchior and Peregrine are characters in Dora's fiction, their stories told 'inadvertently' (11) in 'the course of assembling notes towards my own autobiography'. Peregrine supplies the pulp romance and Melchior is no more substantial. After the great reunion at the novel's end Dora, discussing their father with Nora, wonders: 'If we haven't been making him up all along . . . if he isn't just a collection of our hopes and dreams and wishful thinking in the afternoons' (230).

Peregrine is not the only fabulist in this tale. It is not coincidental that Dora has an identical twin called Nora, but Dora distances herself from the Joycean female. 'She [Nora] said, "Yes!" to life and I said, "Maybe . . ." ' (5). Dora is no Molly Bloom then, but a variety of Joycean female roles are suggested. Her description of Peregrine in terms of 'pulp romance' can be read as a kind of retort by Gerty McDowell. The 'Nausicaa' episode in *Ulysses* parodies certain elements in the 'demon lover' motif: 'She could see at once by his dark[8] eyes that he was a foreigner' (Joyce, 1986 [1922]: 293). This episode is on one level the epitome of the feminization of popular culture and the appropriation of the aesthetic to the masculine 'author'. It is the implication of such an authorial presence that ironically frames Gerty's fantasy and makes her story and particularly her way of telling it the debased opposite of that authority. There is a double irony, however, for the distance from which the avant-garde artist views Gerty's 'marmalady drawsery' (Joyce, 1966 [1957]: 135) prose is also the distance from which Bloom views Gerty. In effect, Joyce's parody of 'women's fiction' is identified as a male masturbatory fantasy, an identification which not only undermines the hierarchy of prose style and gender initially proposed, but also opens up the possibility of reciprocity. 'Still it was a kind of language between us', thinks Bloom. Karen Lawrence has recently claimed that 'in "Nausicaa", Joyce opened up the possibility of female desire', though she must admit that 'the fantasy was rooted in the patriarchal view' (Lawrence, 1990: 252).

Wise Children inverts the terms of the parody. Peregrine plays 'demon lover' to Dora's demystified version of both the heroine and narrator of women's fiction. There are strong parallels with

Heroes and Villains. Ironic distance is a property of literary authority, but in both these novels it is improperly centred on feminine
protagonists, Marianne and Dora. In the wedding scene in *Heroes
and Villains* this prevented the frank exchange of women and
signifiers, was linked with incest and challenged the sacrifice
which instituted the thetic. It presaged the end of language and
the approach of death. In *Wise Children*, the consequence of transgression is suspended, the threat of madness or death replaced by
a 'laughing apocalypse' (Kristeva, 1982: 206) that never quite
happens.

MYTHS OF WRITING

In *Bearing the Word* the discussion of Eliot, so concerned with the
loss of legitimate fathers, is interrupted by a lengthy analysis of
Elizabeth Gaskell's *My Diary: The Early Years of My Daughter
Marianne*. Homans makes clear that the title of that text is not
Gaskell's own, but is none the less indicative of a confusion of
identity between mother and daughter which permeates Gaskell's
record of three and a half years of her own and her daughter's
lives. The diary format in itself suggests a strict, linear and
chronological record of Marianne's development and her mother's
'plans' and instructions. Yet, as Homans points out, there is
a tension between the mother's desire to induct her daughter
successfully into the symbolic order and the mother's desire to
repeat her own 'happy daughterhood' (Homans, 1986: 153)
through her relationship to her daughter. Homans points out that
Gaskell is quite aware of the dangers implicit in this desire for
repetition, yet neither endows the mother–daughter relationship
with the nightmarish qualities it has for Irigaray and Lessing. In
turning aside from Eliot, who 'became the figurative mother of
George Lewes's adolescent sons at the same time that she began
writing fiction', to Gaskell, who 'raised four daughters while
writing', Homans rewrites the dilemma of the feminine subject
as she had delineated it in *Middlemarch*. At this point *Bearing
the Word* substitutes the search for an empowering mother for
Dorothea's quest for a 'legitimate' father:

> Allowing her text to be a conduit for maxims, laws, and biblical
> quotations, Gaskell at once yields to the paternal order's
> requirements and finds a strategy for reconciling motherhood

and writing, albeit a minimal sort of writing. That Gaskell has in mind a myth of writing and of authorship as she writes her relation to her daughters (and, briefly, to her foster mother) is suggested at the very start of the diary in a series of passages that implicitly compare the 'formation of her little daughter's character' to a novelist's formation of literary characters, a comparison that originates in Marianne's being called in the text of the diary, the 'little subject,' both of Gaskell's maternal attention and of her text.

(Homans, 1986: 169)

Gaskell's 'reconciling' of motherhood and writing differs from Eliot's reconciliation of sisterhood and originality in that it is a myth of woman as writer constructed in exclusively female terms. The 'little subject' in this myth is constructed in terms of a pre-Oedipal relation to the mother. More importantly, the literary subject writes, at least in part, to preserve that relationship (with her daughter and her mother).[9] Indeed the text becomes a place where that pre-symbolic relationship is preserved – in the symbolic, in a diary, in language and time: 'I sometimes think I may find this little journal a great help in recalling the memory of my darling child if we should lose her' (quoted in Homans, 1986: 163).[10] *Bearing the Word* displaces the daughter/writer's relationship to the father/brother from the centre of its discussion of Eliot. (When Homans returns to discuss Eliot it will be to discuss the novelist as the author of 'Madonna Romola') (1986: 189). The shift of focus to Gaskell substitutes for the loss of 'paternal legitimation' (Kristeva, 1986: 158) a myth of feminine 'authority' rooted in the author's relationship to her mother and daughter. *Wise Children* explores the relationship between these two myths of writing.

LANGUAGE AND LEGITIMACY

In *Bearing the Word* Homans defines her 'mother–daughter' language in terms of 'literalization' (as opposed to figurative language). Homans distances herself from Julia Kristeva's work and distinguishes 'the mother–daughter language I am discussing' (Homans, 1986: 19) from Kristeva's semiotic, which Homans identifies with the mother–son dyad. There is also an implicit critique of Kristeva's emphasis on the 'central linguistic element in the writing of such modern male writers as Joyce, Céline and

Artaud' (18), in contrast to Homans's exploration of the upsurge
of maternal language in Woolf. This constitutes a significant departure on Homans's part from her distrust of the concepts of
women's language and particularly of 'literal' language in *Women
Writers and Poetic Identity*. Her arguments in the earlier work against
the association of the feminine and the literal and her insistence on
the necessarily representational and 'artificial' nature of language
are far more convincing than the acceptance of the possibility of
'literal' language in *Bearing the Word*. Identification of feminine and
literal language recurs even in the work of a critic acutely aware
of the dangers of that identification.

In *Wise Children*, by contrast, the artificiality of language is
inextricably linked with the artificiality of maternity. Carter
rejects the concept of women's language as 'the lust for the real
thwarted by the necessary artifice of language'. In this she is in
sympathy with Kristeva's suspicion of the 'semi-aphonic corporeality' which makes of some contemporary women's writing
merely a support for 'phallocratic power' (Kristeva, 1986: 207).
Kristeva is here obviously alluding to '*écriture féminine*' and to
Cixous's injunction to women to 'write the body'. While it is
true that Kristeva herself is far from advocating 'writing with
mother's milk', she does posit a special relationship between the
maternal, the subversive and the poetic:

> The force of *writing* lies precisely in its return to the space-time
> previous to the phallic stage – indeed previous even to the
> identifying or mirror stage – in order to grasp the becoming
> of the symbolic function as the drive's *différance* faced with the
> absence of the object.
>
> (Kristeva, 1984: 142)

Such a 'return', the recoil, 'in order to grasp the becoming of
the symbolic function' occurs in *Heroes and Villains*. Marianne's
predicament could readily be described as that 'wedding to a
torrent' (1981: 162) which Kristeva describes as the (inter)action
of 'the novel as polylogue', the polyphonic text. In this respect
it foreshadows the fate of Paul in *The Hothouse by the East River*.
In Kristeva's own engagement with the 'ever-widening margin
of undifferentiated and nameless matter surrounding the outposts
of man' (Carter, 1969: 136), she has always fought a rearguard
action against the return of 'the most archaic death drive' (Kristeva, 1986: 158), through the primary narcissism precariously

harnessed by the symbolic, not least through the idealization of the relationship to the mother (161). The semiotic is inextricable from madness, regression and death:

> The invasion of her speech by these unphrased, nonsensical, maternal rhythms, far from soothing her, or making her laugh, destroys her symbolic armour and makes her ecstatic, nostalgic or mad. . . . She can take pleasure in it. . . . But she can just as easily die from this upheaval.
>
> (Kristeva, 1986: 150)

The female subject here is the daughter, who must choose, 'Daughter of the father? Or daughter of the mother?' (151). This is a reformulation of Cixous's 'Castration or decapitation?' (1981) and, as Kristeva's litany of female literary 'suicides without a cause' (1986: 157) points out, this 'impossible dialectic' (156) has produced spectacular texts of the id most ambiguously uttered (Cixous, 1976: 889) but also the desire 'not to be' (Kristeva, 1986: 156–8).

There seems to be little option but to stage the occasional raid and fleeting ambush on the border which defines this conflict, and rapidly retreat. The risks involved in any attempt to redefine the territory are perilously high for the woman writer. Kristeva warns in *About Chinese Women*, 'if no paternal legitimation comes along to dam up the inexhaustible non-symbolized drive, she collapses into psychosis or suicide' (158). Explicitly referring to Joyce and a number of his modernist counterparts, Kristeva comments that:

> In an analogous situation a man can imagine an all-powerful, though always insignificant, mother in order to 'legitimize' himself: to make himself known, to lean on her, to be guided by her through the social labyrinth, though not without his own occasional ironic commentary.
>
> (Kristeva, 1986: 158)

The 'unreadable' (42) *Finnegans Wake* legitimizes itself through its engagement with that unrepresentable excess represented by the feminine. *Wise Children* misreads it as a resource for the woman writer renegotiating her relation to origin, biological and literary. The demon lover scenario is played out with far more intensity at this metanarrative level than it is within the narrative in the relation between Dora and Peregrine. Joyce's fiction is posited as the non-identical double of *Wise Children*. Carter foregrounds the presumption implicit in the appropriation of this icon of the avant-garde and postmodernism. Illegitimacy is not only the subject, but also the condition of the narrative:

> I, Dora Chance, in the course of assembling notes towards my own autobiography, have inadvertently become the chronicler of all the Hazards, although I should think that my career as such will go as publicly unacknowledged by the rest of the dynasty as my biological career has done for not only are Nora and I, as I have already told you, by-blows, but our father was a pillar of the legit. [sic] theatre and we girls are illegitimate in every way – not only born out of wedlock, but we went on the halls, didn't we?

> (Carter, 1991: 11)

Dora frequently acknowledges the derivative quality of her writing. She owes her literary knowledge and aptitude to an affair with a novelist turned scriptwriter, Ross O'Flaherty, referred to throughout as 'Irish': 'He didn't have sufficient cash to buy me a mink. Therefore he gave me Culture' (123). This 'Irish' is no more Joyce than Will Ladislaw is Wordsworth. He is described as 'American to the core' (120) and the parallels to F. Scott Fitzgerald are striking. It is, however, with 'Irish' that Peregrine is first discovered singing 'Finnegan's Wake'. The down-at-heel scriptwriter enables Dora to illegitimately become the chronicler of all the Hazards and the relationship between these two illuminates Carter's resourcing of *Finnegans Wake* in *Wise Children*. On the one hand, 'Irish' empowers Dora to tell her own story: 'He did wonders for my grammar, not to mention my grasp of metaphor, as witness the style of this memoir' (120). When he tells her story, makes her a character in *his* fiction, however, she is

> bound to say my best friend wouldn't recognize me in the far-from-loving portrait he'd penned after I'd gone. I'm the treacherous, lecherous chorus girl with her bright red lipstick that *bleeds* over everything. . . . Vulgar as hell. The grating Cockney accent. The opportunism. The chronic insensitivity to a poet's heart. And you couldn't trust her behind a closed door. Such turned out to be the eternity the poet promised me, the bastard.

> (Carter, 1991: 119–20)

Even if, at the novel's close, the authority of tradition is overcome by modern carnival, the modern and carnival figures, 'Irish' and Peregrine, are deeply implicated in patriarchal tradition. This is evident in Peregrine's introduction of 'Irish': 'I want you to meet my dear friend, *mon semblable, mon frère*, my collaborator, just he and I, and William Shakespeare, working on the script. Irish, meet Floradora' (118). (The two men are scripting the film version of *A Midsummer Night's Dream*.) Peregrine's medley of literary reference indicates the continuity of the traditional and modern, but also confounds the distinction between cultural legitimacy and the culture industry. Carter's use of popular forms is part of a trend in which her Joycean resources partake,[11] but for her, as for Spark, these forms becomes the instrument, not the object, of ironic distance. It is worth speculating on whether the simultaneous derision and feminization of such forms has promoted women writers' active recuperation of them. Such inversion creates a different kind of ironic distance, one necessary to any renegotiation of literary difference. It pre-empts the possibility of becoming the faithful daughter in a discourse which, however radical in its potential, is limited by its Oedipal trajectory. For Lessing the greatest threat to the woman's position as 'author' was the maternal and material in language. For Carter, the threat seems to be that the maternal and material in language are already a resource at the disposal of the (literary) masters. This is related to her scepticism about the valorization of maternity. In both instances, there is a danger of returning the feminine to an image of alterity, a 'figure' for an other's desire:

> The phrase 'misses in print' suggests the errancy and waywardness of language which for Joyce, particularly in his later works, is figured by women. Biddy Doran's midden heap in *Finnegans Wake* is an image of the uncontaminated, uncontrollable material of language. . . . (The female figures the comic, almost slapstick potential in language that eludes patriarchal control.
>
> (Lawrence, 1990: 244)

As Cixous, in her celebration of those who 'slip . . . something by . . . of woman' (1976: 877) makes clear, such a figuring is a resource, an escape route for the woman writer. While the impossibility of representing the feminine is acknowledged in the texts of Joyce and others, however, engagement with this impossibility becomes a touchstone for a new kind of literary authority,[12] which, once again, is symbolized, not exercised, by women. 'Anna Livia is a thief, a retriever and interpreter of other people's language' (Lawrence, 1990: 244), but for Lawrence, her theft of language can only serve

> as a model for its citationality. She provides a figure for an illegality, something outside of the patriarchal rebellion that is a killing of the literary forefather by the male heir apparent. She offers, metaphorically, a way out of the discourse of Freudian rebellion, offers instead a term for the Derridean 'drift' in language.
>
> (Lawrence, 1990: 244)

Much of Lawrence's defence of Joyce against feminist critique centres on his anxiety about his representation of women and his anticipation of that feminist critique. 'Scorching[13] my hand and starving my famine to make his private linen public' (Joyce, 1992a [1939]: 196), complain the washerwomen in *Finnegans Wake*. There are parallels here with Dora's complaint about her misrepresentation in 'Irish' 's publication of his private linen in 'the last flame of a burned out case', his final collection of stories (Carter, 1991: 119). *Finnegans Wake* does raise the possibility that women may be more than figures for 'something outside' the patriarchal agonistics of literary succession. The text never vanquishes the spectre of 'the mother of the book with a dustwhisk tabularasing his obliteration done upon her involucrum' (Joyce, 1992a [1939]: 50). Dora, who 'never rates more than a footnote in the biographies' of her literary mentor (Carter, 1991: 119), turns that prestigious figure into a minor character in her own story. This story is of a quest familiar in its form, but with an other hero: 'The urge has come upon me before I drop to seek out an answer to the question that has always teased me, as if the answer were hidden somewhere, behind a curtain: whence came we? Whither goest we?' (11). This question of identity is at the heart of all the riddles in *Wuthering Heights, Heroes and Villains, Landlocked* and even perhaps *Finnegans Wake*. But *Finnegans Wake* is itself a riddle. In *Heroes and Villains*, the question of female identity, repudiation of the patrilinear and exploration of that 'wilderness of unknowability' (Carter, 1991: 12) that constitutes the maternal, foreclose 'the frank exchange of women'. Joyce's epical forgery (Joyce, 1992a [1939]: 181) performs the same function in relation to words.

Wise Children imitates this only in its extravagant intertextuality, but *Finnegans Wake* none the less facilitates the comic approach to the thetic boundary. Joyce's excess and exhaustion of language themselves become a 'figure' in *Wise Children*, the unconscious of the text, its demonic other. The intertextual relation between *Wise Children* and *Finnegan's Wake* is a 'passage from one sign system to another' of the type described by Kristeva in *The Revolution in Poetic Language* (1984: 59). Kristeva there expresses a preference for the term *transposition* over the term *intertextual* precisely because 'it specifies a new articulation of the thetic' (60). Transposition is crucial to the relation between 'signifying process' and 'social practice' (61). For Kristeva, 'mimesis and poetic language . . . question the very principle of the ideological because they question the *unicity* of the thetic (the precondition for meaning and signification) and prevent its theologization' (61). She premises the right of mimesis and poetic language to enter into social debate on 'their confrontation with signification and denotation but also with all meaning'. Carter (re)turns to a text which is a highly significant site of the modernist confrontation with meaning and a site of infinite transposition between sign systems in order to produce a new articulation of the thetic.

The collapse of this project into chaos seems ecstatically and dangerously close when Dora briefly contemplates the possibility that her carnivalesque coupling with Peregrine might have brought her father's house down, 'sent it all sky high, destroyed all the terms of every contract, set all the old books on fire, wiped the slate clean' (Carter, 1991: 222). This is the tragic conclusion of *Heroes and Villains* replayed as comedy. But at this point, when all boundaries appear to have been transgressed, Dora acknowledges she can go no further: 'There are limits to the power of laughter and though I may hint at them from time to time, I do not propose to step over them' (220).

Wise Children draws back from the limit where carnival ends (222). For inextricable from the novel's celebration of the irrelevance of biological origin is the denial of death implicit in all resurrection stories. In answer to her 'Wither goest we?', Dora initially answers 'Oblivion' (11), but by novel's end she and Nora have realized that 'if we've got those twins to look out for, we can't afford to die for at least another twenty years' (230). Carter draws attention to these limitations in her attempt to exceed the law of the father and the rebellion of the son. 'The carnival's got

to stop, some time,' Dora admonishes Peregrine (222). Claiming
affinity with yet another literary predecessor, a female one this
time, Dora passes over the war in her memoir: 'Let other pens
dwell on guilt and misery. A., for Austen, Jane. *Mansfield Park*.
I do not wish to talk about the war. Suffice to say it was no
carnival, not the hostilities. No carnival' (163). In her use of
Bakhtin, as well as Joyce, Carter has found a mode of celebrating
difference, releasing its subversive potential. In one sense she
has gone further than Kristeva, who associates carnival with a
subversive undercurrent within the patriarchal tradition: 'Rabelais,
Swift and Dostoevsky . . . Joyce, Proust, Kafka' (Kristeva, 1986:
42). But there is still a limit. Dora leaves her father's house
standing, her story pauses before the possibility of a trangression
from which there could be no recovery:

> But truthfully, these glorious pauses do, sometimes, occur in
> the discordant but complementary narratives of our lives and if
> you choose to stop the story there, at such a pause, and refuse
> to take it any further, then you can call it a happy ending.
>
> (Carter, 1991: 227)

TEXTUAL DOUBLENESS

Wise Children can envisage the comic collapse of the symbolic
order, because it has appropriated a powerful, illegitimate
paternity while celebrating an exuberantly non-essentialist
maternity. That vision is recognized as a glimpse of the impossible, however. Kristeva's 'Stabat Mater' takes a very different
route towards that 'limit' and undertakes the transgression Dora
imagines. A damming up (Kristeva, 1986: 158) does occur, of
course, but it is of a different and redefining sort. This is achieved
primarily by the shift in the conception of the border itself. It is
not 'surrounding the outposts' (Carter, 1969: 136), but at the
heart of the text. This centrality is not thematic but physical.
'Stabat Mater' is centred on an empty space. The essay is split,
the double columns a technique shared with Derrida's *Glas* (1974).
The fusion and separation of these columns in Kristeva's text
enacts the drama of separation and the desire for compensation
for that separation with which the essay concerns itself:

A mother is a continuous separation, a division of the very flesh. And consequently	Moreover, when Freud analyses the advent and transformation of

a division of language – and it has always been so.

monotheism he emphasizes that Christianity comes closest to pagan myths by integrating . . . a pre-conscious acknowledgement of the maternal feminine.

(Kristeva, 1986: 178)[14]

'Stabat Mater' separates and fuses, is poetic and analytical. Maternity is celebrated through the only discourse available to it, but that discourse is put into question. If there is a danger of 'collapse' into the semi-aphonic corporeality which would support the same old abstractions, it is counterpointed, in the manner of the baroque music to which the title refers, by a rigorous interrogation of that discourse, by its disruption and by a negation which establishes no alternative hegemony. It is an open text which, advertising its openness and ambiguity by resort to typographical innovation, parodies its own refusal of closure.

In an observation parallel to and extending Carter's comment on the function of the womb as symbol of eternity, a place outside time which guarantees time, Kristeva comments:

In asserting that 'in the beginning was the Word', Christians must have found such a postulate sufficiently hard to believe, and, for whatever it was worth, they added its compensation, its permanent lining: the maternal receptacle, purified as it might be by the virginal fantasy. Archaic maternal love would be an incorporation of my suffering that is unfailing, unlike what often happens with the lacunary network of signs.

The *Stabat Mater* which in the text attributed to Jacopone da Todi, enthralls us today through the music of Palestrina, Pergolesi, Haydn and Rossini.

Let us listen to the baroque style of the young Pergolesi (1710–36) who was dying of tuberculosis when he wrote his immortal *Stabat Mater*. His musical inventiveness, which, through Haydn, later reverberated in the work of Mozart, probably constitutes his one and only claim to immortality.

(Kristeva, 1986: 176)

A strong contrast in style between the two parallel passages is not consistent throughout 'Stabat Mater', but in general a distinction is observed between the left-hand column, which is more poetic, lyrical, saturated with the language of Christian myth and of the myths of 'maternality', and the right-hand column, which is an erudite, precise and scholarly exposition of the development and function of the myth of the Virgin Mother. The relationship of the columns varies. There are frequent contrasts and even contradictions, interrogation by their juxtaposition of the assumptions prevalent in either column at any given point. A complementary relation may also be established, as is apparent in the passage above. Here the left-hand column is engaged in the ironic exposure, through the very language which seeks to conceal it, of the mutuality of womb and word. This play on 'the Word' as myth and mythical origin is counterpointed by a play on the word as fact. Names, dates, references abound in the right-hand column. The maternal compensation can become a threat, however.

Belief in the mother is rooted in fear, fascinated with a weakness – the weakness of language.

Christianity, it is true, finds its calling in the displacement of that bio-maternal determinism through the postulate that immortality is mainly that of the name of the Father.

(Kristeva, 1986: 175)

The litany of proper names, 'Palestrina, Pergolesi, Haydn and Rossini', the erection of the male canon of 'great' artists 'enthralls us'. This glamorous patrilinear tradition surely proclaims that 'immortality is mainly that of the name of the father'. The ambiguity of 'enthrall' alerts us to the ironies of these passages, however.[15] The 'claim to immortality' of the name of the father is mocked even while it takes on the status of 'historical fact' sanctified by those absolute names, numbers – Pergolesi (1710–36). It is a mere 'postulate' and so 'hard to believe' that the displacement which is Christianity's (name) 'calling' can be reversed. Not only is the 'young Pergolesi (1710–36) . . . dying of tuberculosis' (and subject to linear time) contrasted to 'his immortal *Stabat Mater*'. The probability that 'his one and only claim to immortality' is 'his musical inventiveness, which, through Haydn, later reverberated in the works of Mozart' is counterpointed by a declaration that this 'lacunary network of signs', the names of the fathers, fails. The reassurance which accompanies this, 'Archaic maternal love would be an incorporation of my suffering that is unfailing', is itself undermined, however. The other immortality offered by the reluctance to acknowledge that the mother or the music are themselves mortal is more challenge than compensation, a question not an answer. Can the cry to the 'mother, source of love', be 'merely a remnant of the period' (1986: 176)? And if it is not? If the immortality of the naming game is a paltry shadow of a 'bio-maternal determinism'?

Any belief, anguished by definition, is upheld by the fascinated fear of language's impotence. Every God, even including the God of the Word, relies on a mother Goddess . . .

When this cry burst forth, referring to Mary facing her son's death *'Eia Mater, fons amoris!'* ('Hail mother, source of love!') – was it merely a remnant of the period?

(Kristeva, 1986: 176)

'Every God, even including the God of the Word, relies on a mother Goddess' not to exercise the power with which the word has of necessity endowed its guarantor. It is on this complicity that the powerful alliance of word and womb is based. By, fraudulently (as Jane Gallop points out [1982]) assuming the impossible power of the mother as the place of the speaking subject, 'Stabat Mater' uses that alliance against itself. 'Mary defying death' must contend with the maternal body as the place of 'borders, separations, vertigos' (1986: 176).

THE MOTHER AND DEATH (OF THE WORD)

'Stabat Mater' does more than explore maternity as the 'compensation' for the Word and the denial of death. The audacious fraud at its heart is explicated in the opening sentences of the essay:

If it is not possible to say of a *woman* what she *is* (without running the risk of abolishing her difference), would it perhaps be different concerning the *mother*, since that is the only function of the 'other sex' to which we can definitely attribute existence?

(Kristeva, 1986: 161)

The irony of this apparently tentative opening emerges as textual play of the kind which restores poor Pergolesi to tuberculosis. Mortality proliferates. 'Stabat Mater' uses the maternal 'fantasy' against itself, but 'the actual world is constantly present in fantasy, by negation' (Russ, 1973: 52). The myth of maternity is the fantasy which negates death, particularly death as the limit of language. The myth therefore implies that life and death are at the disposal of the mother.

Jane Gallop in *The Daughter's Seduction*, her work on feminism and psychoanalysis, has identified the residual belief in 'the phallic Mother, in command of the mysterious processes of life and death, meaning and identity', as a lingering problem in the work of Luce Irigaray (Gallop, 1982: 115). Such belief paralyses the daughter in a relation of eternal minority, according to Gallop. The question must then of course be immediately asked, why is paralysis not also the fate of the son, who shares this fantasy?

The answer must lie in the differing fantasies available to men and women of *return* to this 'ideal' mother, who can make everything all right.

Jane Gallop's commentary on 'And the one doesn't stir without the other' and on 'Stabat Mater'[16] juxtaposes these two texts, which she hesitates to classify as discourse of the daughter and of the mother respectively, and thereby shifts the emphasis of 'Stabat Mater' from that of the relationship of mother and son to that of mother and daughter. In this respect Gallop's discussion imitates developments within 'Stabat Mater' itself. In order to trace the changing emphasis in the description of the 'child' it is necessary to examine the structure of the interplay between the essay's two columns.

'Stabat Mater' commences as a straightforward historical analysis of the cult of the Virgin Mother, in particular as it has been described by Marina Warner as a key to understanding the absorption of femininity into motherhood in western culture (1976)[17]. This prosaic analysis is suddenly interrupted by a literally 'bold' intrusion from a new left-hand column. In a much earlier essay, on Bakhtin's *Problems of Dostoevsky's Poetics*, Kristeva had celebrated Bakhtin's transformation of diachrony into synchrony, his situating of 'the text within history and society, which are then seen as texts read by the writer, and into which he inserts himself by rewriting them' (Kristeva, 1986: 36). The analysis of such interrelations reveals '*linear* history . . . as an abstraction' and 'the only way a writer can participate in history is by transgressing this abstraction'. Carter's fiction tends to transgress this abstraction at the level of narrative itself, in her use of the speculative mode, in the anachronic elements of her fiction, in her related use of chance/Chances[18] and of 'adventure-time' (Bakhtin, 1981: 93):

> this time usually has its origin and comes into its own in just those places where the normal, pragmatic and pre-meditated course of events is interrupted – and provides an opening for sheer chance, which has its own specific logic. This logic is one of random contingency [*sovpadenie*], which is to say *simultaneity* (meetings) and *chance rupture* (nonmeetings), that is a logic of random disruptions in time.
>
> (Bakhtin, 1981: 92)

'Stabat Mater' follows the logic of random disruption, not as a process of narrative, but as a process of writing. The dialogical relationship between columns is also an anachronic relationship. Kristeva criticizes feminism for identifying maternity with the 'idealization of primary narcissism' which has absorbed both maternity and femininity into a fantasy of 'a lost territory' (161). The result of perpetuating the confusion has been

> A negation or rejection of motherhood by some avant-garde feminist groups. Or else an acceptance – conscious or not – of its traditional representations by the great mass of people, women and men.

FLASH – instant of time or of dream without time. . . . Photos of what is not yet visible and that language necessarily skims over from afar, allusively. Words that are always too distant, too abstract for this underground swarming of seconds, folding in unimaginable spaces.

Christianity is doubtless the most refined symbolic construct in which femininity . . . is focused on *Maternality*. Let us call 'maternal' the ambivalent principle that is bound to the species, on the one hand, and on the other stems from an identity catastrophe that causes the Name to topple over into the unnameable, that one imagines is femininity, non-language or body.

> (Kristeva, 1986: 161–2)

After the flash of 'WORD FLESH'[19] a single discursive column resumes which quotes biblical and apocryphal sources and traces the scholastic development of Mariology to the point where 'the path that would lead to Mary's deification was then clear' (166). At this point the double columns return, a strong contrast emerging between the description of the process of deification and an exploration of the pain of separation in childbirth:

My body is no longer mine, it doubles up, suffers, bleeds, catches cold, puts its teeth in, slobbers, coughs, is covered with pimples and it laughs. And yet when its own joy, my child's, returns, its smile washes only my eyes. But the pain, its pain – it comes from inside, never remains apart, other.

It fell upon Duns Scotus to change the hesitation over the promotion of a mother goddess within Christianity into a logical problem, thus saving them both, the Great Mother as well as logic. He viewed Mary's birth as *praeredemptio*, as a matter of congruency.

(Kristeva, 1986: 166–7)

A challenge to this logical solution of the problem emerges in the incongruousness of this reversal of the problem of separation.

Gallop points out that the presumption that the mother controls the processes of separation and identity and the resentment felt at either her desertion or refusal to let go locks the mother 'into the classic role of receiver of the child's discourse' (Gallop, 1982: 115). In 'And the one doesn't stir without the other' (Irigaray, 1981), 'the distinction of second and first person pronouns gives the daughter whatever fragile separateness she has. As long as she speaks there is a distinction' (Gallop, 1982: 115). Gallop does not emphasize sufficiently here the fragility of that separateness[20] and is too hasty in making a distinction within Irigaray's essay which she hesitates to make between it and 'Stabat Mater'. This context does illuminate, however, the significance of the attempt in 'Stabat Mater' to speak of the mother's pain, to speak of separation as experienced by and out of the control of the mother. Now that 'she speaks there is a distinction', at the very place which was to deny all distinctions, 'wreck partitions, separations, classes' (Cixous, 1976: 886). Speaking from the mother's place, Kristeva is also usurping 'the lost territory' of the extra-historical and playing out the fantasy of a place beyond time where history is (paradoxically) instituted. Alice Jardine, commenting on the 'space' outside history which western culture has constructed as history's opposite, notes:

> The woman-subject usually becomes a kind of 'filter' for questioning this space ('a place of passage, a threshold where "nature" confronts culture').[21] But that is another problem: in fact, the mystification produced by imagining 'that there is *someone* in that filter' *is* the problem
>
> (Jardine, 1985: 89)

Jane Gallop initially suspects that Kristeva succumbs to such a mystification in 'Stabat Mater'. The form of Gallop's abandonment of that suspicion is interesting, particularly in its use of spatial metaphors:

> To assign Kristeva the mother's place is to ignore much of what she has said out of some desire to make things simple and secure, some desire to locate the mother and have her there. Although she has spoken from the mother's place, Kristeva has also announced that place as vacant: '. . . And no one is there, in that space both double and foreign, to signify it.'
>
> (Gallop, 1982: 117)

In the context of *The Daughter's Seduction*, and Kristeva's own exploration of the mother-daughter relationship, 'the legitimation crisis' (Habermas, 1976) is transformed by the replacement of the mother-son by the mother-daughter relationship as the 'primary' relationship constitutive of the 'little subject'.[22] What Jardine identifies as the source of a pervasive sense of loss in contemporary (masculine) discourse becomes, in these women's texts, the source of a sense of freedom, even if that freedom is qualified and fragile. Gallop points out that in 'Stabat Mater' there is a dual insistence on speaking from the place of the mother and on the impossibility of speaking from the place of the mother, which by forgery unmasks forgery and pares 'a good deal of the fraudulent magic from the idea of women' (Carter, 1979: 109). It might be added that Kristeva's double text also insists on writing the transgression of history and the impossibility of transgressing history. 'Stabat Mater' simultaneously undermines maternal omnipotence by assuming it and parodies legitimacy, rendering explicit its dependence on (denying) the power of the maternal. As a text preoccupied by the thetic boundary, it situates itself at the threshold of history and language. Speaking from that inter-dict place parodically, illegitimately, it confronts and exhausts 'the mystification produced by imagining that there is *someone* in that filter' (Jardine, 1985: 89). In 'Stabat Mater' the woman-subject moves out of the position of ' "filter" *for* the questioning of that space' to usurp the space and its legitimizing function, as Kristeva does in writing such a text, or to question it, as Gallop does in her daughterly reading of it.

MOTHER-OF-THE-SON, DAUGHTER-OF-THE-MOTHER

After a long, contrapuntal, double-column exposition of maternal power and the power of the 'Word', 'Stabat Mater' moves on to a single-column analysis of the myth of the Virgin Mother as 'image of power' and of that image as 'the underhand double of explicit phallic power' (Kristeva, 1986: 170). When the left-hand column resumes after this exposition of the maternal as 'a kind of substitute for effective power . . . but no less authoritarian', it is to commence a eulogy to the child, 'My son'. There ensues a more harmonious relation between columns than previously, as an historical analysis of the cult of the mother and son, particularly as a linchpin of western humanism, is initially accompanied by a veritable litany of the son's praises. This harmony is soon interrupted, however:

The wakeful tongue quietly remembers another withdrawal, mine: a blossoming heaviness in the middle of the bed, of a hollow, of the sea . . . Recovered childhood, dreamed peace restored, in sparks, flash of cells, instants of laughter, smiles in the blackness of dreams, at night, opaque joy that roots me in her bed, my mother's, and projects him, a son, a butterfly soaking up dew from her hand, there, nearby, in the night. Alone: she, I and he.

She knows she is destined to that eternity (of the spirit or of the species) of which every mother is unconsciously aware, and with regard to which maternal devotion or even sacrifice is but an insignificant price to pay. A price that is borne the more easily since, contrasted with the love that binds a mother to her son, all other 'human relationships' burst like blatant shams.

(Kristeva, 1986: 172)

The shock of 'contrasted with the love that binds a mother to her son, all other "human relationships" burst like blatant shams', taken in isolation would more than justify Jane Gallop's objection: 'It is simply too reminiscent of a "vulgar but oh how effective trap" of motherhood' (Gallop, 1982: 128).[23] This very passage, however, confounds Gallop's suspicion that Kristeva has 'forgotten that a mother is also a daughter' (123).

For at this point the subjection to the son/husband/father is undermined by the implication that this relationship, far from being an end, is accepted in its self-abnegatory form only as a mediation, as the necessary sublimation of the desired return to the mother. Despite the 'sweetness of the child' (Kristeva, 1986: 171), 'a hunger remains' (174). Not surprisingly, for the result of deification is that 'we are entitled only to the ear of the virginal body, the tears and the breast' (172–3). Following the exposure of the complex identity of the mother of the son as daughter of the mother, a strong contrast emerges between the lyricism of anguish, addressing maternity as painful alienation, and a lucid exposition of the myth of 'the Mother and her attributes' as 'representatives of a "return of the repressed" in monotheism' (174):

> The law of the same . . . requires that the little girl abandon her relation to the origin and her primal fantasy so that henceforth she can be inscribed into those of men which will become the 'origin' of her desire. In other words, woman's only relation to origin is one dictated by man's. . . . The tropism, as well as the rivalry, is in fact between the man and (his) mother. And woman is well and truly castrated from the viewpoint of this economy.
>
> (Irigaray, 1985a: 33)

Were it merely to attempt another return to the origin, 'Stabat Mater' would again privilege the maternal, perpetuating the myth of the total mother. In her attempt to elucidate such dangers, Gallop discusses the relation between the semiotic and imaginary:

> Both are associated with the pre-Oedipal, pre-linguistic maternal. But whereas the imaginary is conservative and comforting, tends toward closure, and is disrupted by the symbolic; the semiotic is revolutionary, breaks closure, and disrupts the

symbolic. It seems there are two kinds of maternals; one more conservative than the paternal symbolic, one less.

(Gallop, 1982: 124)

In the conjunction of the mother of the son and daughter of the mother, 'Stabat Mater' sets these two categories against each other. This becomes clear as the two columns again converge. The 'paranoid logic' of the 'wrenching between desire for the masculine corpse and negation of death' (Kristeva, 1986: 175) is shattered by a speculation which transforms the 'imaginary' Pietà, 'conservative, comforting', the insurance against death, by a 'semiotic' 'revolutionary' disruption. Could it be that the 'love . . . of mourners for corpses', and particularly 'Mary's outburst of pain at the foot of the cross' (175), expresses the mother's 'desire to experience within her own body the death of a human being, which her feminine fate of being the source of life spares her?' It is at this point that the case of Pergolesi's *Stabat Mater* is specifically addressed and the precariousness of the name of the father is exposed in a textual wantonness on the part of the 'Virgin Mother', which betrays not only the fraudulence of language, but also that of 'the Great Mother' herself. *'Eia Mater, fons amoris!'* is addressed to 'only a massive *nothing*' (179), 'one seeks in vain for mothers' (178).

Where do we seek at this point in the text? In the writings of Freud, another son betrayed, exposed in his inadequacies. Kristeva on the one hand seems to delight here in impersonating 'Mamma', betraying her sons, Freud and Jung, by exercising the terrible power, not least of laughter, with which they have endowed her. Just as they are robbed of authority, however, so is she. For she becomes the mother's daughter, herself a child attempting to explore the continent of the maternal body, 'a very black one indeed' (179). That exploration by the daughter counterpoints the son's dangerous confrontation with 'motherhood':

Concerning that stage of my childhood, scented, warm and soft to the touch, I have only a spatial memory. No time at all. Fragrance of honey, roundness of forms, silk and velvet under my fingers, on my cheeks. Mummy.

Jung was the first to rush in, getting all his esoteric fingers burnt, but not without calling attention to some sore spots of the imagination with regard to motherhood, points that are still resisting analytical rationality.

(Kristeva, 1986: 179–80)

At the comic denouement of Carter's *Nights at the Circus* Fevvers reveals that the unlikely virginity, which centuries of myth, folktale and tradition have taught us to believe to be the source of her magical powers, is a fraud. 'Stabat Mater' (de)mythologizes another fraudulent virginity. 'Kristeva is acting out the Virgin Mother while writing about her' (Gallop, 1982: 129–30) and in the process discovers infidelity at the very heart of the myth. For what in 'this maternal representation' 'was able to attract women's wishes for identification' (Kristeva, 1986: 180)?

Mummy. . . . Almost no voice in her placid presence. Except, perhaps, and more belatedly, the echo of quarrels: her exasperation . . . her hatred. Never straightforward, always held back, as if although the unmanageable child deserved it, the daughter could not accept the mother's hatred – it was not meant for her. A hatred without recipience or rather whose recipience was no 'I' . . . Women doubtless reproduce among themselves the strange gamut of forgotten body relationships with their mothers. . . . No communication between individuals but connections between atoms, molecules, wisps of words, droplets of sentences. The community of women is a community of dolphins.

There might doubtless be a way to approach the dark area motherhood constitutes for a woman; one needs to listen, more carefully than ever, to what mothers are saying today. . . . What is it then in this maternal representation that, alone of her sex, goes against both sexes and was able to attract women's wishes for identification as well as the very precise interposition of those who assumed to keep watch over the symbolic order? . . .

The Virgin assumes her feminine denial of the other sex (of man) but overcomes him by setting up a third person: *I* do not conceive with *you* but with *Him*. The result is an immaculate conception (therefore with neither man nor sex), conception of a God with whose existence a woman has indeed something to do, on condition that she

acknowledges being subjected
to it.
(Kristeva, 1986: 179–80)

There are comic analogies in *Wise Children*. The novel concludes
with the 75-year-old sisters repetition of their Grandma's non-
essentialist, voluntary version of maternity and their adoption of
the twin children of their lost half-brother, an erring Jesuit: 'To
add to the hypothetical, disputed, absent father that was such a
feature of our history, now you could add a holy father, too.
Put it down to liberation theology' (Carter, 1991: 227), comments
Dora, gleefully deconstructing the mystical underpinning of the
legal fiction.

That the (eternal) child's fantasy of a relation to the mother
should banish the rival father is not surprising. To translate this
into a 'feminine denial of the other sex' is, however, and it is
just such a translation which is effected in 'Stabat Mater'. This
disconcerting of the Oedipal formulation of the 'holy family'
creates a fissure in which the implications of the simultaneous
observations on the mother-daughter relationship can register.
The attraction of the Virgin Mother myth for women is rooted
in the relation of these two. Feminine complicity in her own
exile from history springs here from the pain of rejection by
the mother. The desire to have a son is presented in the interplay
of these columns as the desire to (re)enter the mother-of-son,
daughter-of-mother nexus, to mother the (feminine) self in the
son that the mother would not have rejected.

This becomes even more obvious as the relation between the
columns themselves becomes that of sibling rivalry. 'Maternal
aversion' is counterpointed by the image of the Madonna pros-
trate before 'the child-god'. Counter to the mother's adoration of
the son in this essay there runs the daughter's resentment of this
rival, a resentment which runs through *Heroes and Villains* also,
where Marianne can survey her brother's murder with such
equanimity.

ANOTHER READING OF 'STABAT MATER'

There is a danger here that any reading of 'Stabat Mater', particularly one which concentrates as this one does on the interaction
between its different elements, will homogenize, will refuse to

accept the disparities and attempt to establish a comfortable, closed version of the text. In praising Kristeva's dialogical columns one immediately is challenged to follow suit, to write the commentary on 'Stabat Mater' in the style of 'Stabat Mater'. This is not an option I have chosen to adopt. One reason for this is that Kristeva's use of the double columns is a sublime fraud. No reader will read both columns exactly simultaneously: it is the reader's disorientation that is sought and effected. The double columns signify the doubleness of every text, the inextricable strands of poetry and analysis, womb and word, semiotic and symbolic, which are the texture of writing. It is not necessary to imitate its doubleness when writing of 'Stabat Mater': that doubleness already imitates our writing and the ambivalence of our responses to Kristeva's text.

While it may not be necessary to write in double columns, it is important to keep the central gap in the text open, to generate rather than exclude other possibilities, other readings. It is therefore useful to establish a contrapuntal relationship, between my emphasis on the recurrence of the voice of the daughter within the text and within the mother and Jane Gallop's emphasis on the imposture practised by the mother on the daughter.

The discussion of 'Stabat Mater' in *The Daughter's Seduction*, as Gallop herself points out, returns 'again and again to a similar suspicion, a mistrust of the Mother, of the occupant of the Mother's place' (Gallop, 1982: 130). That suspicion perpetuates the 'eternal minority' of daughter *as opposed to* mother in *The Daughter's Seduction*, perhaps more emphatically than in 'And the one doesn't stir without the other'. It is precisely the insight encapsulated in Irigaray's title and quoted repeatedly by Gallop herself that such a suspicion functions to ignore. Gallop argues that in 'The one doesn't stir without the other' the first-person voice is that of the daughter: the second person, the addressee, is the mother. She inverts this in relation to 'Stabat Mater': the mother speaks and we, the readers, are, with Gallop, the daughters to whom the text is addressed. This unwillingness to confront the different voices within 'Stabat Mater' (and within one 'subject') leaves Gallop, after a detour through 'Polylogue', at first 'stuck, stymied, paralysed' (127), symptoms that indicate once again the operation of mother as Medusa.

The 'doubly duplicitous' nature of that Medusa emerges in Gallop's response to this paralysis, however. 'There are two paths of inquiry that beckon. But I cannot choose one.' This is not an inability to choose equivalent to the inabilities of the early Martha Quest, for example. It is instead an inability to choose one which is the ability to choose more, despite the anxieties:

> The right path to take leads to the mother and something that worries me.[24] But in planning to proceed down the right path, there remains a desire or a need or a compulsion for the path which is left. The one left leads to the lesbian and something that worries Kristeva.
>
> (Gallop, 1982: 127)

'Forgive me, Mother, I prefer a woman to you' (Irigaray, 1981: 67). Gallop's attempt to come to terms with 'Stabat Mater' articulates an anxiety which the more readily pervades contemporary feminism for being so rarely articulated. Obviously the terms of the paradox, mother or lesbian, are imposed from far outside the feminist culture which *The Daughter's Seduction* explores. That they should still so crudely (re)present themselves within such a sophisticated feminist text makes it obvious that they cannot simply be dismissed. As Gallop describes how she will confront this paradox there is an echo of the old paralysis: 'The only way I can move from this spot is to do both – "never one without the other" ' (Gallop, 1982: 127). The 'eternal minority' she saw implied in that phrase earlier is outgrown as she emulates Kristeva in writing a double text. 'Me too. Just like Mummy' (119).

But different. For the similarity to 'Stabat Mater' ends with the use of double columns. Gallop's columns do not quarrel in style, nor in their object. They launch a double (duplicitous) attack on mother. The terms of the dilemma are used against each other. Kristeva as mother was worried by these lesbians from the start. So Gallop uses them to frighten her so successfully that she cannot be frightening herself: 'as she faces the East, brave in the encounter with the Oriental other, a threat sneaks up from behind' (130). Meanwhile, there is a simultaneous attack on 'the maternal scandal' (129):

> Upon becoming a mother, the woman, like a Queen Bee, loses all interest in her husband, in heterosexuality, and derives her gratification in maternity. I fear that both the mother-child relationship and the experience of one's own otherness can be

more easily contained in the imaginary . . . than can a relation
to another adult.

The old fears, so familiar from the work of Lessing and Carter,
resurface: that maternity will rob the woman of her sexuality,
her adulthood, confine her to 'a stagnant representation'. The fear
that maternity will deprive her even of 'humanity' perhaps offers
some excuse for Gallop's own scandalous complicity in the
dehumanization of the mother and so, always potentially, the
woman, 'a mother . . . like a Queen Bee'. (Particularly since
'human' is so infrequently applied as a descriptive term for any
experience so specifically feminine as childbirth.)

The dual defence against maternity proceeds to a conclusion
which far exceeds the terms of the initial paradox, however,
towards an option which has been sneaking up from behind all
along. For Gallop uses both the categories, mother *and* lesbian,
against each other to bring her back to what she thought she had
found in 'Polylogue'. The homosexuality which she does not
wish to reject in itself bears traces of the phallic mother and of
the conservative imaginary: mother, finally, does bear traces of
heterosexuality:

> *As she faces the East, brave in the encounter with the Oriental other, a threat sneaks up from behind. Have we found, here,*[25] *the phallic mother with whom Kristeva cannot identify and who thus paralyzes her rigid defences?*
>
> I am relieved to find a trace of the previous heterosexual encounter. Kristeva has made up a word, *'Heréthique,'* to name her maternal textual production. The word is rich in connotations: a condensation of *'heretique'* (heretic) and *'éthique* (ethics). But although altered in spelling, in speech the made up word in no way differs from 'heretique'. What has been added is a silent 'H', the name of the Sollers text in 'Polylogue'.

(Gallop, 1982: 130)

At the point when the voice of the daughter is finally recognized
in Kristeva's writing, the mother's sexuality is also restored.

A strong strand within 'Stabat Mater' itself parallels this development in Gallop's reading. Kristeva moves on from her dis-

cussion of the attractions of the myth of the Virgin Mother for women to a discussion of 'the aspects of the feminine psyche for which that representation of motherhood does not provide a solution or else provides one that is felt to be too coercive by twentieth-century women' (1986: 183).

Among things left out of the virginal myth there is the war between mother and daughter. But the preceding pages of 'Stabat Mater' have read that very relation as the sub-text which gives the myth its allure for women.

(UN)LIKE SUBJECTS: NEW WAYS OF BECOMING

Drawing on the mother-of-son/daughter-of-mother relation she has explored earlier, Kristeva goes on to practise an inversion in the mode of Rousseau and Engels, though for quite contrary ends:

> Motherhood opens out a vista: a woman seldom (although not necessarily) experiences her passion (love and hatred) for another woman without having taken her own mother's place – without having herself become a mother, and especially without slowly learning to differentiate between same beings – as being face to face with her daughter forces her to do.
>
> (Kristeva, 1986: 184)

The convolution of the sentence indicates how tortuous a route 'Stabat Mater' has followed to arrive at a different relation of mother and daughter. The mutual recognition described here refuses the concept of mother and daughter as interchangeable, one self merely a trajectory between the two. It therefore dispenses with the necessity of mediation through the distant son and substitutes the possibility of a relationship between (un)like subjects for that between like objects.

'Promoting Mary as universal and particular, but never singular – as "alone of her sex" ' (1986: 183) – promotes, as Kristeva points out, a 'war' between mother and daughter. More is at stake, however, than a simple policy of divide and rule:

> The exchanges upon which patriarchal societies are based take place exclusively among men. Women, signs, commodities and currency always pass from one man to another; it it were otherwise, we are told, the social order would fall back upon

exclusively endogamous ties that would paralyze all com-
merce.[26]

(Irigaray, 1985b: 192)

The exchangeability of women which Lévi-Strauss posits as basic
to society depends on their interchangeability. That interchangeability can only break down, 'when the goods get together' as
Irigaray points out. If, as both Carter and Kristeva argue in their
different ways, the relationship between mother and daughter is
no longer a chain of reproduction, the possibility of that getting
together occurs. And with that, the 'repudiation of the other sex'
and the mediation of all sexual relations through 'the child, the
third person, the non-person', becomes instead

*Discontinuity, lack and
arbitrariness: topography of
the sign, of the symbolic
relation that posits my
otherness as impossible.
Love, here, is only for the
impossible.*
an acknowledgement of what
is irreducible, of the
irreconcilable interest of both
sexes in asserting their
differences, in the quest of
each one – and of woman,
after all – for an appropriate
fulfillment.

(Kristeva, 1986: 184)

It must be added that the model for this 'acknowledgement' of
difference is no longer the relation of mother and son, of loss,
but of mother and daughter 'slowly learning to differentiate
between same things'.

THE SPACE AND TIME OF THE THETIC

Does 'Stabat Mater' then open up the path to

Exchanges without identifiable terms, without accounts, without end. . . . Without additions and accumulations, one plus
one, woman after woman. . . . Without sequence, without
number . . . enjoyment without a fee, well-being without pain,
pleasure without possession . . . Utopia? Perhaps.

(Irigaray, 1985b: 197)

That there is a danger of homogenizing 'Stabat Mater' to a bland
idealistic utopianism in the name of radical textual heterosexuality
is evident in Gallop's reading. *The Daughter's Seduction*'s attempt

to break out of the 'imaginary' relation of mother and child, the 'stagnant representation', arrives at the same point as Carter's inverse exploration of the 'female imaginary' in *Heroes and Villains*. Indeed it could be argued that Gallop's recourse to a double text in emulation of 'the mother' actually precipitates a return to 'paternal legitimation', 'the mark', the name of the father, for she proposes that 'written language is a further mediation over oral, and it is in the written, mediated, more symbolic dimension that we find the mark of the father' (Gallop, 1982: 130). Gallop's discussion of 'Stabat Mater' and *About Chinese Women* thus becomes involved in an attempt to reinstitute the symbolic. It re-enacts the thetic.

It therefore immediately poses a question: to what extent is such a re-enactment inevitable in the space created in 'Stabat Mater' by the disruption of the relation between the maternal body and representation? To what extent will the form of (hetero) textuality based on the slow differentiation of same things inevitably succumb to a 'further mediation'?

Such an inevitability certainly exists in any space bounded by Gallop's serial equation, 'the written, mediated, more symbolic dimension', 'the mark of the father'. 'Stabat Mater' is structured by the rejection of those equations, however. The body of the mother and the body of the text are repeatedly presented in Kristeva's writings as having common allegiances to the spatial and material, rather than the temporal and symbolic. The interweaving of simultaneous columns in 'Stabat Mater' shatters any notional temporality.

The split text is self-consciously a spatial and material artefact. Presenting itself as one essay, though centred on an empty space, it produces the effect of simultaneous separation and refusal of separation. This effect the text discusses as a crucial component of the experience of maternity, but also of 'the topography of the sign, of the symbolic relation that posits my otherness as impossible' (Kristeva, 1986: 184). The occasionally converging columns enact, repeatedly, 'a division of the very flesh. And consequently a division of language' (178).

The thetic rupture? But in this spatial economy place supersedes event and the topography of the sign remains just that.

In *Nights at the Circus* Fevvers, 'the impossible squared' (Carter, 1984: 15), defrauds time and an empiricist reporter determined to prove her a liar. What he has been 'seriously discomposed' to

consider a magical suspension of time at midnight and has accord-
ingly mystified in his narrative, turns out to be a matter of
backstage trickery with clocks (Carter 1984: 42).

Fevvers's transgression has much in common with that practised by 'Stabat Mater'. It irreverently denies the 'linear abstraction', time, history, not through retreat to myth, whether of
maternity or 'femininity', but by harnessing the power of those
myths through self-conscious artifice:

It seems to me that there is only one way to go through the religion of the Word, or its counterpart, the more or less discreet cult of the mother: it is the way of the 'artists', those who make up the vertigo of language weakness by the oversaturation of sign systems.

Such a love [maternal] is in fact, logically speaking, a surge of anguish at the very moment when the identity of thought and living body collapses. The possibilities of communication having been swept away, only the subtle gamut of sound, touch and visual traces, older than language and newly worked out are preserved as an ultimate shield against death.
(Kristeva, 1986: 177)

The Fraudian mother constructs herself, through language, at the
place where language fails. The 'subtle gamut of sound, touch
and visual traces, older than language' are 'newly worked out' in
language: the 'maternal representation' which 'normally' makes
up for 'the vertigo of language weakness' is swept aside in 'the
oversaturation of sign-systems' that is 'art' (177).

In the passage above and in the course of 'Stabat Mater' the
'Word' and the 'Mother' are overwhelmed by 'an overabundance
of discourse' and a 'demented *jouissance*' (179). Thus a negation
occurs of the inversion 'through expenditure in the wealth of
signs which constitutes the baroque'. The cult of the Virgin did
not oppose the cult of the Mother, according to Kristeva, but
rendered it 'useless', exhausted by excess (177). Such is the operation of the textual excess of 'Stabat Mater' in relation to the
alliance of womb and word which it exposes.

The fraudulent assumption of an impossible subjectivity, the
imposture of speaking from the 'outside language' through which
language defines itself, are allied to the text's other 'transgression'.

Where Rousseau and Engels sought by 'sleight of hand' to conceal that gap in representation, the thetic, by situating it at an 'imaginary' time, Kristeva seeks to expose it by presenting it in space. The socio-symbolic contract cannot be dissolved, but in this landscape it can never occur either.

'Stabat Mater' (im)poses, at least in part, as a return to the 'womb . . . domain of futurity' (Carter, 1979: 107–8). The thetic cannot be said to be postponed indefinitely there. It has and will recur, but in the space opened up by its transgression, perhaps an herethical reformulation of its terms can take (a) place. In such a new topography of the sign, 'the symbolic relation which posits my otherness as impossible' also concedes, 'impossible, that is just the way it is. . . . The other is inevitable' (Kristeva, 1986: 184–5).[27]

In speaking of 'herethics' at the end of 'Stabat Mater', Kristeva appears to be moving towards a new form of ethics, an ethics divorced from morality, but firmly wedded to politics. Access to the other *and* to 'that which in life makes bonds' (185), herethics would be a discourse of the motherhood on which silence has weighed so heavily (183) and simultaneously a rejection of the god of the word and the mother goddess.

It therefore bears a strong resemblance to modern art as described in 'Stabat Mater'. The modern writer joins the saint and the mystic in escaping the erection of a maternal representation in the place where death is and the symbolic order would collapse. Such a writer

> Through the power of language, nevertheless succeeds in doing no better than to take apart the fiction of the mother as mainstay of love, and to identify with love itself and what he is in fact – *a fire of tongues*, an exit from representation.
>
> (Kristeva, 1986: 177)

'Stabat Mater' is structured around that particular exit, *Wise Children* pauses before it, *Heroes and Villains* posits its inevitable recurrent closure. The herethical *Hothouse by the East River* concludes by going through it.

It is inappropriate to attempt to reach 'conclusions' about Kristeva's open text. Her own concluding comments, however, will aptly open the discussion of Spark's problematic novel and the discussion of the novel may extend the horizon of heterotextuality explored in 'Stabat Mater'.

Chapter 5

Unknowing the true-real

REMEMBERING/DISMEMBERING

The Hothouse by the East River and 'Stabat Mater' are both written in the space where the maternal body impinges on representation. 'Stabat Mater' concerns itself primarily with the not necessarily complementary functions of that maternal body as source of life and guarantee of the symbolic order. The concluding comments change the focus to the relation of the maternal and death.

> *The 'just the same' of motherly peace of mind . . . it is there, too, that the speaking being finds a refuge when his/her symbolic shell has cracked and a crest emerges where speech causes biology to show through: I am thinking of the time of illness, of sexual-intellectual-physical passion, of death . . .*

> An *herethics* is perhaps no more than that which in life makes bonds. Herethics is undeath [*a-mort*], love . . . *Eia Mater, fons amoris.* . . . So let us again listen to the *Stabat Mater*, and the music, all the music . . . it swallows up the goddesses and removes their necessity.

(Kristeva, 1986: 185)

On the one hand the power of the maternal is rooted in the fear of death, the necessity to deny mortality. On the other hand the denial of death is also the denial of the mother – she is swallowed up in a-mort, a love with no object but the negation of death. On the one hand there is a speech which causes biology to show through, the semiotic closeness to the mother as source of life.

On the other there is music masking that other unavoidable aspect of biology, death.

The Hothouse by the East River is written at the limit where 'a-mort' becomes death. In this as in other novels Spark focuses on the feminine as death and the end of representation. In general Spark is more concerned with the woman as other rather than mother, with the feminine stripped of its function as reassurance. In her discussion of melancholia, Kristeva argues that:

> The feminine as image of death is not only a screen for my fear of castration, but also an imaginary safety catch for the matricidal drive, that without such a representation would pulverize me into melancholia if it did not drive me to crime.
>
> (Kristeva, 1989: 28)

Such a safety catch poses very specific problems for the feminine subject, problems which may explain the intensity of the matricidal drive and the concomitant drive to take the mother's place in Lessing's fiction, for example.

> For a woman, whose specular identification with the mother as well as the introjection of the maternal body and self are more immediate, such an inversion of matricidal drive into a death-bearing maternal image is more difficult if not impossible. Indeed, how can She be that bloodthirsty Fury, since I am She (sexually and narcissistically), She is I? Consequently the hatred I bear her is not oriented towards the outside but is locked up within myself. There is no hatred, only an implosive mood that walls itself in and kills me secretly.
>
> (Kristeva, 1989: 28–9)

I am She, She is I. Once again the feminine subject seems to find in the mother-daughter relationship the evidence of her non-existence. *The Hothouse by the East River* deals with this impossibility by assuming it. I am Death. This identification is at the heart of Spark's myth of 'the author'. Spark's treatment differs from Lessing's preoccupation with the maternal as engulfment and Carter's ambition to secularize 'Woman'. *The Hothouse by the East River* celebrates the uncontrollable destructive powers of the spectacular and sacred 'Woman' invented by the self in search of a mirror.

BREAKING THE ICE

The Hothouse by the East River pushes to its inevitable conclusion
the specular logic which dominates western thought. At its heart
is the image of a shadow cast against the light, a shadow which
suggests another 'origin' from the One and the Same, an other
source and different light from that which has been already bent
to his logos by the philosopher (Irigaray, 1985a: 276). The philosopher in question is Plato and the final section of *Speculum of
the Other Woman*, 'Plato's hystera', analyses Plato's allegory of the
cave (Plato, 1974: 316–25). 'Plato's hystera' analyses the abro-
gation of 'origin' from the (maternal) cave of Nature to the pure
(sun)light of Reason and the Ideas, which are postulated as
reflected in, not conceived in, matter: 'On the one hand the
"amorphous" but insistent anteriority of the *hystera*, that irrepres-
entable origin of all forms and all morphology, and on the other
hand, the dazzling fascination of the Sun – image of God' (Irigaray, 1985a: 253).

Irigaray speaks of the 'mother-mirror' which is 'silver-backed',
an ocean which is frozen over to become '*Une Mère de glace*'
(302). Its

> water serves as a reflecting screen and not as a reminder of the
> depths of the mother; it sends back the image of the sun, of
> men, of things, even of the prisoner-child. Those *appearances*
> veil the risk of falling back, of returning into the darkness of
> those chasms.
>
> (Irigaray, 1985a: 289)

By positing a source of light behind the mirror and underneath
the ocean, one which casts a shadow against the light of the sun,
The Hothouse by the East River opens up those chasms. It turns
the mirror against those who have made it and exploits the hor-
rific powers of life and death which the subject projects on to
the (m)other in whom he finds his image. It disturbs the trajectory
of the gaze of the one at the other and stages as a literary performance the collapse of the specular economy through which the
opposition of subject and object is constituted. *The Hothouse by
the East River* is therefore close in its project and effect to *Speculum
of the Other Woman*.

Speculum of the Other Woman is a treatise on invisibility written
in the spaces between the sayable. 'The feminine must be

deciphered as *inter-dict:* within the signs or between them, between the realized meanings, between the lines' (Irigaray, 1985a: 22). The crucial role of the hegemony of sight in the economy of 'representation' and its identification between what can be seen and what can be said are at the heart of *Speculum of the Other Woman.* Irigaray analyses the specular economy which makes of woman the object of the gaze. In this she continues a project which has been undertaken by women's writing at least since Mary Wollstonecraft wrote *A Vindication of the Rights of Woman* and fuses it with analysis of the mode in which language functions to exile the feminine from the realm of the sayable, the knowable, from existence itself. *Speculum of the Other Woman* moves beyond analysis of this as a problem and attempts to interrupt the return of the gaze to its proper owner. In a way Irigaray reinvents the castration/decapitation problem, subject of or subject to, the problem posed by Lessing and Cixous and, to a lesser extent, by Kristeva and Carter. She situates those options within the specular economy of patriarchy and so within the economy of representation itself. The politics of representation are in one way or another central to all the women writers under discussion: by focusing on the politics of the gaze Irigaray allows us both to reinvent the Medusa and to move beyond her.

In compressing the milestones of western philosophy into one unannotated, puzzling book, Irigaray parodies the idea of the absolute and total book, an ideal which is inscribed in the veneration of bibles, dictionaries, encyclopaedias and textbooks. *Speculum of the Other Woman* is an epilogue to all those other books, to 'the whole western, speculative history' (Kristeva, 1988: 375).[1]

AHISTORICAL OR ANACHRONIC?

> These women's stories are not inscribed in a void or an ahistorical time where their repetitions would be identical.
>
> (Cixous and Clément, 1986: 6)

Spark's narrative practice is rooted in her insistence that a story can only be told when its end has come. Irigaray attempts to tell the story of western culture – through its recurrent 'end', its encounter with the feminine. *Speculum of the Other Woman* concurrently explodes the simple chronology of beginning, middle and end and is written as a ring of interlinking concentric circles. Its very structure is a challenge to the linear; linear thought, linear time, the line beyond which 'she' cannot go. It is a misreading to see this critique of 'history' as a foreclosure or denial of change.[2]

Speculum of the Other Woman starts with a discussion of Freud and ends with a discussion of Plato. It is a circular text, a speculum rather than a speculation. It holds up a mirror to western thought and shows it in reverse and distorted. It marks the return of the gaze of the Medusa. That reflection is more than a statement, a reiteration which reinstitutes the exile of woman from history, from language and thought. It is not ahistorical: it is an anachronic transgression of history, an attempt like Carter's and Kristeva's to redefine and dislocate a history and culture which have been constituted by the exclusion of women. It exposes the unity of that culture as partial, partial in the sense that it is not objective but dedicated to the interest of one party, interest accruing through the speculation appropriated from the Medusa.

Speculum of the Other Woman does not present western culture as a seamless and timeless whole. The historical significance of Descartes' *Cogito*, for example, is not occluded though it is presented as a development of a trend constitutive of western philosophy from its inception (Irigaray, 1985a: 180–201). Irigaray does not deny history or present western thought and misogyny as static and changeless. She dis(re)members it. That disremembering is made possible by a specific historical moment: that is obvious even without reference to the recurrence in the writing of Kristeva, Spark, Carter, Cixous and Lessing of elements found in her work.

DISREMEMBERING

Irigaray even borrows the techniques of the discredited science of certitude. She dissects. The two short essays at the centre of her circle, 'Une Mère de glace' (Irigaray, 1985a: 168–79) and 'Taking the eye of a man recently dead' (180–90), are both concerned with a change of focus. Both essays deal with 'reflection' and with the specular economy which underlies both science and philosophy. The subjects of these two essays, the fourth-century neo-Platonist Plotinus and the seventeenth-century sceptical rationalist Descartes, also feature in Julia Kristeva's *Tales of Love* (1988). *Tales of Love* traces the (historical) development of 'amatory discourse'. In tracing that development it also traces the transition from the concept of self as one-in-relation-to-an-Other, the *Ego affectus est* which Kristeva identifies in the writings of Plato, the Song of Solomon and a variety of Christian and pre-Christian sources, to the concept of the self as one, as self-defining and autonomous unit. This latter concept reaches an apotheosis in Descartes, but Kristeva sees the origin of this modern concept of the subject's relation to itself in the writings of Thomas Aquinas and of Plotinus. Kristeva draws heavily on the myth of Narcissus, who fell in love with his own image, to elucidate the construction of 'internality' (109) and internalized psychic space as the condition of the (thinking) subject in Plotinus' work.

PLOTINUS, NARCISSUS AND DIONYSUS

Irigaray identifies two conflictual strands in Plotinus' tractate on 'The impassivity of the unembodied' (MacKenna, 1956: 201–22).[3] The dominant strand asserts that 'Matter has no reality and is not capable of being affected' (Irigaray, 1985a: 168). A muted but persistent strand is uneasy and defensive in the realization that the assertion that Matter is an immutable mirror which reflects 'the Authentic Existents' poses a question:

> But this would mean that if there were no Matter nothing would exist?
> Precisely as in the absence of a mirror or something of similar power, there would be no reflection.
>
> (Irigaray, 1985a: 175)

Plotinus denies that the absence of its reflection would in any way affect 'Reality': 'what appears in Matter is not reality'.

The necessity of insisting on this absolute independence of 'Reality' in the realm of Ideas from its manifestation in Matter poses another, less tractable problem than the relation of Ideas to the mirror which reflects the shadows of Ideas. The 'Authentic Existents', as Plotinus postulates them, do not need the mirror, nor do they need to enter into the process of reflection. The philosopher or, more precisely, the philosophical subject does need the mirror, however, in order to turn away from its images towards 'Truth'. Without the mirror there is no opportunity to speculate. Without speculation there is no philosophy and the philosophical subject becomes as 'destitute' as the Matter he denigrates:

On the one hand . . . the perceptible world is for Plotinus the result of a reflection in a mirror; as if the pernicious effect that is today pejoratively called 'narcissistic' were, logically and quite normally, the necessary creator of the world. In short, the soul produces a reflection when it encounters inert matter, just as a body is reflected in a shining surface. On the other hand and nevertheless, it would be a serious error to take for solid reality what is merely a reflection – as Narcissus does. Narcissism is thus condemned, but that condemnation has no bearing on the origin of the reflection process; according to Plotinus, the error would simply set in at the moment when the individual being grants reality to such images instead of examining its own intimacy.

(Kristeva, 1988: 106)

Kristeva identifies the same two strands in Plotinus' writings which Irigaray foregrounds, but Kristeva sets them in a somewhat different context. *Tales of Love*, in which Plotinus is discussed, is an analysis of the discourse of love in western philosophy and literature. Plotinus' writings are identified by Kristeva as marking a crucial stage in the transition from *Ego affectus est* to *Ego cogito*:

Platonic dialogism is transformed, with Plotinus, into a mono-logue that must indeed be called speculative: it leads the ideal inside a Self that, only thus, in the concatenation of reflections, establishes itself as an *internality*. To the narcissistic shadow, a snare and a downfall, it substitutes autoerotic reflection, which leads ideal Unity inside a Self that is illuminated by it.

(Kristeva, 1988: 109)

Both Kristeva and Irigaray suggest that the creation of the 'Ideal' and the opposition between Ideal and Matter is, for Plato as for his neo-disciple, an opening up of the space where philosophy and a discourse which assumes philosophy can take (a) place.

Irigaray does not greatly distinguish between Plato's and Plotinus' project in this respect: Kristeva sees a definite distinction between them. She reads Plato as opening up a space where a relationship to the (One) other is possible, Plotinus as internaliz-ing that space, opening up the possibility of a relationship with (One's) Self. This relationship to oneself constitutes self-consciousness and assumes that the other is always a reflection (of One self). Kristeva emphasizes the 'concatenation of reflections' (109) while Irigaray forces us to pay attention to the mirror itself. Both Kristeva and Irigaray would none the less concur that the consequence of the creation and internalization of the space between the 'Authentic-Existents' and their perceptible 'Reflections' must be an 'elimination of otherness' (Kristeva, 1988: 120). An other One must be introduced to execute this elimination and it is in keeping with the self-reflexive process that this One be identifiable with 'Reality' which was initially postulated 'elsewhere' as the *origin* of the images reflected in its material opposite:

> The blending love with the One is elimination of otherness. The soul's merging with the One is described by Plotinus in visual terms: 'seeing oneself whole' (*Enneads* V, 5, 10) rather than 'being whole'. The soul then loses its specificity, it is no longer completely itself, it is outside itself in *extasis*. It has pushed aside otherness in order to reach, beyond the grasp of otherness, the steadiness of rest.
>
> (Kristeva, 1988: 120)

'One may well wonder at the inherent contradictions in Plotinus' theory of otherness.' Plotinus still posits One who by His/Its existence guarantees that the self is and that nothing else is, nothing will come between the self and its self, nothing will open the perfect enclosure of self-reflection. The neo-Platonist trusts his philosophical inheritance and so cannot yet say, 'God is, but it is the "I" that by thinking has granted him that essence and existence that the "I" expects from God' (Irigaray, 1985a: 187). It was a long time before the self became destitute and resourceful enough to speculate on its own reflection as the sole guarantee of its existence. Because he cannot go this far, there is a chink in the glittering armour of refraction and auto-reflection which for Plotinus constitutes the thinking subject. At the point where the other (One) intervenes to save the 'soul' from discord, an other origin is posited:

> The other, that is, the eye, sees only because it reflects the light of a single source. The loving soul must therefore give up its otherness, and give in to the sameness of the single light where it loses itself as other, in other words, for Plotinus, as nonbeing. Narcissus' error would lie in his having reversed the perspective: he mistook his eye for the solar source, for the One, and believed there could be an other for that other.

Plotinus knew that the soul is always already an other, but it can emerge from its solitude, its nothingness, its possible downfall, by means of the amorous return to the Single Source. After having been barely sketched out, the soul's otherness is thus reintegrated into the mystical, initiatory path of non-dualistic neoplatonism.

(Kristeva, 1988: 121)

Plotinus may eventually resolve the dilemma of the soul's otherness posed by his positing of a 'single source', but his route to that solution is monological and exclusionary: 'The Narcissan Plotinian divinity is love, but it is a love of self and in itself' (113). Being one self at one with such a divinity entails not merely a rejection of all else, but a *denial* of all else. Matter is systematically stripped of all attributes save its reflective surface:

Matter has no reality and is not capable of being affected. Matter must be bodiless – for body is a later production, a compound made by Matter with some other entity.

Matter is not Soul; it is not Intellect, is not Life, is no Ideal-Principle, it is not limit or bound, for it is mere indetermination; it is not a power, for what does it produce?

(Irigaray, 1985a: 168)

One might answer, 'Images', but then one remembers that it does not produce those of itself, but reflects images of Ideas and Forms whose 'Reality' is elsewhere and which are projected on to Matter by a light which emanates from 'a single source', a source for which the sun is a metaphor. Matter is 'utter Non-Being', absolutely without part in Reality (175). Matter retains nothing but the power of reflection, a power which is not a power, since it is merely the result of Matter's powerlessness and poverty: 'Matter is destitute of The Good. The claimant does not ask for all the giver's store, but it welcomes what it can get; in other words, what appears in Matter is not reality' (175). Matter's function in relation to 'Authentic Beings' is to reflect and its ability to do so is a function of its inauthenticity, its Non-Being.

This impoverishment of Matter until it has nothing but 'imaging skill' (175) has ambiguous consequences. The duality of Authentic Existence and Matter is destabilized, for one side of the opposition is emptied of significance until everything is an attribute, category, or reflection of Authentic Existence, and Matter is nothing. Since only one function or attribute of Matter remains, the function of reflecting its opposite, that function is fore-grounded and the necessity of Matter to the philosophical enter-prise is exposed. At the point of construction of self-reflexive internality, the fragility of that construct is manifest. The space (between Reality and Matter, Being and Non-Being) into which the philosophical subject will insert himself and which will hence-forward be the inner psychic space of the subject exists only as long as the opposition which structures it can be sustained. The 'existence' of the subject and the stability of that space are inter-dependent. The self thinks, distinguishes, separates itself from Matter and mother by postulating another Origin. The fragile basis of that other origin is protected first by the process of inversion: Matter is described as derivative, a mere reflective sur-face the origin of whose images are the Ideas and Forms which the subject derives to escape determination by Matter. A second defence of the other origin is conducted by gradually paring down Matter, denial to it of attributes or the power to change, until the mirror becomes paradoxically a vanishing-point, greedy Non-Being which seeks to contain everything, but possesses nothing, which threatens Being with annihilation as surely as it keeps Being in existence as its opposite.

The need to deny material origin and postulate another *source* is an extension of the displacement of accent identifiable with traditional renderings of the Medusa myth. A displacement of origin occurs which allows western philosophy to constitute itself in relation to another and superior source which will rescue the (philosophical) subject from its status as derivative of matter and posit it as an original, a soul which predates its entry into the (maternal) body. That originality is guaranteed and granted by a first Origin, a prime mover from which matter derives. The independence of that first Origin (divinity or idea) is asserted to deny that dependence of the (philosophical) subject which can never be less than subject to a body (and to death as well as birth).

A backlash from the denied maternal is always to be feared. Kristeva points out that the myth of Narcissus is linked by Ovid and Plotinus with that of Dionysus. The spring in which Narcissus sees his image is identified by Kristeva as maternal (Kristeva, 1988: 113). Confronted with the maternal mirror, Narcissus' 'error lies . . . in failing to see that the reflection is of none but the self' (107). The penalty for that failing is the anguish of a desire which can never be satisfied.

Narcissus dies when he realizes his beloved image can disappear, a realization which comes when his tears of frustrated desire cause ripples in the reflecting water (Ovid, 1955: 86–7). Those who fail to acknowledge that reflection is 'of none but the self' risk annihilation of selfhood. The initial error is, moreover, the cause of the tears which link him to the watery element which his parentage tells us was his origin: Narcissus' parents were the river Cephissus and the nymph Liriope (Kristeva, 1988: 103; Ovid, 1955: 83).[4] In her work on melancholy, Kristeva focuses on this aspect of the Narcissus myth. It is failure to separate from the maternal 'spring', 'denial of negation' (1989: 63), that determines the 'depressive structure'. Denying the loss of the mother,

> The melancholic subject then freezes his unpleasant affects . . . and preserves them in a *psychic inside* thus constituted once and for all as distressed and inaccessible. This painful innerness, put together with semiotic markings, but not with signs, is the invisible face of Narcissus, the secret source of his tears.
>
> (Kristeva, 1989: 63)

This is yet another reminder from Kristeva that, while subversion of the symbolic and release of semiotic potential is linked with *jouissance*, inability to identify with the symbolic is the sign of a wounded narcissism, a threat even to the biological survival of the self, since the desire 'not to be' is unleashed in the absence of symbolic safeguards (Kristeva, 1986: 158).

Narcissus' tears denote his perilous affinity with the spring, but they also disturb its surface, forcing him to realize that the existence of the (self) image is dependent on the stability of the mirror in which it is reflected. We see why Plotinus must insist on the immutability of Matter: 'Mirrors and transparent objects . . . are quite unaffected by what is seen in or through them: material things are reflections and the Matter in which they appear is further from being affected than is a mirror' (Irigaray, 1985a: 169–70). This immutability is a trait which, for Plotinus, renders Matter maternal: 'The Ideal Principles entering into Matter as to a mother affect it neither for better or worse' (Irigaray, 1985a: 179). The immutability of the mother is assumed and submerged in a strategic inversion, familiar from the writings of Freud and

Lévi-Strauss. The manifest point, that Matter is immutable, displaces emphasis and attention from a 'secondary' point which is assumed, the immutability of the mother. Through this immutability motherhood is identified with Matter and Non-Being and physical maternity becomes a metaphor for the concept 'Matter'.

Narcissus' reflection in this reflection is unstable. It is significant that the myth gives him a spring as a mirror, for water, unlike glass, has depth. Irigaray entitles the Plotinus essay '*Une Mère de glace*'.[5] If the frozen ocean melts and moves then the (self) image is dispersed, perhaps destroyed. The ripples in Narcissus' spring dissipate, fragment and multiply his image so that it becomes something other than the 'true' image he loves.

This disintegration of the self (image) is precipitated by the tears which signify Narcissus' parentage. Those tears dropping back into the water drop Narcissus back into his material/maternal origin. They close the gap in which the subject was able to originate the concept of its own existence by observing itself. When that gap closes Narcissus dies: 'When he realises . . . that the other in the spring is merely himself, he has put together a psychic space – he has become subject. Subject of what? Subject of the reflection and at the same time subject of death' (Kristeva, 1988: 116).

THE MIRROR OF DIONYSUS

> Better than the gaze of the other, which is necessarily threatening because of its different viewpoint, is the subject's self-observation, the protective and reflexive extension of his own gaze.
>
> (Irigaray, 1985a: 81)

Even though she links the Narcissan element in Plotinus with the 'mirror of Dionysus' (Kristeva 1988: 107) Kristeva does not foreground the threat of disintegration through confrontation with the maternal. This threat does, however, surface in Ovid's integration of the story of Narcissus with that of Pentheus and is discernible in Plotinus' identification of the mirror of Dionysus with the Narcissan error of 'image-laden dispersion' (107).

The story of Pentheus immediately follows that of Narcissus in Ovid's *Metamorphoses*. The two are linked by reference to the powers of the blind seer Tiresias, who predicted that Narcissus would live long 'if he does not come to know himself' (1955: 83) and told Pentheus: 'How lucky it would be for you if you too were to be deprived of sight, so that you could not behold Bacchus' sacred rites. . . . This thing will come to pass: You will lament that in my darkness I saw all too clearly' (87–8). The motif of sight and seeing is clearly a common factor in both stories. Like Narcissus, Pentheus would not see what he ought to see – in his case that he should worship and defer to the gods – and saw what he ought not to have seen, the sacred rites of Bacchus. The superiority of moral or second sight over sense perception is the lesson which links Tiresias' prediction with the presentation by Plotinus of the eye as a metaphor for the superior sight of the soul (MacKenna, 1956: 202):

> Withdraw into yourself and look. . . . Do you purely dwell within yourself without any obstacle to unity, does *nothing foreign anymore*, by its submixture, *alter the simplicity of your interior* essence? . . . you shall then have become light itself . . . Then you must observe carefully, for yours will be the only eye that is able to perceive supreme beauty. For the eye will first have to be rendered analogous and similar to the object it is to contemplate. Never would the eye have seen the sun unless first it had assumed its form.
>
> (Kristeva, 1988: 108)

Plotinus replaces the Narcissan eye which thinks that it is the sun, with an eye that knows it can take the form of the sun but that it must turn its light inward and never mistake anything in the external world for more than an image of the inner reality:

> Whoever would let himself be misled by the pursuit of those vain shadows, mistaking them for realities, would grasp only an image as fugitive as the fluctuating form reflected by the waters and would resemble that senseless man who, wishing to grasp that image himself, according to fable, disappeared, carried away by the current. Likewise he who wishes to embrace corporeal beauties, and not release them, would plunge, not his body, but his soul into the gloomy abysses, so repugnant to intelligence: he would be condemned to total blindness.
>
> (Kristeva, 1988: 106)

To leave the 'inner sanctuary' and look outward is to risk 'image-laden dispersion' (107), disintegration:

According to one version of the myth, Dionysus as a child allows himself to be seduced by Hera by means of a mirror, before undergoing the ordeal of the Titans, who cut him into pieces that are then put back together again by Athene and Zeus, or Demeter, or Apollo.

(Kristeva, 1988: 107)

Pentheus was also torn apart. Like Narcissus and Dionysus he was led astray by what he saw. Like Medusa's his crime, according to Ovid, was sacrilege. He offends against Bacchus, but the penalty and the perpetrators of it, together with the link to the story of Narcissus, suggest that it is looking directly at the (wrong) origin which is his crime. Pentheus is an atheist and blasphemer who scorns the gods and scorns any injunction or limit on his gaze (Ovid, 1955: 87–9): 'Pentheus looked upon the mysteries with uninitiated eyes. The first to see him, the first to make a frenzied rush, the first to hurl her thyrsus and wound him, was his own mother' (93). Pentheus appeals for clemency in the name of Actaeon, another who gazed on the prohibited and was torn apart,[6] but his plea goes unheeded by the women who celebrate the secret rites. Pentheus appeals to his mother, Agave: 'Agave uttered a wild shriek, tossed her head till her hair streamed through the air, then tore his head from his shoulders' (93).

The link between gazing on the prohibited (maternal) mystery and being torn apart is consistent with the Narcissus myth. To disrupt the 'concatenation of reflections' which constitute the self as One is to risk disintegration. To maintain the concatenation of reflections, it is necessary to *look away*. In the light of Irigaray's reading of Plato it is significant that Actaeon saw what was forbidden because he wandered into a cave by accident (78).

To gaze on the forbidden is linked to transgression of the incest taboo: this is, however, only one element in Ovid's tales of death by seeing. The tearing off of Pentheus' head by his mother reminds us of the threat of decapitation which Cixous identified as the penalty for the woman who refuses to be castrated (Cixous, 1981: 41–55). It appears that the man who refuses to be (properly) blind faces the same penalty:

To decapitate = to castrate. The terror of Medusa is thus a terror of castration that is linked to the sight of something . . . a boy, who hitherto has been unwilling to believe the threat of castration, catches sight of the female genitals, probably

those of an adult, surrounded by hair, and essentially those of
the mother.

(Freud, 1955: vol. 18, 273)

The appropriation of Medusa's head by Perseus and Athene was
the appropriation of the power of the gaze which would henceforward be a masculine agency, 'one of Perseus' means of killing
his enemies' (Laing, 1960: 79). Woman would become the object
of the gaze in this context. The myths of Narcissus, Pentheus
and Actaeon allow us to extend this: 'Woman' is the object of
the gaze, but it is forbidden to look on her as (being) origin or
(having) existence. To do so is to risk annihilation for it is to
risk the conflation of psychic space, which needs the origin to be
elsewhere and the mirror to be still and empty, in order to
constitute itself between the One and its image. Alienation from
material and maternal origin 'initiates the speculative space of
psychic ideal and contemplative internality' (Kristeva, 1988: 116).
To seek to be reunited with it or to bridge the gap between the
self as subject and object of the (internal) gaze is to risk fading
away like Narcissus or being torn apart like Pentheus or
Dionysus.

Irigaray plays on that threat in *Speculum of the Other Woman*,
'taking the eye of a man recently dead' (1985a: 180). Descartes
has dissociated the organ from the body, the sense from the
perception. Irigaray's text cuts out this retina of Descartes's
corpus and reconnects it with the metaphysics which conditioned
its responses and the psychology which underlies the fetishization
of this one part.

In '*Une Mère de glace*' Irigaray dissects Plotinus. Cutting up
his words and putting them back together again, she treats the
philosopher as Dionysus. The monstrous female author of this
atrocity thus adopts the position of the devouring mother goddess
who demands the blood of the hero. Sated on the divine nurture
which is 'himself', the mother in this fantasy risks becoming the
quiescent matter Plotinus describes. The symbolic offers the
power of devouring (the inversion of her power of nurture) as
the *imaginary* compensation for the appropriation of feminine
power. All the women writers under discussion are aware of the
attractions of this role of power available to them as women.
Irigaray, like all the others, is engaged in a struggle with that
'feminine' power which is the support of the symbolic order.

'*Une Mère de glace*' is the ultimate mimicry of philosophy, but the mere mirror also mimics herself, the woman philosopher. She uses the only words available to her – the already said. She borrows the words of the male philosopher. Her 'originality' is in daring to say anything at all, to posit herself as origin of an utterance. Hers is a travesty of origin and utterance. Her adventure into philosophy breaks up the very tradition which gives her something to say.

THE ANACHRONIC NOVEL

The transgression of linear history is a recurrent feature of contemporary women's writing. The writings of Carter and Kristeva are engaged in such transgression and it is a structural principle in *Speculum of the Other Woman*. *The Hothouse by the East River* is even more emphatically anachronic. It produces in narrative fiction the structural disjunctions which *Speculum of the Other Woman* produces in philosophy. Spark's use of plot can to some extent be described as anti-narrative. Such a reading is very much at odds with what most critics have said of Spark's work over the years. Frank Kermode argued that her work constituted a renewal of the concordance fictions which sustain meaning, (Kermode, 1967 [1966]: 131–3). Spark's novels systematically interrogate these metanarratives, however, and in the later fiction the interrogation destabilizes them. *The Hothouse by the East River* engages with the great twentieth-century metanarrative, psychology, the last resort of the enlightenment belief in knowledge, particularly scientific knowledge, as mode of liberation (Lyotard, 1984: 131). Spark ridicules the viability of this or any other explanatory fiction. 'He's looking for causes and all I'm giving him are effects', Elsa comments on her long-suffering analyst. 'It's lovely' (Spark, 1973: 48). The function of fiction for Spark is to resist explanation, to refer the reader 'elsewhere for reality' (Spark, 1967: 283).

The Hothouse by the East River is a story of life after death lived by those who will not accept their non-existence. It is not surprising that they are 'troubled by reminiscences' (Freud, 1981a: vol. 2, 221).[7] This novel is one of a number of anachronic novels by Muriel Spark. It contracts temporality into a dislocated present, 'the instant that includes eternity but may also be pulverized by death' (Kristeva, 1988: 331):

That was three years ago. But now it is long years ago, when they are recently engaged and are working together in England.

(Spark, 1973: 22)

Spark consistently uses tense in a manner quite alien to the traditions of narrative fiction. *The Hothouse by the East River* opens in the past perfect, switching immediately to the present tense. Spark's preferred mode of 'story-telling' is in a present tense punctuated by jumps into the future: 'Her mind is not dreamy as she absorbs each face, each dress, each suit of clothes, all blouses, blue-jeans, each piece of hand-luggage, each voice which will accompany her on the flight now boarding at Gate 14' (Spark, 1970: 36), ends chapter 1 of *The Driver's Seat*. Chapter 2 begins:

She will be found tomorrow morning dead from multiple stab-wounds, her wrists bound with a silk scarf and her ankles bound with a man's neck-tie, in the grounds of an empty villa, in a park on the edge of the foreign city to which she is now travelling on the flight now boarding at Gate 14.

(Spark, 1970: 37)

The description of this narrative device as flash-forward (Lodge, 1971: 126) is an attempt to appropriate it to the familiar model of fictional time as continuous and sequential and to contain the logic of Spark's narratives within the framework of a linear chronology. The cinematic connotations of 'flash-forward' transform the concept of time as a sequence of events into time as a series of images. The underlying concept is that of an *actual* beginning, middle and end which are cleverly transposed.

Spark's distortion of narrative convention is far more radical. The reader is stranded outside chronology. 'What's done is about to be done and the future has come to pass' (Spark, 1971c: 9). In *Not to Disturb* the author figure, Lister, disdains to 'split hairs between the past, present and future tenses' (58). The author to whom past, present and future are one and the female protagonists who collaborate with this fateful figure are, among other things, witches, sorceresses. They have the gift of second sight.

The image of the sorceress, Catherine Clément points out in *The Newly Born Woman*, is a residue of the primitive past which contains within it the promise of a different future (Cixous and Clément, 1986: 25). The sorceress has much in common with the hysteric (10–22) and both sorcery and hysteria have an anachronic disposition.

HYSTERICAL OR SCHIZOPHRENIC?

The temporal maze that defines Clément's exploration of what she calls 'the imaginary groups' (8) – 'madmen, deviants, neurotics, women, drifters, jugglers, tumblers' (9) – echoes the confusion of tense and time in Spark's novels. Clément asks if these 'abnormal ones' 'anticipate the culture to come, repeat the past culture, or express a constantly present utopia'? (Clément and Cixous, 1986: 9). Clément's question is asked of groups which exist only in interstices which the disjunctions of symbolic systems force those systems to surrender to the imaginary (8). Since time has no meaning in such a space the question is unanswerable in its own terms.

Clément's hysterics and sorceresses are invested with the power of the repressed. The return of the repressed is explicitly identified by her as 'anachronism' (9). 'The hysteric is troubled mainly by reminiscences' (Freud, 1981a: vol. 2, 221) and is troubling because she will not distinguish between reminiscence and reality, past and present, internal or external. The hysteric and the sorceress breach those boundaries.

Despite or perhaps because of this, Clément considers anachronism to be 'limited to imaginary displacements': 'It is a matter only of individual symbolism and not communicable, the culture cannot take it into account and make it the object of a transmission' (Cixous and Clément, 1986: 9). The anachronic return of the repressed as hysterical symptom cannot act upon the symbolic. It aspires to disorder, but collapses into anomaly.

Anomaly is outside of regularity and pattern. It is fragile and transitory and at the point where it is integrated into the prevailing structure it ceases to be an anomaly and becomes part of the structure which will define new anomalies as deviant:

> In their attempt to define the cultural function of the *anomaly*, both Lévi-Strauss and Sartre, who elsewhere contradict each other, seek to situate it in the fault-lines of a general system where some correlative structures do not successfully harmonize all their correlations.
>
> (Cixous and Clément, 1986: 7)

Contemporary women's writing tends to explore the fault-line where woman is simultaneously excluded from and subjected to the 'general system'. Spark and Irigaray expand the fault into a gaping hole in representation (Irigaray, 1985a: 50) which renders signification amorphous and poses a very distinct threat to the 'harmonization' and correlation of general systems and structures.

Anomaly is a deviation rather than a challenge (Clément and Cixous, 1986: 9), yet it has the potential to change the rules. It is freakish and of its nature cannot order the shape of change, but it can dislocate structures and make difference a viable possibility. An analysis of anomaly, as Clément presents it, provides an insight into the limitations and potential of the anachronic as a way out of the dilemma posed by Carter and Kristeva's analysis of the feminine subject's relation to history. The anachronic will affect systems in unpredictable ways. Anomalous by definition, it gives none of the guarantees of progress we would wish to find in a model for the rereading or production of history. Instead, as is apparent in *The Hothouse by the East River*, anomaly and anachronism threaten madness and death. Anomaly offers no more than a space or an anachronic instant outside of logical causality where 'a history read differently' (Cixous and Clément, 1986: 6) anticipates different 'relations between the Imaginary, the Real and the Symbolic' (9).

ELSA'S PROBLEM

Anachronism is the major narrative device of that hysterical fiction, *The Hothouse by the East River*. It is not surprising therefore that the plot of *The Hothouse by the East River* is the history of an anomaly. Elsa, the main female protagonist, has a peculiar 'problem', one which constitutes an anomaly in the strict scientific sense of 'deviation from the natural order' (OED). Elsa's shadow falls the wrong way.

The Hothouse by the East River is structured as the conflict of two novels. Paul, Elsa's husband, is the typical modern literary hero, the interpreter of an enigmatic reality. He attempts to come to terms with such obtuse contingencies as the contravention of the laws of physics by his wife's shadow. Paul differs from this modern archetype, however, in that he competes for control of the narrative with a 'character' whose perception is both reliable and, eventually, communicated. For Paul is a dead man, an egoist whose terrible dreams (Spark, 1973: 95) of jealous power have temporarily defied death itself. And Elsa, the woman, the other, trapped in his dreams tells 'the truth'. In other words, she is the agent of death.

EXTERNALIZATION AND THE CONCRETIZATION OF THE SIGNIFIER

Externalization, 'a technique of purely sharp-edged photography of events', has been adapted by Spark from the work of the anti-novelists (Kemp, 1974: 128–9). Bernard Harrison, in an essay comparing Spark and Jane Austen, has commented that we recognize the existence of a 'reality' outside ourselves only through its resistence to our will (Harrison, 1976: 246): 'The purpose of Muriel Spark's technique I think is to construct novels that have to be read with the same sense of engagement with a perpetually obstructing reality.'[8] Certainly this is the technique of Elsa in *The Hothouse by the East River*. 'He's looking for causes and all I'm giving him are effects' (Spark, 1973: 48). In this she achieves that separation, 'of a signifier from its signified and referent', with which Kristeva associates the irruption of the true-real in language.

Before discussing the 'true-real' it is useful to recapitulate the Lacanian concept of the 'Real'. It is the third term of the 'Borromean knot' identified by Lacan: Imaginary, Symbolic and Real (Lacan, 1977: ix-x). The 'Real' is distinct from the other two strands. These constitute 'reality' as the interaction of the relation between the subject and language (the Symbolic) and that between the ego and its images (the Imaginary). This 'reality' is the fiction achieved by the complicity of subject and society and it is perfectly knowable. The unknowable 'Real' is what that comfortable fiction cannot accommodate. It is 'other' than reality and so already bears some relation to philosophical definitions of 'truth'. It is also, tellingly, referred to by one distinguished commentator on Lacan as 'the umbilical cord of the Symbolic'. (Lacan, 1977: x)[9] The real becomes the place where truth and mat(t)er coalesce as the limits of language and of language's function as an 'identification circuit' (Cixous, 1974: 385).

Kristeva's writing undertakes the exploration of such limits, discovering them particularly in poetic discourse, in the language of madness and 'woman'. 'The true-real' brings together these liminal discourses under a new category. Lacan has described the Real as 'the impossible': the true-real is the impossible become, momentarily, possible. The irruption of the true-real in psychosis can be identified with the denial of death, that 'only radical "historical" reality' (Kristeva, 1986: 224). It is not denial of death, but insistence on it, which is identified with the irruption of the true-real in *The Hothouse by the East River*.

THE 'HALLUCINATORY ICON'

Elsa's 'truth'-telling takes the form of a radical disruption of all discourse. She follows Irigaray's programme for the woman who would bring about 'unparalleled interrogation, revolution' in the 'dominant ideology – that is of hom(m)osexuality and its struggles with the maternal . . . which still constitutes the sense of history also':

> Insist also and deliberately upon those *blanks* in discourse which recall the places of her exclusion and which, by their *silent plasticity*, ensure the cohesion, the articulation, the coherent expansion of established forms. Reinscribe them hither and thither *as divergencies*, otherwise and elsewhere than they are expected, in *ellipses* and *eclipses* that deconstruct the logical grid of the reader-writer, drive him out of his mind, trouble his vision to the point of incurable diplopia at least.
>
> (Irigaray, 1985a: 142)

Elsa's shadow defies the laws of physics and disrupts the specular economy in which power resides in the gazing subject rather than the object gazed upon. 'Her shadow falls the way it wants' (Spark, 1973: 63). Her extravagant gestures, her unwillingness to confirm or deny any statement and her anti-logical logic all follow the pattern outlined by Irigaray above. The deconstruction of the logical grid of her reader-writer, her husband Paul, reaches its apotheosis as the novel draws to a close:

> 'Go back, go back to the grave,' says Paul, 'from where I called you.'
> 'It's too late,' Elsa says. 'It was you with your terrible and jealous dreams who set the whole edifice soaring.'
> 'You're not real. Pierre and Katerina don't exist.'

'Don't we?' she says. 'Well then that settles the argument.
Just carry on as if nothing has happened all these years.'

(Spark, 1973: 95)

Paul is in the position of the 'dominant ideology' which finds
that

There where we expect to find the opaque and silent matrix
of a logos immutable in the certainty of its own light, fires
and mirrors are beginning to radiate, sapping the evidence of
reason at its base.

(Irigaray, 1985a: 144)

That Elsa's challenge is launched visually (by her shadow) rather
than verbally links it to Irigaray's emphasis on 'fires and mirrors'
and is crucial to the enterprise of sapping the evidence of a
'reason' based on the privilege of sight and identity. That privilege
eliminates the woman at the start, suppressing the possibility of
a 'feminine libido' (Irigaray 1985a: 43, 50–2) under the sign of
castration:

Nothing to be seen is equivalent to having no thing. No being
and no truth. The contract, the collusion between *one* sex organ
and the victory won by visual dominance, therefore leaves
woman with her sexual void, with an 'actual castration' carried
out in actual fact.

(Irigaray, 1985a: 48)

In the concluding section of *Speculum of the Other Woman*, 'Plato's
hystera', Irigaray explores the relationship between this specular
economy and the linguistic economy also supported on the
absence of woman. The two are identified through the interplay
of 'echo' and reflection as the twin fates of 'Woman' (256–66).
Supported by the logos which 'connotes' his wife 'as castrated,
especially as castrated of words' (142), Paul spins webs of words,
protecting the explanatory fictions which convince him of his
own existence:

'Mother is no fool', says Pierre. 'Mother is intelligent. More
than one can possibly calculate, she's intelligent, it gives one a
jolt sometimes.'

The father feels a sudden panic because it is infinitely easier
for a man to leave a beautiful woman, to walk out and leave
her and be free, than to leave a woman of intelligence beyond

his calculation and her own grasp. 'No', Paul shouts. 'She's crazy. I have to think for her, I have to do her thinking all the time.'

'All right, Father. All right.'

'She's cunning that's all. When she wants to be.'

(Spark, 1973: 37)

Across Paul's normative fictions, his 'reality', Elsa casts her shadow. 'You've externalized, Elsa,' her excited analyst tells her (47). Her anomalous shadow is thrown perpetually against the light, against logic, law and the most basic forms of order. According to Paul, desperate to term her mad, this means that 'Her delusion, her figment, her nothing there has come to pass' (15). According to Kristeva, the true-real is found in the hallucination of the psychotic, where verbal and visual collide, the signifier becomes real and so, for example, the word green becomes a vision of the colour green. 'Nothing there' comes to pass.

Elsa's laughter echoes through this 'excessive' text: the irruption of the true-real indicates 'an unutterable *jouissance*' (Kristeva, 1986: 230). Elsa's shadows and symbols challenge and eventually precipitate the disintegration of Paul's fictions of self, sanity and society. 'The hallucinatory icon . . . challenges what may be structured as a language: it obliterates reality and makes the real loom forth as a jubilant enigma.' Kristeva's reference to this 'jubilant enigma' echoes the 'lithe cloud of unknowing' (Spark, 1973: 140) Elsa trails through the homogenizing fictions which would confine her and deny the 'real'. The hallucinatory icon's conflation of the categories of the specular and the linguistic brings us back to Irigaray's play on the relationship of Echo and Narcissus: it upsets representation and reflection. Precisely because it does not allow the space for signification to take place, because it short-circuits representation, the hallucinatory icon prevents the return of the echo and the gaze. In the imagery of Plato's allegory of the cave analysed by Irigaray, the shadow becomes substance.

The 'true-real' of the 'psychotic text', as Kristeva describes it, is precipitated by the foreclosure of the phallic, the denial of castration, of lack and of sexual differentiation (Kristeva, 1986: 224). It is more than a residue of the pre-linguistic and the refusal of separation from 'mother', however. It is a fold in discourse (233), a point where that which is normally excluded finds its way into language without losing itself. This makes it a powerful and dangerous anomaly.

Elsa terrorizes the symbolic, incidentally frightening the life out of psychoanalysis and modern New York. Her 'meaningless' gestures, her 'femininity' and madness gradually acquire the status of 'truth'. They reveal Paul's explanations of 'her problem' as truly meaningless, as a doomed attempt to impose power and order on the intractable forces of the real: on life and death and on Elsa herself.

By the end of *The Hothouse by the East River* the woman, Elsa, is no longer the object of language and fiction. Nor is she the subject who speaks, again determined by language. The novel launches an effective attack on the symbolic order. It situates the feminine speaking subject on a 'border zone' (228), allying herself with the true-real, that stumbling block of discourse, but also using language, subverting it to her own ends. Elsa is more reckless and more dangerous than Dora Chance. She does not hesitate to step over 'the limits of the power of laughter' (Carter, 1991: 220).

THE POWER OF THE ENDING

At the beginning of the novel it is Elsa who appears to be the source of the madness within the novel: 'The schizophrenic has imposed her will. Her delusion, her figment, her nothing-there, has come to pass' (Spark 1973: 15). She presents the psychotic symptom of the hallucinatory icon. It is Paul, however, who denies death.

Elsa accuses Paul of responsibility for the shape of their story: 'It was you with your terrible and jealous dreams who set the whole edifice soaring' (95). It is Paul who has imposed *his* delusion. Since his terrible dreams are the source of this nightmare existence and it is imposed by his will, it is he who has made 'nothing there' come to pass. He is the schizophrenic. He is also one of a series of delinquent author figures in Spark's fiction. As such, he casts considerable light on the 'schizophrenic' desire for authorial omniscience – pursued in Lessing's later fiction, for example. Paul follows the pattern of attempting to create an alternative reality in which he can be omnipotent, a fictional universe where he knows all and sees all. In other words, he wants to be God, as did Anna Wulf in *The Golden Notebook*.

(How else can one describe her desire to create and name all things?) Anna unites the cosmos (her cosmos) under the auspices of a central, perceiving self. Paul attempts to do likewise. He is countered by another kind of authority. This is the power of the ending, a power quite different from that of the 'nightmare of repetition' which characterized ideological and biological reproduction for Lessing and, more ambivalently, Carter.

During the seven-year period when she was writing *The Hothouse by the East River*, Spark wrote three novellas (Kemp, 1974: 157), all of them concerned with the conflict between these two forms of 'authority'. *The Public Image* recounts the successful attempts of Annabel, an actress, to combat the story of her life and marriage which her husband has engineered through his suicide. Annabel has to wrest power from the dead to continue living.

In *The Driver's Seat* Lise organizes her own murder. She is the antithesis of the 'character' as its function is described by Cixous (1974). Aware that she has not written the plot of her life, Lise becomes co-author of her story through her co-operation with its inevitable end. This agency is of course completely artificial since Lise is a character in a novel, a fiction, 'only some hundreds of words, some punctuation, sentences, paragraphs, marks on a page' (Spark, 1981: 61). She is also the author's surrogate in the novel and her attempt to take 'the driver's seat' indicates how Spark's treatment of 'authority' differs from Lessing's. Lise's attempt to write her own script is defined by an acceptance that her fate is predetermined and that she is subject to a structure outside her control. Lise finds that her aspiration to 'authority' can be fulfilled only through complicity in the story of her own murder. She is a figure for the feminine subject whose options are no options. She can either choose a subjectivity which kills her or lose subjectivity and all ability to act.

Spark is often read as a novelist who revitalizes and validates the assumption of authorial omniscience. *The Driver's Seat* insists on quite a different reading. In the figure of Lise, Spark parodies the aspiration to authority, particularly her own aspiration to authority as a woman writer. Spark's fiction is full of female protagonists (Lise, Elsa, the Abbess of Crewe, Jean Brodie, Annabel) who act out the role of the 'hysteric' as described by Irigaray:

Woman's special form of art would be to 'mimic' a bad work

of art, to be *a bad (copy of a) work of art*. Her neurosis would be recognized as a counterfeit or parody of an artistic process. It is transformed into an aesthetic object, but one without value, which has to be condemned because it is a *forgery*. It is neither 'nature' nor an appropriate technique for re-producing nature. Artifice, lie, deception, snare – these are the kinds of judgements society confers upon the tableaux, the scenes, the dramas produced by the hysteric.[10]

(Irigaray, 1985b: 125)

Artifice, lie, deception, snare – these are also the techniques which Spark insists are at the root of her own 'artistic process': 'I don't claim that my novels are truth,' she once said in an interview. 'I claim that they are fiction, out of which a kind of truth emerges' (Kermode, 1971: 273). Spark's mimicry and parody of 'bad works of art' are noteworthy in *The Driver's Seat* where the gory thriller and the holiday romance are mockingly combined with the tragic scenario of the inevitably doomed heroine. In a 1971 interview she commented that glossy magazines and paparazzi had begun to provide her with material for her fiction (Spark, 1971a: 73).

Not to Disturb was published directly after *The Driver's Seat* and addresses similar issues. In *Not to Disturb* the Klopstocks imagine that they are directing their own lives. Lister, their sinister butler, knows better. 'Playing at erotic situation games the Klopstocks are ultimately trapped inside one. The fictional stereotypes they have perversely toyed with close vengefully round them' (Kemp, 1974: 135). The servants' participation in these games has been purchased and they are therefore already aware that the actors act under compulsion and do not determine their own roles. This understanding of the inevitability of plot ironically places the servants in a position of power. They exploit the Klopstocks' sordid end to their own advantage: the banality of the story is the guarantee of its commercial success. They therefore acquire a vested interest in a tragic outcome.

Spark expressed her impatience with tragedy and with realistic tragedy in particular in her address to the American Academy of Arts and Letters in 1971 on 'The desegregation of art'. The art of pathos 'cheats us into a sense of involvement with life and society but in reality it is a segregated activity' (Spark, 1971b: 24).

A great number of the audience or of the readers feel that their moral responsibilities are sufficiently fulfilled by the emotions they have been induced to feel. A man may go to bed feeling less guilty after seeing such a play [of pathos]. He has undergone the experience of pity for the underdog. Salt tears have gone bowling down his cheeks. He has had a good dinner. He is absolved, he sleeps well. He rises refreshed more determined than ever to be the overdog.

(Spark, 1971b: 23–4)

This use of art to transform emotion into commodity is savagely mocked in *Not to Disturb*. Lister, the purveyor of the Klopstock tragedy as mass entertainment, is cultured, literary and callously exploitative. His victims are petty pornographers. In the conflict between novelist and pornographer, art is portrayed as more deadly than pornography. The plots of both are in this case utterly meaningless and absolutely inevitable. The end of both is violent death.

FORGETTING AND UNKNOWING

Spark's novels are dominated by a struggle for authority, a struggle between conflicting models of authority. The struggle is not that between God, the novelist, and his/her creatures, as is sometimes suggested (Kemp, 1974; Bradbury, 1972; Kermode, 1967 [1966]). It is between the authority of the autonomous creating subject derived from a universal origin (the model of the creator) and an authority which has no origin. This authority without origin is a radical contingency which is neither motivated nor intelligible, which has no pattern, only the power of its own intractability. In *The Driver's Seat*, in *The Public Image*, in *Not to Disturb* and *The Hothouse by the East River* it is the power of the predetermined and terrifying ending. It is, simply, death: 'In this proliferating desire of the same, death will be the only representative of an outside, of a heterogeneity, of an other: woman will assume the function of representing death . . .' (Irigaray, 1985a: 27). Elsa's relation to death differs from that of Lise in *The Driver's Seat*. Lise allies herself with the forces which propel her towards her *own* death. Elsa forces those around her to accept *their* death. She is not simply an 'anti-myth of mothering' (Carter, 1977: 113). Nor is she the antithesis of the Virgin Mother in 'Stabat Mater'. *The Hothouse by the East River* operates on the basis that the maternal no longer supports the fragile Word. Elsa is a mother only in the deranged fiction of her husband. 'Katerina is a vagary of your mind', Elsa tells Paul of their daughter, 'that's all' (Spark, 1973: 127). Katerina in this scenario is a kind of Athene, a product of her father's mind and an absurd realization of the displacement of origin from Matter to Idea. It is interesting that Elsa is exasperated by Katerina – 'so bloody literal' (21). Paul's daughter is a woman of the Word unmediated by the matter of language.

Elsa's shadow is a play on the word 'negative'. It is the negation of life and the agent or sign of death, but is also a photographic negative (it reverses the image). It is described as a 'cloud of unknowing' (Spark, 1973: 140). *The Cloud of Unknowing* (Wolters, 1978 [1961]) is an anonymous fourteenth-century mystical work which stresses the perils and temptations of the contemplative way. Most of its instructions to those who would wish to be contemplatives are in the negative (Burrow, 1977). The first phase of contemplation, according to *The Cloud of Unknowing*, must be forgetting. The contemplative soul must put a 'cloud of forgetting' between itself and everything which is not God:

> Everything must be hidden under the cloud of forgetting.
>
> For though it is sometimes useful to think of particular creatures, what they are and do, in this case it is virtually useless. For the act of remembering or thinking about what a thing is or does has a spiritual effect. Your soul's eye concentrates upon it, just as the marksman fixes his eye on his target. Let me say this: everything you think about, all the time you think about it, is 'above' you, between you and God. And you are that much farther from God if anything but God is in your mind.
>
> (Wolters, 1978 [1961]: 67)

The process to which Elsa subjects those around her in *The Hothouse by the East River* is a paradoxical reversal of the 'forgetting' advocated in *The Cloud of Unknowing*. Bombarded by confusing detail, Paul (and the reader of *The Hothouse by the East River*) is, like the contemplative, stripped of specifics, disorientated in his relation to 'effects' (Spark, 1973: 48). When Elsa exults in the bewilderment of her analyst, she, like the author of *The Cloud of Unknowing*, repudiates causality, logic, evidence. Paradoxically, the way to apprehend the cause is to forget the effects. For the author of *The Cloud of Unknowing* this means that contemplation must not even pause on the attributes of its supreme object:

> No man or woman can hope to achieve contemplation without the foundation of many such delightful meditations on his or her own wretchedness, and our Lord's passion, and the kindness of God, and his great goodness and worth. All the same, the practised hand must leave them, and put them away deep down in the cloud of forgetting if he is ever to penetrate the cloud of unknowing between him and God.
>
> (Wolters, 1978 [1961]: 69)

At the end of *The Hothouse by the East River* Paul must forget her bewildering effects and simply follow Elsa: 'She turns to the car, he following her, watching as she moves how she trails her faithful and lithe cloud of unknowing across the pavement' (Spark, 1973: 140). The soul which fails to forget and which 'deliberately conjures up the memory of somebody or something or other' is lost (Wolters, 1978 [1961]: 75, 78). It is just such a failure to forget which has left Paul after death in a dark nightmare world, a kind of purgatory. The shades around him are the inflated caricatures which his imagination has made of old acquaintances. These creatures of his jealous dreams bear some resemblance to the different kind of memories which in *The Cloud of Unknowing* threaten the perpetual exile of the contemplative soul from God: 'If it is a thing that grieves or has grieved you, then you rage and want revenge – and that is *Wrath*' (Wolters, 1978 [1961]: 75). The first character we meet in the novel is Helmut Kohl, whom Paul has betrayed and from whom he fears revenge, but on whom he has and would again revenge himself. (Paul suspected Helmut of having an affair with Elsa during the war and the affair and its aftermath of suspicion and paranoia are repeated in the dream landscape of the 1970s.)

Paul's rescue from his own nightmare comes about by means of a spiritual trick advocated in *The Cloud of Unknowing*, which suggests:

> When you feel that you are completely powerless to put these thoughts away, cower down before them like some cringing captive overcome in battle, and reckon that it is ridiculous to fight them any longer. In this way you surrender yourself to God. . . . Such knowledge and experience is humility. And this

humility causes God himself to come down in his might, and
avenge you of your enemies and take you up.

(Wolters, 1978 [1961]: 99)

Exhausted by the effort of interpreting Elsa's 'signs', Paul simply
gives in.

SOMETHING OTHER

Commentary by critics such as Malcolm Bradbury (1972), Frank
Kermode (1967 [1966]; 1971) and Peter Kemp (1974) celebrates
Spark's novels as metafictional musings on metaphysics. Her
novels are described as unique among contemporary fiction in
their ability to combine a self-reflexive insistence on their own
fictionality with insistence on their right to reflect on or postulate
the existence of something beyond fiction and outside language.
'Positing the existence of that other language or even of an other
of language, indeed of an outside-of-language, is not necessarily
setting up a preserve for metaphysics or theology' (Kristeva, 1989:
66). But Spark is very much identified as a Catholic novelist and
her exploration of the novel form has been consistently linked by
her with that faith. So it has perhaps been inevitable that that
'something' other, other than and to fiction and language, has
been identified as a deity. The consistent metaphor of the author
as God within her own text has lent weight to such an identification. That the author is a woman and that her relationship to
the novel form is one of radical interrogation already puts the
metaphor into question, however. Spark's attempt to breach the
self-reflexive circularity of metafiction confronts a similar impasse
to that confronted by the woman who must speak, but finds
subjectivity in language entails subjection.

If the author is God in Spark's novels, then the author surrogates would indicate that God is female, omniscient, violent and
unreliable. Effie is the divine author in *The Only Problem*. She is
absent from the action, but she determines the plot. She is also
an unfaithful wife and a member of a Baader-Meinhof style gang.
In *The Hothouse by the East River* Elsa is not a political terrorist
– more a metaphysical guerrilla.[11] Marriage is not an unusual
metaphor in religious writings for the relationship of the soul to
God (Kristeva, 1988: 83–100). Spark's use of the image draws
attention to the conflict between the two meanings of God which

the author of *The Cloud of Unknowing* submerges in 'unknowing'. The concept of a God constitutes a recognition of a radical and non-human Otherness, but also an attempt to name and humanize that Otherness, to make of it a support for the law of the one and the same. On the one hand, 'God' is 'that thing which I cannot think' (Wolters, 1978 [1961]: 68). On the other, *The Cloud of Unknowing* presents this God 'just as a father' (99). These two conceptions of God, unthinkable *and* human, correspond to the two kinds of authority explored in Spark's fiction, the authority of inexplicable contingency and that of the ego-centred 'identification circuit' (Cixous, 1974: 385). The former always wins in Spark's fiction, but it is striking that in *Symposium* (1990) contingency is no longer characterized. Margaret, the character who comes closest to the roles played by Elsa and Effie, has no truth to offer. She is overtaken by the contingency she interpreted as a fate in which she had a catalytic function. Whatever the initial impulse behind Spark's analogy of God and novelist, one must ask whether the woman novelist and her surrogates are any longer the representatives of an arbitrary and unknowable 'God' or whether that 'God' has become a metaphor for the woman who can find no other place in which to signify herself (Irigaray, 1985a: 27):

It becomes clear that the supreme Being . . . the immobile sphere from which originates all movements . . . is situated in the place, the opaque place of the *jouissance* of the Other – that Other which, if she existed, the woman might be.

(Lacan, 1982: 153)

Chapter 6

The abject and the
absence of the ideal

THE ABJECT AND THE SUBLIME

The Hothouse by the East River and *Speculum of the Other Woman*
exhaust logic, language and the law. What is left? 'If I take time
off from thinking, what then?' (Carter, 1969: 98). The answer at
the end of *The Hothouse by the East River* is death. 'Non-meaning'
(Kristeva, 1989: 49). Or, the Truth of the real. *The Hothouse
by the East River* points towards a different relation between the
true-real and death than that put forward by Kristeva in
her essay 'The true-real' (1986: 214–37). The true-real of *The
Hothouse by the East River* is deathly. It is also both abject and
sublime.

Kristeva's concepts of the abject and sublime are outlined in
Powers of Horror (1982), which was first published in 1980, one
year after 'Le vréel' appeared as part of the seminar material
published as *La Folle Verité* (1979). The abject, like the true-
real, is linked to the maternal body. Abjection marks the first
differentiation of the subject from that body. It precedes the
opposition of self and other and even of subject and object. The
abject is a pre-object of the pre-subject: abjection precipitates the
process by which subject and object take (their) place(s):

> When I am beset by abjection, the twisted braid of affects and
> thoughts I call by such a name does not have, properly speak-
> ing, a definable *object*. The abject is not an ob-ject facing me,
> which I name or imagine. Nor is it an ob-jest, an otherness
> ceaselessly fleeing in a systematic quest of desire. What is abject
> is not my correlative, which providing me with someone or
> something else as support, would allow me to be more or less

detached and autonomous. The abject has only one quality of the object – that of being opposed to *I*.

(Kristeva, 1982: 1)

The abject is consistently linked in *Powers of Horror* with the sublime. The concept of the sublime has a lengthy history which is generally perceived to have its roots in Longinus' work *On the Sublime*. For Longinus the sublime was primarily a matter of style: 'The Sublime, whenever it occurs, consists in a certain loftiness and excellence of language' (2). The work of Edmund Burke and Immanuel Kant has been most significant for modern formulations of the sublime and it is on modern formulations that this chapter will focus. Two formulations of the sublime have emerged since the eighteenth century, the metaphysical and the psychological sublime. Edmund Burke's essay 'A philosophical enquiry into the origin of our ideas of the sublime and beautiful' was published in 1757 and appeared in a revised and enlarged edition two years later. For Burke the sublime was an emotional state in which all reasoning and agency on the part of the mind or soul are suspended (598) due to the powerful emotional impact of the terrible:

> Whatever is fitted in any sort to excite the ideas of pain and danger, that is to say, whatever is in any sort terrible, or is conversant about terrible objects, or operates in a manner analogous to terror, is a source of the *sublime*; that is, it is productive of the strongest emotion which the mind is capable of feeling (585).

Kant's theory of the sublime was outlined in his *Critique of Judgement*, first published in 1790. The sublime is defined therein in contrast to and through differentiation from 'the beautiful' (1892 [1790], 1.1.24: 102–10). This classic differentiation is not observed in Kristeva's work: 'Artifice, as sublime meaning, for and on behalf of the underlying implicit non-being, replaces the ephemeral. Beauty is consubstantial with it' (Kristeva, 1989: 99). Kant's formulation of the sublime owes much to Burke, but Kant introduces a metaphysical dimension which changes the significance of the sublime and makes the inadequacy of emotive perception the source of the sublime pain which Burke perceived as originating in terror:

The feeling of the Sublime is therefore a feeling of pain, arising

from the want of accordance between the aesthetical estimation
of magnitude formed by the Imagination and the estimation of
the same formed by Reason. There is at the same time a
pleasure thus excited, arising from the correspondence with
Rational Ideas of this very judgement of the inadequacy of our
greatest faculty of Sense.

(Kant, 1892 [1790], 1.1.27: 119–20)

Burke's sublime is an emotional state in which the subject loses
itself in 'its object':[1]

The passion caused by the great and sublime in *nature*, when
those causes operate most powerfully, is astonishment: and
astonishment is that state of the soul in which all its motions
are suspended, with some degree of horror. In this case the
mind is so entirely filled with its object, that it cannot entertain
any other, nor by consequence reason on that object which
employs it. Hence arises the great power of the sublime, that,
far from being produced by them, it anticipates our reasonings
and hurries us on by an irresistible force.

(Burke, 1852 [1759]: 598)

The sublime is thus a state of total identification with an other,
not unlike the state of love described by Kristeva in *Tales of Love*:
'in love', as in the sublime state, ' "I" has been an *other*' (1988:
4). For Kant 'the feeling of the Sublime' is, by contrast, 'a want
of accordance' (1892 [1790], 1.1.27: 119). Burke's sublime is predicated on a collapse (or perhaps an infinite expansion) of Narcissan
internality into an Other. Kant's sublime is metaphysical in the
sense observed in Plotinus: it opens up internal space by postulating an other origin (elsewhere). The sense of the sublime for
Kant is a sense of the distance between the perceptual, material
world of 'Sense' (120) and the 'Rational Ideas'. The painful
internal discord between the philosophical subject's perception
and the Idea it reflects is compensated for by the pleasure of being
able to identify such a discord. For Burke's identification of subject with object, Kant substitutes the object's lack of identity with
the Idea it represents. This lack is then displaced by a new identity, between subject and Idea. This is a variant of the displacement
of origin constitutive of the philosophical subject in Plotinus and
in Plato. It is also a variant of Rousseau's and Engels's postulation

of a primary alienation which can be transformed into an antidote to alienation.

The repetition of these moves in Kant's formulation of the sublime would indicate that the sublime itself constitutes a threat to the security of the subject (of the displaced origin or alienation). The sublime is at the 'edge' of something (Kristeva, 1982: 11).

For Kristeva, that something is the abject. Like the abject, the sublime partakes of oblivion (in this case as an excess of memory) and of the prehistory of subject and object:

> For the sublime has no object either. When the starry sky, a vista of open seas or a stained glass window shedding purple beams fascinate me, there is a cluster of meaning, of colors, of words, of caresses, there are light touches, scents, sights, cadences that arise, shroud me, carry me away, and sweep me beyond the things that I see, hear, or think. The 'sublime' object dissolves in the raptures of a bottomless memory. It is such a memory, which from stopping point to stopping point, remembrance to remembrance, love to love, transfers that object to the refulgent point of the dazzlement in which I stray in order to be. As soon as I perceive it, as soon as I name it, the sublime triggers – it has always already triggered – a spree of perceptions and words that expand memory boundlessly. I then forget the point of departure and find myself removed to a secondary universe, set off from the one where 'I' am – delight and loss. Not at all short of but always with and through perception and words, the sublime is a *something added* that expands us, overstrains us, and causes us to be both *here* as dejects, and *there*, as others and sparkling.
>
> (Kristeva, 1982: 12)

Kristeva's explication of the sublime through abjection problematizes any distinction of the psychological and metaphysical sublime. This (abject) sublime is Kantian and metaphysical in that it is 'something more'. It is psychological by virtue of its association with the abject and shares with Burke's psychological sublime the feature of 'loss' of one self as subject, though in the Kristevan case the subject is lost in 'no object' (12). The sublime as edge of the abject is the experience of being one's self Other, an experience closer to Burke's than Kant's theory of the sublime, though the effect of doubling is intrinsic to both Kristeva's and Kant's concepts of the sublime.

The metaphysical sublime is of the timeless realm of 'Rational Ideas' (Kant, 1892 [1790], 1.1.27: 120) but the psychological sublime is anachronic, 'it anticipates our reasonings, and hurries us on by an irresistible force' (Burke, 1852 [1759]: 598). The abject sublime, as I will refer to Kristeva's concept of the sublime, is anachronic also. It expands 'memory boundlessly' and postulates another (spatial) dimension which breaks up the here and now and substitutes the '*here* . . . and *there*' (Kristeva, 1982: 12).

DEATH – THE BORDER – THE ABJECT

Cixous, Lessing, Kristeva and Carter are all centrally if differently concerned with the relation of the maternal and death, with that which is outside language and thought where the parameters of language and thought are defined by and united under the sign of the One, Being. For Kristeva the maternal is the threat of death and the compensation for that theat (1986: 185). Irigaray emphasizes feminine difference as occupying the same (extra)symbolic space as death:

> In this proliferating desire of the same, death will be the only representative of an outside, of a heterogeneity, of an other: woman will assume the function of representing death . . .
>
> (Irigaray, 1985a: 27)

Spark is closer to Irigaray's viewpoint. *The Hothouse by the East River*, like much of Spark's fiction, dematernalizes death. The alliance between death and the woman which she celebrates is no consolatory fiction. It does nothing to make 'the thought of death bearable' (Kristeva, 1986: 185). The existence of the unbearable, the unthinkable, is the point of Spark's fiction.

In their radical alterity death and the woman mark the end of signification, its border with the unspeakable. *The Hothouse by the East River* crosses that boundary. A story of life after death, it is written 'beyond the ending' (du Plessis, 1985). Peter Kemp has criticized the 'excess' of *The Hothouse by the East River*:

> The cool elegancies of distaste, the razor-blade finesse, and damning, finely attuned mimicry so notable in the preceding books here coarsen into strident overkill. Dealing with rampant imbecility, extreme crassness, gross stupidity, Mrs Spark

disappointingly allows her style to slip towards a corresponding flagrancy.

(Kemp, 1974: 151)

Kemp further comments in relation to *Hothouse by the East River* that Spark's 'reluctance to specify seems merely perverse', 'sphinx-faced' (149). Flagrant, crass, strident: the use of such 'moral' and sexual categories to police the writing of women is too well documented to require comment here (Russ, 1984; Gilbert and Gubar, 1979; Moi, 1985; etc.). The importance of Kemp's distaste for *The Hothouse by the East River* is that it highlights the operation of the 'abject' in the novel. Abjection is the rejection by which 'I' become. I give birth to myself (Kristeva, 1982: 3) through the exclusion of not-I, 'that which is not me' (2). In abjection 'not me' has not yet stabilized into an Other. 'The abject has only one quality of the object – that of being opposed to I' (1). Abjection takes place on the margin where subject and object differentiate themselves. In other words, abjection may be mapped on to the thetic. In *Powers of Horror* abject and sublime are developed as another inextricable couple with a relationship to Kristeva's earlier 'couple', semiotic and symbolic. Abject and sublime, however, are not identifiable with or components of the earlier terms, and *Powers of Horror* marks an important development in Kristeva's work.

As in the case of semiotic and symbolic, one term of the abject-ideal pair is given priority: *Powers of Horror* is subtitled *An Essay on Abjection*. The new couple are an inextricable as semiotic and symbolic: 'To each ego its object, to each super-ego its abject' (2).

The abject and the semiotic share a relationship to the death drives. In the semiotic these drives are powered by a resistance to separation which is fundamentally a resistance to separation from the mother:

> Drives involve pre-Oedipal semiotic functions and energy discharges that connect and orient the body to the mother. We must emphasise that 'drives' are always already ambiguous, simultaneously assimilating and destructive. . . . The mother's body is therefore what mediates the symbolic law organizing social relations and becomes the ordering principle of the semiotic *chora* which is on the path of destruction, aggressivity and death.
>
> (Kristeva, 1984: 27–8)

In abjection, the death drives are powered by a loathing which is intrinsically a loathing of the maternal body (Kristeva, 1982: 100–1). Separation from the maternal body is still crucial.[2] 'The ultimate of abjection' is 'the birth-giving scene . . . something *horrible to see* at the impossible doors of the invisible – the mother's body' (155).

The 'vortex of summons and repulsion' which constitutes abjection is also constitutive of the pre-subject's relation to the 'Mother' (1). The semiotic is pre-verbal, 'musicating' (1981: 185), it thrives in the register of touch and colour (216–22, 243–50). It is 'Desire in Language'. In abjection, 'Apprehensive, desire turns aside; sickened, it rejects' (1982: 1). 'The vision of the abject' (154)

> is indeed a vision, to the extent that sight is massively summoned to play a part in it, broken up by the rhythmic sound of the voice. But it is a vision that resists any representation, if the latter is a desire to coincide with the present identity of what is to be represented.[3] The vision of the ab-ject is, by definition, the sign of an impossible ob-ject, a boundary and a limit.
>
> (Kristeva, 1982: 154)

A sign of an impossible ob-ject, a boundary and a limit, all existing in a prioritized register of vision where the desire for representation no longer exists; the abject offers us another context in which to interpret Elsa's shadow. *The Hothouse by the East River* does not approach the relationship of woman and death through the maternal terms of the semiotic. Instead it approaches it through the failed abjection of Paul.

'The one by whom the abject exists' is 'the deject' (8). Kristeva's description of the deject illuminates the operations of the anachronic and true-real in *The Hothouse by the East River* and the obsessive nightmare quality of the novel:

> Instead of sounding himself as to his 'being' he does so concerning his place. '*Where* am I?' instead of '*Who* am I?' . . . A deviser of territories, languages, works, the *deject* never stops demarcating his universe whose fluid confines – for they are constituted by a non-object, the abject – constantly question his solidity and impel him to start afresh. A tireless builder,

the deject is in short a *stray*. He is on a journey during the
night, the end of which keeps receding.[4]

(Kristeva, 1982: 80)

Like Paul, the deject has a sense of the danger and the loss that
the pseudo-object which attracts him represents for him. Unlike
Paul, the deject draws a pleasure bonus from his/her abjection,
'it is out of such straying on excluded ground that he draws his
jouissance' (8). This straying on excluded ground is similar to the
transgression of forbidden boundaries (by the gaze) which caused
the disintegration of the self in the myths of Actaeon and
Pentheus. The constant putting into question of his 'solidity' by
the 'fluid' universe in which the deject finds himself also suggests
analogies with Narcissus. The deject and his abject are not sufficiently stable or separate to construct the self-reflexive space of
subjectivity:

The abject from which he does not cease separating is for him,
in short, a *land of oblivion* that is constantly remembered. Once
upon blotted out time the abject must have been a magnetized
pole of covetousness.

(Kristeva, 1982: 8)

Covetous Paul with his jealous dreams (Spark, 1973: 95) is a
'tireless builder' (Kristeva, 1982: 8). The 'land of oblivion' he has
conjured up as an afterlife is described as an edifice. The architec-
tural metaphor is complete when the apartment block with which
his will and fantasy are identified collapses as he and Elsa depart
for death (Spark, 1973: 139–40). Paul has created a place outside
time where death can be denied. His relation to time is thus
anachronic and within that relation there occurs a 'flash' (back-
ward) which will illuminate the relation of sublime and abject in
The Hothouse by the East River.

The clean and proper . . . becomes filthy, the sought-after turns
into the banished, fascination into shame. Then forgotten time
crops up suddenly and condenses into a flash of lightning,[5] an
operation that if it were thought out would involve bringing
together the two opposite terms but on account of that flash
is discharged like thunder. The time of abjection is double: a
time of oblivion and thunder, of veiled infinity and the movement when revelation bursts forth.

(Kristeva, 1982: 8–9)

The Hothouse by the East River situates itself in that flash between time and its double. It takes (a) place between oblivion, the veiled infinity of death and the limbo of New York now, on the one hand, and thunder, revelation and a bomb in 1945, on the other. The novel's two central protagonists are a couple and perhaps even doubles. They constitute a double protagonist, Paul, the deject 'by whom the abject exists' (8), and Elsa, who is again double, the locus of abjection *and* the one who experiences the deject's *'jouissance'* (9) as she strays into 'a territory I can call my own because the Other, having dwelt in me as alter ego, points it out to me through loathing' (10). Who is abject, who deject? Which is alter-ego in a text where ego is fragile and false? 'We may call it a border; abjection is above all ambiguity' (9) and Paul and Elsa are not characters, but positions of the subject which is ceaselessly giving birth to itself (3) and giving itself simultaneously up to death: 'Abjection preserves what existed in the archaism of pre-objectal relationship, in the immemorial violence by which a body becomes separated from another body in order to be' (10).

THE SUBLIME: MODERN AND POSTMODERN

The Hothouse by the East River is centrally concerned with the abject. How important is the abject's non-identical double, the sublime, in Spark's novel? I will concentrate very specifically on the contrasting contemporary theories of the sublime to be found in the work of Kristeva (1982, 1988) and Jean François Lyotard (1984: 77–82). This concentration is motivated by two related factors. Lyotard posits an aesthetics of the sublime as definitive of modernism and postmodernism. (He is concerned with the metaphysical sublime.) Kristeva links the sublime inextricably to the abject, and problematizes the distinctions between the metaphysical and psychological sublime. Through a discussion of the sublime as it is put forward by these two writers it is possible to read *The Hothouse by the East River* in the context of modernism and postmodernism (as Lyotard has influentially described them). The postmodern, as thus defined, turns out to operate within *The Hothouse by the East River* in a manner remarkably similar to that of the true-real. Analysis of the relationship of postmodern and true-real in *The Hothouse by the East River* puts into question the relation of the abject to the sublime and ultimately that of the abject sublime to the true-real.

There are specific problems for feminist critique in such use of Lyotard's work.[6] *The Postmodern Condition* accomplishes a most extraordinary exclusion. A 'report on knowledge' in the late twentieth century which fails to examine changing sexual roles, feminist research and the impact of both on representation and the construction of knowledge is an anachronism, in the nostalgic, not the subversive, sense. Despite these reservations, Lyotard's work does offer interesting mediations between the writing of Spark and of Kristeva.

LOOKING ELSEWHERE FOR REALITY

Interpretations of Spark as a 'metaphysical' writer have stressed her exhaustion of language, causality and plot, her attempt to make us look 'elsewhere for reality' (Spark, 1967: 283). The direction to an 'elsewhere' shrouded in unknowing situates Spark's fiction in the context of modernist art as described by Lyotard: 'I shall call modern the art which devotes its "little technical expertise" . . . to present the fact that the unpresentable exists' (1984: 78).

In so far as *The Hothouse by the East River* is 'modern' in Lyotard's terms, it is also sublime. The sublime sentiment occurs 'when the imagination fails to present an object which might, if only in principle, come to match a concept' (78) and is triggered by a confrontation with the unknowable, the impossible, the Real.

The relationship of the sublime to the modern's acknowledgement of 'the unpresentable' is not straightforward. Like *The Cloud of Unknowing* (Burrow, 1977: 283) modern art operates by 'negative presentation' (Lyotard, 1984: 78):[7]

> Modern aesthetics is an aesthetics of the sublime, though a nostalgic one. It allows the unpresentable to be put forward only as the missing contents; but, the form, because of its recognizable consistency, continues to offer to the reader or viewer matter for solace and pleasure.
>
> (Lyotard, 1984: 81)

In *The Hothouse by the East River* this modernism is eclipsed by the postmodern component which according to Lyotard always subsists within the modern: 'The postmodern would be that which, in the modern, puts forward the unpresentable in presentation itself' (81). Presenting the unpresentable, postmodern art makes 'nothing there' 'come to pass' (Spark, 1973: 7). Lyotard's comments on the postmodern apply specifically to the visual arts, but a more general application is obviously invited. The minimalism of some of the work Lyotard describes is echoed in the habitual sparseness of Spark's prose. That sparseness is itself one of *The Hothouse by the East River*'s excesses. Too much is withheld. In their resistance to interpretation Spark's 'sphinx-faced' (Kemp, 1974: 149) novels 'enable us to see only by making it impossible to see' (Lyotard, 1984: 78).

If modern aesthetics can be said to be an aesthetics of the sublime, postmodern aesthetics can be said to be an aesthetics of the true-real. Reading *The Hothouse by the East River* one can trace the analogous operations of the postmodern and the hallucinatory icon. Elsa's shadow, the hallucinatory icon, makes the true-real 'loom forth as a jubilant enigma' (Kristeva, 1986: 230). When the same shadow is described as a 'cloud of unknowing' it becomes literally an 'allusion to the unpresentable' (Lyotard, 1984: 78). This allusive quality is an indicator of the sublime for Lyotard.

The true-real is quite explicitly associated by Kristeva in her essay 'The true-real' with the pre-Oedipal and with the foreclosure of castration and separation from the maternal body (1986: 215, 218):

> We shall be led to consider how the *foreclosure* that decapitates the name of the Father and snatches the subject away, into the real, is *contained* within different types of discourse at the very point at which each speaks its *true-real*. We shall therefore have to envisage certain *kinds* of foreclosure (specific to the limits of each discourse), if we accept that psychosis is the crisis of truth in language.
>
> (Kristeva, 1986: 218)

In *Tales of Love* (1988) the true-real itself is not predominant, but it bears important affinities with the abject and the sublime, the linked couple which are crucial to Kristeva's discussion of love and amatory discourse. It is important before discussing the relation of this couple with the true-real to stress how similar is the effect of the abject with the sublime, specifically the Kantian sublime.

Kristeva appropriately titles the first chapter of *Powers of Horror* 'Approaching abjection'. 'It lies there quite close, but it cannot be assimilated' (Kristeva, 1982: 1). The abject cannot be defined: it already resembles the Kantian sublime in being 'unsuited to our presentative faculties' and doing 'violence to the Imagination' (Kant, 1892 [1790], 1.1.24: 102–3). Abjection is 'directed against a threat that seems to emanate from an exorbitant outside or inside, ejected beyond the scope of the possible, the tolerable, the thinkable' (Kristeva, 1982: 1). The abject

> is a brutish suffering that 'I' puts up with, sublime and devasta-
> ted, for 'I' deposits it to the father's account (*verse au père –
> père-version*): I endure it, for I imagine that such is the desire
> of the other.
>
> (Kristeva, 1982: 2)

Sublime and abject both operate 'like an inescapable boomerang' (1). 'A vortex of summons and repulsion places the one haunted by it [the abject] literally beside himself.' The mind 'moved' by the sublime is subject to what 'may be compared to a vibration i.e. to a quickly alternating attraction towards and repulsion from the same object' (Kant, 1892 [1790], 1.1.27: 120).

> As the mind is not merely attracted by the object but is ever
> being alternately repelled, the satisfaction of the sublime does
> not so much involve a positive pleasure as admiration or
> respect, which rather deserves to be called negative pleasure.
>
> (Kant, 1892 [1790], 1.1.24: 102)

The satisfactions of the sublime are negative: the abject is also defined in terms of negation and qualification:

> Not me. Not that. But not nothing, either. A 'something' that
> I do not recognize as a thing. A weight of meaninglessness,
> about which there is nothing insignificant, and which crushes
> me.
>
> (Kristeva, 1982: 2)

THE OBSCURE SUBLIME

If the abject and sublime are so close in effect, the force of the abject in *The Hothouse by the East River* would indicate that the sublime is also operative in that text. The novel's consistent attack on reason, form and the imposition of an 'Idea' is very much at odds with the context in which Kant elaborates his theory of the sublime. 'Sublimity . . . does not reside in anything in nature, but only in our mind' (Kant, 1892 [1790], 1.1.28: 129), according to the *Critique of Judgement*. The 'sublime' components of *The Hothouse by the East River* are precisely those which exceed 'mind' and specifically the mind of Paul. Contrary to Spark's emphasis on 'absolute truth' as intractable to human will and understanding, Kant asserts:

> Only by supposing this Idea in ourselves, and in reference to it, are we capable of attaining to the Idea of the sublimity of that Being, which produces respect in us, not merely by the might that it displays in nature, but rather by means of the faculty which resides in us of judging it fearlessly and of regarding our destination as sublime in respect of it.
>
> (Kant, 1892 [1792], 1.1.28: 129)

This supposing, referring, judging and regarding subject which regards a sublime Being as the guarantor and measure of its own sublime quality is in marked contrast to the forgetting, desiring soul in search of its God in a cloud of unknowing. Yet *The Cloud of Unknowing*'s God does have the sublime characteristic of exceeding thought (Wolters, 1978 [1961]: 68). Kant emphasizes *resistance* to external immensities as the sublime faculty:

> Bold overhanging, and, as it were, threatening rocks; clouds piled up in the sky, moving with lightning flashes and thunder peals; volcanoes in all their violence of destruction; hurricanes with their track of devastation; the boundless ocean in a state of tumult; the lofty waterfall of a great river, and suchlike; these exhibit our faculty of resistance as insignificantly small in comparison with their might. But the sight of them is the more attractive, the more fearful it is, provided only that we are in security; and we willingly call these objects sublime, because they raise the energies of the soul above their accustomed height, and discover in us a faculty of resistance of a quite different kind, which gives us courage to measure ourselves against the apparent almightiness of nature.
>
> (Kant, 1892 [1790], 1.1.28: 125)

Kant is rather like Spark's deplorable theatre-goer (1971b: 23–4), the observation of catastrophe from a position of security serves

simply to elevate self-importance to a sublime status. The stormi-
ness of this paragraph from Kant indicates how closely fought is
the battle between self and mighty otherness. Its lightning flashes
echo those which herald the collapse of ideal (the ideals of self
and of sublime) into abject.

Kant does not give the same prominence to terror as some
other philosophers of the sublime. A more precise picture of the
operations of the sublime in *The Hothouse by the East River* can
be derived from reading the novel in the context of a twentieth-
century (but traditional) philosopher of the sublime, George
Santayana. Santayana deals with the psychological sublime and,
though *The Hothouse by the East River* is in many senses a 'metaphysical' novel, it, like Kristeva's abject sublime, makes any clear-
cut distinction between the psychological and the metaphysical
difficult to sustain.

Santayana's descriptions of the sublime bear striking resemblances to elements of Spark's fiction. Nicholas Farringdon, the
anarchist poet in Spark's 1963 novel, *The Girls of Slender Means*,
declares in his 'Sabbath Notebooks':[8]

> There is a kind of truth in the popular idea of an anarchist as
> a wild man with a bomb in his pocket. In modern times this
> bomb, fabricated in the back workshops of the imagination,
> can only take one effective form: Ridicule.
>
> (Spark, 1963: 59)

Nicholas's 'notebooks' are to some extent parody, but the parody
is of theories close to Spark's own. Ideas very similar to those
recorded in the 'Sabbath Notebooks' are expressed in equally
similar terms eight years later by Spark herself. In her 1971
address to the American Academy of Arts and Letters, ridicule
was described as a weapon, one that could leave 'a salutary scar'
(1971b: 25). Two of Spark's author surrogate figures, Effie in
The Only Problem and Robert in *Territorial Rights*, are political
terrorists, Robert being also a blackmailing author. George Santayana would concur with Spark's linking of literature and terror:

> So natural is the relationship between the vivid conception of
> great evils and the self-assertion of the soul which gives the
> emotion of the sublime, that the sublime is often thought[9] to
> depend upon the terror which these conceived evils inspire . . .

this subdued and objectified terror is what is commonly regarded as the essence of the sublime.[10]

(Santayana, 1979: 179)

Santayana's comments have a specific application to the Eichmann trial incident in *The Mandelbaum Gate*, which for Barbara Vaughan 'rolled away the stone that revealed an empty hole in the earth, that led to a bottomless pit. So that people drew back quickly and looked elsewhere for reality, and found it' (Spark, 1967: 282). The passages both from *The Mandelbaum Gate* and from Santayana allow of two viable readings; one which emphasizes the validity of the sublime alternative to evil and terror, a second which emphasizes the status of the sublime as a reaction formation, a turning away from the pit of abjection. These alternatives are subjected to a further twist at the conclusion of *The Hothouse by the East River*. Paul's terror gives way to an acceptance of the sublime 'cloud of unknowing'. His sublime destination (Kant, 1892 [1790], 1.1.28: 129) is none the less death. In his contrast of sublime and beautiful, Santayana speaks of two modes of 'securing harmony'

> One is to unify all the given elements, and another is to reject all the elements that refuse to be unified. Unity by inclusion gives us the beautiful: unity by exclusion, opposition and isolation gives us the sublime. The one identifies us with the world, the other raises us above it.

(Santayana, 1979: 178)

Frank Kermode's description of Spark's novels as concordance fictions identifies them with Santayana's aesthetic 'unity' (1967 [1966]: 132). In *The Mandelbaum Gate*, the novel as Jerusalem, that 'unity' is *inclusive* (Kermode, 1971: 272). Like its heroine, Barbara Vaughan, it is 'a social and religious anthology' and like her 'it is composed of very varied elements which cohere, however, into a harmony, so that she is "all of a piece" '[11] (Kemp, 1974: 104). In *The Hothouse by the East River*, where everything is finally dismissed as 'a figment of your imagination' (Spark, 1973: 95), that unity is *exclusive*. Further, a unity expressed in terms of exclusion, opposition and isolation is the fragile unity of the deject, the self as other of abjection where

> The 'unconscious' contents remain *excluded*, but in strange fashion: not radically enough to allow for a secure

differentiation between subject and object and yet clearly enough for a defensive *position* to be established – one that implies a refusal but also a sublimating elaboration.

(Kristeva, 1982: 7)

Santayana was obviously heavily influenced by Burke and having identified the operations of the psychological sublime in *The Hothouse by the East River* it is necessary to analyse the relevance of Burke's concept of the sublime to Spark's novel. Burke argued that 'whatever . . . operates in a manner analogous to terror, is a source of the sublime' (1852 [1759]: 585). Burke's theories on the role of terror (598) and obscurity (599) in the creation of 'the sublime sentiment' are particularly useful for an analysis of the operation of the sublime in *The Hothouse by the East River* since they emphasize (lack of) vision as the medium of the sublime: 'Whatever is therefore terrible with regard to sight, is sublime too' (598). Terror is best invoked by obscurity and darkness:

> To make any thing very terrible, obscurity seems in general to be necessary. When we know the full extent of any danger, when we can accustom our eyes to it, a great deal of the apprehension vanishes.
>
> (Burke, 1852 [1759]: 599)

Burke almost defines terror as an effect of sight or rather of not seeing. One is tempted to make a connection here with the horror of nothing to see. However, for Burke terror – and, indeed, the sublime sentiment it evokes – is not the product of seeing nothing or of having no object of vision. These are effects of not knowing what one sees and of the disjunction between one's (psychological or intellectual) conception of what the obscure object of vision *might* be and the object itself which one cannot identify. Sublime terror is a matter of confronting the limits of the faculty of sight through which the (thinking) subject constitutes itself as subject and as origin. Elsa's shadow can thus be seen not only as positing an alternative 'source' of light (Irigaray, 1985a: 276), but as the threat (of death) which is posed by distortion of vision. The supreme example of sublime and 'judicious obscurity' (Burke, 1852 [1759]: 599) for Burke is Milton's description of Death at the gates of hell:

> The other shape
> If shape it might be called that shape had none

Distinguishable, in member, joint, or limb;
Or substance might be called that shadow seemed;
For each seemed either; black it stood as Night,
Fierce as ten Furies, terrible as hell,
And shook a dreadful dart; what seemed his head
The likeness of a kingly crown had on.

(*Paradise Lost*: book 2, 666–73)[12]

In the specular economy in which seeing (reason) and being are indistinguishable, confrontation with the limits of vision is confrontation with death:

As pain is stronger in its operation than pleasure, so death is in general a much more affecting idea than pain. . . . When danger or pain press too nearly, they are incapable of giving any delight and are simply terrible: but at certain distances and with certain modifications they may be, and they are delightful.

(Burke, 1852 [1759 585])

Distance, however, is precluded by the nature of the sublime as Burke himself describes it: 'The mind is so entirely filled with its object, that it cannot entertain any other, nor by consequence reason on that object which employs it' (Burke, 1852 [1759]: 585). Recalling the identification of Reason with light and vision in the texts of Plato, Plotinus and Descartes discussed by Irigaray, it is not surprising that the place where there is no room for reason is also a place where vision is occluded. The identification of subject with object, the loss of self in other, which is the sublime state, is the collapse of the space which western philosophy has constructed as the space in which 'I' exist and as the internal space which is 'I'.

The sublime is the loss of self in an other which, because it cannot be identified or separated from the self, cannot be constituted as an object (of vision, reason or contemplation) and which therefore prohibits the formation of a subject as its opposite. In its effect (and in the visionary terms in which it is described) it recalls the mystical process of 'forgetting' described in *The Cloud of Unknowing* (Wolters, 1978 [1961]: 67). The object with which the mind identifies in the sublime state, by virtue of that identification, cannot be the object *of* reason. For the contemplative, 'God' is 'that thing which I cannot think' (Wolters, 1978 [1961]: 68). Are the sublime and the divine then variants, interchangeable non-objects of the deject's contemplation? Both are certainly defences against abjection, as is implied in Kristeva's analysis of the 'Semiotics of biblical abomination' (1982: 90–113):

> There is no opposition between material abomination and topological (holy place of the Temple) or logical (holy Law) reference. The one and the other are two aspects, semantic and logical, of the imposition of a *strategy of identity* which is, in all strictness, that of monotheism. The semes that clothe the process of separation (orality, death, incest) are the inseparable lining of its logical representation aiming to guarantee the place and law of the One God. In other words, the place *and* law of the One do not exist without a *series of separations* that are oral, corporeal, or even more generally material, and in the last analysis relating to fusion with the mother.
>
> (Kristeva, 1982: 94)

There is a continuity here with the analysis of the maternal 'lining' of 'the Word' in 'Stabat Mater' (Kristeva, 1986: 176). In the earlier essay there was a textual shift from analysing the maternal as support for the primacy of the Word (of the Father/Son) to postulating the primacy of the relation to the maternal which monotheism only succeeds in displacing by harnessing its *jouissance*. In *Powers of Horror* the primacy of the relation to the maternal is the substance of the 'essay':

> The pure/impure mechanism testifies to the harsh combat Judaism, in order to constitute itself, must wage against paganism and its maternal cults. It carries into the private lives of everyone the brunt of the struggle each subject must wage during the entire length of his personal history in order to become separate, that is to say, to become a speaking subject and/or subject to Law.
>
> (Kristeva, 1982: 94)

The ideal of the sublime in art testifies to its residual desire not to separate. The association between the maternal and writing was the starting-point of this discussion of contemporary women's writing. It is an association which informs all of the key texts and it recurs in the formulation of the sublime, not just by Kristeva, but even by Burke. The eighteenth-century philosopher postulates a rivalry and even an antagonism between the specular economy which sees, identifies, abstracts and knows

('*Ego cogito*') and writing which inscribes, emotes, affects and realizes ('*Ego affectus est . . .* ?'):

> A drawing presents a clear picture, but then (allowing for the effect of imitation, which is something) my picture can at most affect only as the place, temple or landscape [drawn] would have affected in the reality. On the other hand, the most lively and spirited verbal description I can give raises a very imperfect *idea* of such objects; but then it is in my power to raise a stronger *emotion* by the description than I could do by the best painting. . . . The proper manner of conveying the *affections* of the mind from one to another is by words.
>
> (Burke, 1852 [1759]: 600)

Words are the medium of effecting obscurity and obscurity is a precondition of the terror which precipitates the sublime. Elsa obscures and terrifies in *The Hothouse by the East River*, but Elsa is 'some hundreds of words . . . marks on a page' (Spark, 1981: 61). It is necessary here to return to the example of literary 'judicious obscurity' (599) which immediately precedes Burke's contrast of drawing and writing. Milton's Death 'shadow seemed', an association significant for any reading of *The Hothouse by the East River*. Milton's alignment of Death with Sin and Satan, who gave birth to him (*Paradise Lost*: book 2, 727–89), reminds us how unorthodox is Spark's identification of death's obscurity and the divine 'cloud of unknowing' and the indistinction of Death and God in her writing. The Miltonic configuration is not absent from Spark's text, however. Milton's Death is the child of the father of lies: Spark's Death is a character in a novel, 'a pack of lies'. 'There is', Conrad's Marlowe famously and ambiguously tells us, 'a flavour of mortality in lies' (1973 [1902]: 57).

If death's father is Satan in *Paradise Lost*, his mother is the monstrously maternal Sin. Sin and Death, who guard the gates of hell, are ill-distinguished. 'He knows / His end with mine involved', Sin comments (*Paradise Lost*: book 2, 806–7). She is herself the daughter of Satan and the pivot of an incestuous triangle in which she conceived Death by Satan and a horrid assortment of hell-hounds by Death. Her birth is curiously described in terms of the birth of Athene from the head of Zeus. She tells Satan:

> All on a sudden miserable pain
> Surprised thee; dim thine eyes, and dizzy swum
> In darkness, while thy head flames thick and fast
> Threw forth, till on the left side opening wide,
> Likest to thee in shape and countenance bright,
> Then shining heavenly fair, a goddess armed
> Out of thy head I sprung.[13]
>
> (*Paradise Lost*: book 2, 752–8)

In the Puritan version of the semiotics of abomination, the displacement of (maternal) origin is adequate only to a hellish parody of creation, which is properly of the Word alone. Yet this limit-point of patriarchal denial of the feminine and disgust at the maternal is also a point at which that denial returns upon itself. The origin of Sin from the head, or thought, of Satan and their generation of Death, suggest not only that material and sexual 'creation' is an entry into death. In the obscene maternity of Sin, fertility is turned into its opposite. Death is the child, at this stage in the text, not of Eve, but of a devil and his thought. It is masculine displacement of origin (and Satan is, after all, one who seeks to overthrow and invert a prior authority and origin) which produces death here. Gilbert and Gubar have very convincingly read Milton's Satan as feminine and associated with the feminine, as he is with non-representational language. That reading need not be abandoned and indeed can be complemented by a reading which sees Satan's fathering of Sin as an inversion of the displacement of origin which institutes both the philosophical subject and the religion of the God of the Word. As Satan seeks to cross over from hell to earth, *Paradise Lost* finds itself in one of those border regions where the symbolic order is, momentarily, displaced and 'The mother takes up her place, so it once again goes, at the central location' (Kristeva, 1982: 157) of the ultimate patriarchal text. Sin and Death at the gates of hell are 'something *horrible to see* at the impossible doors of the invisible – the mother's body' (155) and, as Burke points out, they are literally sublime. Sin's description of the birth of Death might be an exemplum of Kristeva's identification of sublime and abject, of the scene of writing and the 'primal' scene of giving birth:

> At last this hideous offspring whom thou seest,
> Thine own begotten, breaking violent way
> Tore through my entrails, that with fear and pain

> Distorted, all my nether shape thus grew
> Transformed; but he my inbred enemy
> Forth issued, brandishing his fatal dart
> Made to destroy. I fled, and cried out *Death*!
>
> (*Paradise Lost*: book 2, 781–9)

Gilbert and Gubar identify 'Milton's bogey' (1979: 187–213) as a haunting presence in women's writing. 'Shadow seeming' Elsa in *The Hothouse by the East River* is in some respects Milton's bogey. She explodes 'regulations and codes' (Cixous, 1976: 886), she brings death and madness. Her madness is truth, however. Her shadow is the shadow of the true-real and becomes a cloud of unknowing surrounding the divine. Like Sin and Death she inhabits a liminal area, her window overlooking the East River a parallel to their sentinal at 'hell gate' (*Paradise Lost*, book 2, 725) which Satan reaches having passed 'along the banks / Of four infernal rivers' (book 2, 574–5). Unlike Milton's personifications, however, Elsa's significance is in her intractability to the economy of will and power which seeks to reduce her to 'a figment' of an other's imagination. Paul, whose 'terrible dreams' (Spark, 1973: 95) are the only origin for his world and his children, cannot incorporate his wife into that fantasy of power. Most importantly, it is '*her* figment, her nothing there' (15) which comes to pass. Perhaps, in the later twentieth century, Milton's bogey has been finally vanquished and Elsa is the sign of that victory.

THE TRUE-REAL AND THE SUBLIME

The true-real is the fold in discourse which allows the real to manifest itself in the register of the symbolic (Kristeva, 1986: 230). The post-teleological end of contemporary narrative is, according to Kristeva, 'to communicate the amorous flash' (1988: 368) which is 'the focus where the sublime and the abject . . . come together' (368).[14] Is this the same 'flash' that heralded the 'instant of time or of dream without time' (1986: 162) in which Kristeva discussed the Virgin Mother in 'Stabat Mater'? Not quite, for the spectacular fusion of abject and ideal at the heart of the modern in art marks the psychotic absence of the Virgin Mother as protection from the abject maternal body (1988: 374) and as guarantee of the Symbolic.

Kristeva sees the true-real in the context of a psychotic

disavowal of death. This disavowal of the 'only radical "histori-cal" reality' (Kristeva, 1986: 226) 'places us in the series of the signifier alone' (225). In its minutiae artistic discourse shares this practice:

> I feel more and more that a separate place must be set aside for so-called artistic discourse. If there is any disavowal, it is introduced in the minutiae of such a practice (in each word, sound, colour, rhythm . . .) such that these are never 'pure' signifiers, but always 'word' and 'flesh' and consequently situate themselves at the very heart of the distinction between these extremes and/or their identity to the extent that they are micro-scopic exploration of murder *as* resurrection.
>
> (Kristeva, 1986: 227)

The distinction between the minutiae of artistic discourse and an implied larger framework is the old indistinction of semiotic and symbolic. The inextricable relationship of those two terms is a necessary reminder that the framework of the symbolic remains a necessary support against the death drives which are poetic, 'musicating' (1981: 185), but which threaten total disintegration. The disavowal of death threatens isolation, autism and the very death which is disavowed. The subject which adopts such a posi-tion of disavowal will fester in the wilderness 'trying to get messages out' (Lessing, 1965: 280): 'A woman has nothing to laugh about when the symbolic order collapses' (Kristeva, 1986: 150). Yet Elsa laughs, almost to the end, and her laughter is the agent of the collapse of Paul's egotistical fiction and encroaching death. It is the murderous, revolutionary laughter *Wise Children* kept at bay:

> 'I don't see what there is to laugh at,' Paul tells her and beckons a taxi to the kerb.
>   'When a man's angrily in love with you, it has its funny side,' she says.
>   His heart knocks on the sides of the coffin. 'Let me out!'
>
> (Spark, 1973: 127)

Within Kristeva's framework writing is a disavowal of death. Spark writes Death. In *The Hothouse by the East River* she presents the possibility that the woman who subsumes into herself the role of originator of truth and the authority of the ending *is* Death. This death is not really admitted into Kristeva's account.

It is indisputably the resurgence of biology and of body. It is abject: the incident of the worms hatching from the breast of Princess Xavier could qualify as a parody of the concept of the maternal abject:

> Garven screams. His eyes are on the Princess's bosom. He screams. Under the protective folds of her breast the Princess, this very morning, has concealed for warmth and fear of the frost a precious new consignment of mulberry leaves bearing numerous eggs of silk-worms. They have hatched in the heat. The worms themselves now celebrate life by wriggling upon Princess Xavier's breast and causing Garven to scream.
>
> (Spark, 1973: 45)

The transition from fertility, through corpulence, to the worms' birth from the corpse that is the maternal body brings us through the whole circuit of maternal idealization and abjection. 'The corpse, seen without God and outside of science, is the utmost of abjection' (Kristeva, 1982: 4). Death in *The Hothouse by the East River* is also the ideal or 'God'. The confusion of God and Death in Spark's fiction is true on one level to the economy which turns its abomination of the abject into the indispensable lining of the ideal (Kristeva, 1982: 56–113). *The Hothouse by the East River* exceeds that economy nevertheless.

LOOKING ELSEWHERE FOR REALITY

The process of forgetting, resistance to reading, the induction of abjection: these are characteristic techniques of Spark's fiction. Their effects are consistent with the aim expressed in *The Mandelbaum Gate* of making us look 'elsewhere for reality' (Spark, 1967: 283). The assurance of finding it has evaporated.

Spark initially interrogated fiction from the point of view of its usefulness in communicating 'absolute truth' (Kermode, 1971: 273). In her first novel, *The Comforters*, the main protagonist, Caroline Rose, discovered she was a character in a novel. She could even hear the novelist's typewriter click 'elsewhere'. Caroline, a critic, sets out to discover the meaning of the novel in which she finds herself. The novel's 'obstructions' (Harrison, 1976: 246) convince us of the reality of that meaning because we experience the reality of a mischievous and obtuse novelist playing with our reading responses, integrating those responses into her novel by making the heroine a reader and critic. In the three novellas Spark produced while writing *The Hothouse by the East River* (Kemp, 1974: 156–7) that playful relationship was replaced by something far more sinister. The novelist of *The Driver's Seat* decrees Lise's murder and by anticipating the action herself murders suspense, surprise and the readerly pleasures (Barthes, 1975: 4). In *Not to Disturb* plots are spun for the financial gain of the plotters. In *The Public Image*, almost uniquely in Spark's fiction, the actress protagonist learns to rewrite the script of her life (which a jealous husband tries to determine from beyond the grave). Contrary to some critics' belief, these exposures of fraudulent authority are not maintained as a contrast with a true and absolute authority. The desire for such authority persists. Elsa is the shadow of it: she is the abject woman *and* God. Spark does not simply collapse the abject into the ideal. The faithful and lithe cloud of unknowing trails the desire for the Real through and beyond the text.

According to the author of *The Cloud of Unknowing*, God may be loved 'but not thought' (Wolters, 1978 [1961]: 68). 'It all depends on your desire' (69). The best part of contemplation is 'an urgent love eagerly reaching out into that high cloud of unknowing' (83), a love that is insatiable, a desire that feeds on itself: 'It is characteristic of the true lover that the more he loves, the more he wants to love' (82). God in *The Cloud of Unknowing* is the impossible end of desire.

This limit-point of desire does not, perhaps cannot, survive the interrogation of narrative, authority and the concept of 'Woman' in which Spark's fiction engages. That interrogation brings the interdependence of the ideal and its abject to light. Spark's fiction still points 'elsewhere' (Spark, 1967: 282), but there is no longer anything there. 'A laughing apocalypse is an apocalypse without god. Black mysticism of transcendental collapse' (Kristeva, 1982: 206). *The Hothouse by the East River* exceeds representation and its dual guardians, the womb and the word, it makes us look elsewhere for reality but can only point us towards its absence. The abject-ideal is the substance of the novel: the absence of the ideal is its end. That absence is not sentimentalized nor recovered into a consolatory fiction. Spark's use of impoverished narrative is a function of this. There is no consolation in a linguistic matrix lined with nostalgia for one meaning or a body. 'Knots were not necessarily created to be untied', comments Barbara Vaughan in

The Mandelbaum Gate (1967: 301–2). *The Hothouse by the East River* unravels some frayed edges of the Borromean knot and confronts the Real (Lacan, 1977: ix-x). It is emptied of significance for us when we arrive there. Spark writes a desire to signify it which is so like the mystic's desire for God that it is presumptuous to make distinctions. She collapses the ideal into abjection and writes a desire for an object which is insatiable.

Conclusion

ANACHRONIC HISTORY

In *The Sense of an Ending* Frank Kermode argued that the ultimate narrative structure of beginning, middle and end is simply 'tick-tock' (1967 [1966]: 64). In *The Hothouse by the East River* that tick-tock becomes an infinite stuttering.

Lessing's novel sequences mark the search of the realistic novel for a reality to represent. *Canopus in Argos* to this end produces a model of fictional time which is closer to space-time. This model is one which recurs in some form in all the texts under discussion. It can be read as the last triumph of realism. Fiction and literary theory are keeping pace with scientific theory: relativity and space-time are replacing the telescopic narrative patterns which were moulded in the image of Newton's universe. The harmony between scientific and literary systems may be maintained even while their internal correlations fall prey to the uncertainty principle and become no more than 'probabilities':

> Since human beings have invented history, we have also invented those aspects of our lives that seem most immutable, or rather, have invented the circumstances that determine their nature. Birth and death, the only absolute inescapables, are both absolutely determined by the social context in which they occur.
>
> (Carter, 1979: 11–12)

In *Heroes and Villains* Carter attempted to 'wind back' the clock of history, perhaps to uncover something undetermined. The ending of that novel pauses before such a great task of imagining. The larger narrative pattern acknowledges the power of social and historical determinism. The textual minutiae escape that power in the space which the unwinding creates. Determinism may win and the newly unleashed feminine imaginary succumb to a very old story – neither is quite certain at the end of the novel. That victory, in the context of what precedes it, would in any case be the victory, not of authority, but of absurdity. Within Carter's own framework the only possible authority is that which derives from 'society'. Yet the form of her argument is that a realization of their social derivation relieves so-called 'inevitable' patterns, absolutes, of their 'meaning'. Marianne calls Jewel an 'anachronism,' (Carter, 1969: 56); the old stories of heroes and villains are self-consciously out of place in the post-nuclear world of the novel. Lessing, in *The Golden Notebook* and elsewhere, postulates that our expectations, our view of our selves and our relation to the world lag one generation behind – we have inherited our parents' mind-set and the world and society has moved on while we remain imprisoned in what was their adaptation to a world changed beyond recognition from the world their parents knew. In Spark's *The Hothouse by the East River* contemporary New York is a nightmare of the dead and the present consists of shadows cast awry by the past.

A profound dislocation of history and temporality recurs in the writings of Kristeva, Irigaray and Cixous. All are in their different ways preoccupied with the prehistorical, particularly as it relates to the pre-Oedipal maternal. Irigaray (re)turns to the 'origin' and end of philosophy, its encounter with the feminine. Cixous overturns myth, until its suppressed meanings break forth and the Medusa is 'beautiful and she's laughing'. (Cixous, 1976: 85) Both 'let go the spring of history so that history winds back on itself' (Carter, 1969: 93). Kristeva writes on the horizon of space-time which this undoing of history makes visible.

HERETHICS

Powers of Horror, in its exploration of the horizons of modernism, raises questions which literary theory and literary studies in general must answer and do not seem ready to answer yet. The analysis of an anti-Semitic writer is disturbing in a variety of ways, particularly since Kristeva seems to identify so strongly with Céline's 'laying bare of meaning' (Kristeva, 1982: 154). Nevertheless, Kristeva's claim to locate 'at the doors of the feminine, at the doors of abjection . . . the "drive foundations of fascism" ' is, however differently formulated, an extension and illumination of the feminist perception of the well-springs of fascism in the structures of patriarchy. One could hope for greater elaboration and more circumspection about these drive foundations from Kristeva, but the attempt to identify and confront the psychological and cultural foundations of anti-Semitism and fascism is a brave one. If it is short on moral indignation it is more productive, more timely and much more disturbing than many more indignant texts. Kristeva refuses to treat modernism's relationship to fascism as a sad aberration or an unfortunate consequence of historical circumstance. She situates that relationship at the heart of the modernist project and at the heart of the project of scription as 'the laying bare of meaning' (154). What is so often regarded as the horrible obverse of civilization is seen to be at the heart of what constitutes western culture. Kristeva is not the first to make such a point. The connection made in *Powers of Horror* between horror of the maternal and the worst excesses of power based on exclusive identities does mark a significant progression, however. Kristeva's work on the way in which the West has identified and treated 'strangers' (1991) is a continuation of this. Though *Strangers to Ourselves*, is very much concerned with racism in France, Kristeva's challenge to traditional concepts of communal identity is set in another urgent context by her eastern European background. *Powers of Horror* set the scene for the later work's exposition of

> our disturbing otherness, for that indeed is what bursts in to confront that 'demon', that threat, that apprehension generated by the protective apparition of the other at the heart of what we persist in maintaining as a proper, solid 'us'. By recognizing *our* uncanny strangeness we shall neither suffer from it nor enjoy it from the outside. The foreigner is within me, hence we are all foreigners. If I am a foreigner, then there are no foreigners.
>
> (Kristeva, 1991: 192)

UNLIKE SUBJECTS

The location of the 'primal scene' (Kristeva, 1982: 155), identified as birth, 'incest turned inside out' (155), as not only the ultimate abjection, but also 'the supreme and sole interest of literature', indicates the challenge which women's rejection of their socio-symbolic role poses to the socio-symbolic order. It makes explicit what is assumed and hinted at in all of the writers I have discussed. 'A staggering alteration in power relations' (Cixous, 1976: 882) is at least imaginable, writable. But what will be the consequence of this alteration? If 'I' speak from the body of the one who gives birth, if the distance between primal scene and the one who sees and inscribes that scene, the one who constructs or rejects its primacy, collapses in a flash – where will the inner space of subjectivity be constructed? What kind of subject can function in the storms that those flashes perpetuate? What language can utter this subject?

Contemporary women's writing exposes the sacrifice of the feminine, identifying displacement of origin and denial of difference as constitutive of history, the subject and the socio-symbolic contract. It traces the bonus of maternal '*jouissance*' which ensures the co-option of women into the sacrificial contract and goes on to map the collapse of that economy of sacrifice and compensation. In 'The laugh of the Medusa', *Landlocked*, *Heroes and Villains*, 'Women's time' and 'Stabat Mater', the mother-daughter relationship and the relation of *the subject as woman* to the maternal is central. The analysis of the structures of subjectivity in such terms in contemporary women's writing marks a crisis in the socio-symbolic order. It indicates that the Oedipal narrative has lost the legitimacy of accepted universality.

'And the one doesn't stir without the other', 'Stabat Mater' and *Wise Children* trace the submerged elements of another construction of subjectivity, one no longer predicated upon prohibited desire, the negation of the Other and denial of difference, but exploring the multiple possibilities of differentiation between unlike subjects, of being other to and for an other (Kristeva, 1988: 4) which characterizes the mother-daughter relationship as it begins to surface in the texts of women. The fear of psychosis, of the collapse of subjectivity and alienation from history and action, remain factors in that relationship and its construction of the non-Oedipal subject.

Speculum of the Other Woman subverts a speculative economy which prioritizes vision and introjects the relation of the gaze and its object as the structure of the subject's relation to any(thing) Other. *The Hothouse by the East River* proposes 'another source and different light' (Irigaray, 1985a: 276) which disrupts the self-reflexive circularity of the gaze and the internal certainties of the gazer. Paul is the subject who organizes external experience around the one sun of his own centrality to himself as subject. Elsa, with her shadow cast against this light, destroys the fictions – society, language, science and selves – which keep death at bay.

Heroes and Villains posed the reverberating question, 'If I take time off from thinking, what then?' (Carter, 1969: 98). *The Hothouse by the East River* asks a more truly rhetorical question. If the structures which construct thought and which construct myself as thinking subject collapse, what then but death? Spark's novel posits as the nature of 'the true-real' a totality which, if it is not itself Death, is at least deathly. *The Hothouse by the East River* writes the irruption of the true-real as the irruption of death. It asks its dreadful questions from within the framework of the traditional and religious ideology which *Tales of Love* analyses from its quite different post-theological, post-teleological perspective. Spark's 'anachronistic' framework could be argued to impose limits, to present as either or, life or death, truth or self and society, what in effect are inextricable or contiguous terms. Spark herself describes her Catholicism as a 'norm from which to depart' (1963b). Her destabilization of the self-other opposition in *The Hothouse by the East River*, through Elsa's dual role as product of Paul's will and as autonomous entity intractable to that will, is a move towards the vertigo of kicking away the norms which have sustained earlier voyages into unknowing. Truth erupts as terror, annihilating not just the inauthentic, but also the concepts of selfhood and survival, of will, reason and analysis. And, at the end of the novel, there is only the cloud of unknowing. The norm, the guarantee of safety at the end of the quest, is alluded to, but it is not there.

Of course the absence of the Ideal serves merely to sustain the desire for the Ideal. It is the ineffability of absolute truth which makes it a suitable and sustaining 'meaning' for (Spark's) fiction. To lie like truth is to gain the pleasures of the signifier freed from an economy of representation: the goal of presenting the unpresentable absolves from representation and moreover guarantees endless inspiration for the writing of fiction. The Real will never materialize in words and so the sense of an ending which haunts Spark's work is always thwarted. That is its appeal. It is in this sense that Spark too can be said to write *against* death at the same time as she writes Death. The very nature of the project she has set herself in fiction – 'I am interested in truth – absolute truth' (Kermode, 1971: 272) – ensures that that project can never be completed. The absence of the ideal, the impossibility of realizing it in language, guarantees the proliferation of desire for the ideal and the sublime proliferation of a writing which is secure from defeat by death (or) the ideal precisely because of the 'inadequacy of its greatest faculty' (Kant, 1892 [1790], 1.1.27: 119–20) to present that ideal. In Kristeva's work, the maternal body, from which one is eternally separated, which one eternally desires, fulfils a similar function to that of absolute truth in the work of Spark. Such similarity of function does not suggest that the maternal has become an absolute, but that the 'truth' of contemporary women's writing is the impossibility of the absolute.

My initial project in this book was to ask the question, Is there such a thing as women's writing? As it progressed a more pressing question arose. If we will no longer be party to a socio-symbolic contract constituted by the sacrifice and exclusion of women, how will we henceforward constitute ourselves as women, as thinking, speaking, social subjects? In all of the writers under discussion there is an identification between the institution of the sacrificial contract and accession to language. It is language which marks the maternal out of bounds, which silences the feminine. It is also language which brings us back to the edge of the maternal and the feminine and is resonant with the echoes of what was lost to gain language. Written language, language at the stage of conscious, cultural production and language returning to the material 'marks on a page' (Spark, 1981: 61), has been marked out by women writers as the space in which to restructure what is meant by women and writing. The priority given that space is in part an attempt to pre-empt the 'semi-aphonic corporeality' (Kristeva, 1986: 207) and the horrors of abjection which have always been the threat to those who would renegotiate the socio-symbolic contract.

With the revision and replacement of the Oedipal construction of subjectivity, has come a revision of the values which have governed cultural production in patriarchy. If culture speaks on the basis of women's silence and literature has perpetuated and legitimized that silence, the woman writer must also remake literature and seek a different aesthetic and literary framework. Gynocritics has shown how consistent has been women writers' antipathy to canonical literature and its traditional value, on the one hand, and how consistent has been their exploitation and revision of that literature, on the other. Such revision is still a powerful factor in work as diverse as *Speculum of the Other Woman*, *Landlocked* and *Wise Children*. There has been considerable shift of emphasis, however, away from the misrepresentation to the unrepresentability of women. Cixous, Lessing, Kristeva, Carter, Irigaray and Spark are as diverse as, it is only to be expected, women writers will be. If they have a commonality of experience it is suspended indefinitely in the difference of their writing. Yet all in some way give priority to the unrepresentable as the subject of writing. This is quite different from the modernist and post-modernist projects of Joyce, Céline and Lyotard. For the attempt to realize the unrepresentable, now, in women's writing, is made by those who participate in and inherit the economy of signs and the culture of representation, but who also participate in and inherit silence. It is the self-writing of those who are themselves that which cannot be said, who cannot represent themselves to themselves. The woman writer has often been and is still sometimes torn apart by the need to be on both sides at once. There is, however, more and more vocally and confidently a belief by women artists that their double space, in and out of culture, in-between, is the place where 'a revolt . . . of epochal significance' (Kristeva, 1986: 200) is occurring. Women's space is coming into women's time.

Notes

INTRODUCTION

1 For example, Awkward, 1989; Spivak, 1981, 1987; Smith, 1986. See also Showalter, 1986: 384–5 for an introductory bibliography of Black feminist criticism.

2 All emphases in quotations are original unless otherwise stated.

3 This enthusiasm for demystification is at the heart of Showalter's dislike for *A Room of One's Own* and her disapproval of its 'evasions' and nostalgia for transcendence (1982 [1978]: 263–97).

4 This is particularly true of her more recent *The Female Malady: Women, Madness and English Culture, 1830–1980* (1987) and the collection edited by her, *Speaking of Gender* (1989).

5 Gilbert makes extensive use of the metaphor of the dancing of the tarantella in describing *The Newly Born Woman* where Clément discusses the tarantella at length (19–22).

6 It is interesting to compare Gayatri Spivak's reading of Cixous (1981). Spivak foregrounds the colonization metaphor and draws quite different conclusions about Cixous's work which she perceives as offering opportunities to be developed by Third World feminism. The issue is reopened in Cixous's reading of the Brazilian writer Clarice Lispector (Sellars, 1988).

7 See the section on Structure and Terminology (pp. 13–14).

8 Translated 'Anticipation is imperative' by Cohen and Cohen (Cixous, 1976: 875).

9 *Soleil Noir* (1987) deals controversially with Marguerite Duras. The earlier *Histoires d'amour* (1983; translated as *Tales of Love* [1988]) had discussed the female mystic, Jeanne Guyon.

10 Reading Kristeva in such a context imposes certain limitations, of course. The following study does not deal in detail with negation or melancholia, but concentrates on those aspects of Kristeva's work which most interestingly overlap or challenge the work of Carter and Spark.

11 I am drawing here on her comments to the University of Liverpool

conference, 'Etudes Féminines: Women's Writing and Literary Studies in Theory and Practice', on 21 April 1989.

1 BETWEEN THE MOTHER AND THE MEDUSA

1 See, for example, Rubenstein, 1979; Draine, 1984.
2 See, for example, Vlastos, 1976 and Rubenstein, 1979. Phyllis Chesler puts Laing in the context of a more general feminist overview of psychological theories of the relationship between women and madness. Laing is dealt with exclusively here despite the prevalence among other members of the 'anti-psychiatry' school, particularly Thomas Szasz (1973, 1987), of some of the views Lessing's fiction proposes on madness and its definition. The exclusive concentration on Laing is due partly to the much more specific nature of Lessing's references to Laing's work, but largely to the central position of the Medusa myth in his formulation of his definition of schizophrenia.
3 Cixous, 1976: 878. When she says 'they' in this context Cixous appears to be speaking of 'Men' in general. Elsewhere she will distinguish between 'conventional man' (875) and men 'capable of loving others and wanting them, of imagining the woman who would hold out against oppression' (879).
4 The idea referred to by Freud is his own one, that: 'It seems that women have made few contributions to the discoveries and inventions in the history of civilization; there is. however, one technique which they may have invented – that of plaiting and weaving' (1981b: vol. 22, 132). This is linked to 'concealment of genital deficiency' (132).
5 See Gilbert and Gubar, 1979 for a full discussion on this motif in nineteenth-century women's writing. See Rigney, 1978 for its recurrence in Lessing's fiction.
6 *The Fifth Child* (1988) combines the apocalyptic strain in Lessing's fiction with an analysis of maternity and specifically of the threat which the child can pose to the autonomy and sanity of its mother.
7 Specifically, consummation of her relationship to Poseidon. Poseidon and Medusa were, according to Joseph Campbell, linked with a mythology of horses and the ritual sacrifice of horses, after *c.* 2000 BC. See Campbell, 1974: 154–5.
8 It is typical of Laing that the category of schizophrenia seems to subsume anything which by 'normal standards' is called madness when he is engaged in a general/generalizing discussion. Yet the particular case histories he relates are almost invariably those of clinically diagnosed schizophrenics. While it is feasible that a particular form of insanity should be the key to understanding the general psychic and social condition of late twentieth-century humanity, Laing does not acknowledge that this is the form of his argument and so evades the questions posed by forms of madness which fall outside his own normalizing definitions.
9 This is borne out by the examples of Lessing's borrowings from Laing cited above (pp. 16–17).

10 Like Laing's, Lessing's mysticism is rooted in twentieth-century psychology, particularly its more esoteric variants. The mainstream of psychoanalytical thought is represented in the depiction of the psychic landscape of the narrator's foster daughter, Emily. The narrator's ability to enter that landscape is more suggestive of a collective rather than an individual unconscious, however.

11 Laing's apparent blindness in this area is discussed in Chesler, 1972.

12 My emphasis.

13 'Medusa who suffered a woeful fate: she was mortal' (Hesiod, 1982: 99).

14 Chrysaor sprang from the neck of Medusa. He and Callirrhoe were the parents of Echidna, who was half-nymph and half-snake. Echidna and Orthus gave birth to the Sphinx (Hesiod, 1982: 99).

15 The opposition of Athene and Medusa might be read as a Kleinian split of the mother goddess into good mother/bad mother in western culture. The ambivalent duality of the Indian goddess Kali (who combines both aspects) would then indicate a more sophisticated mythologizing process which corresponds to a later stage in development according to the Kleinian schema. (Joseph Campbell interestingly denigrates the eastern goddesses as more *primitive*.)

16 See de Beauvoir, 1972.

17 Interview, June 1987.

18 Toril Moi has rightly objected to the reinstatement of a 'transcendental signified' (1985: 57–9) in the form of the female author in the work of Showalter and of Gilbert and Gubar in the late 1970s. None the less, the connections they make between women's role as subject of and in writing and women's experience as subject of and in society are, if sometimes too direct, both necessary and useful. Perhaps it would be most productive to read Showalter's heroic woman author as a signifier for women's evasion of and revolt against 'the conventions of the novel and of womanhood' (1982 [1978]: 143).

19 'I don't see any other way to write it. As soon as one has lived through something it falls into a pattern. . . . That is why all this is untrue' (Lessing, 1972: 231).

20 Gilbert and Gubar adopt the term 'non-identical double' from Bersani's reading of *Wuthering Heights* (Bersani, 1976: 208–9).

21 Showalter's analysis of the same motif focuses on Charlotte Brontë's Rochester on the basis that *Jane Eyre* had considerably more influence on women's fiction than *Wuthering Heights*, at least until the end of the nineteenth century (Showalter, 1982 [1978]: 139–42).

22 Catherine had asked her father to bring her a whip from Liverpool, but instead he brings Heathcliff.

23 Gilbert and Gubar make extensive use of Blakeian revisions of the relation of Heaven to Hell as well as reading *Wuthering Heights* as a revision of *Paradise Lost* and orthodox versions of the Fall.

24 This issue will be discussed in greater detail in chapter 5 in relation to Luce Irigaray's work on the economy of the gaze and the relation of 'reflection' to representation.

2 THE MOTHER AS LANGUAGE, LANGUAGE AS MOTHER

1 An excellent bibliography is provided in Showalter, 1986: 390–2.
2 I am grateful to Mairead Hanrahan who, in her presentation to the University of Liverpool colloquium 'Etudes Féminines: Women's Writing and Literary Studies in Theory and Practice', and in conversation, has greatly clarified this aspect of Cixous's work for me,
3 Cixous does name Lacan in the text in order to attack him straight on:

> If psychoanalysis was constituted from woman, to repress femininity (and not so successful a repression at that – men have made it clear), its account of masculine sexuality is now hardly refutable; as with all the 'human' sciences, it reproduces the masculine view, of which it is one of the effects.
>   Here we encounter the inevitable man-with-rock, standing erect in his old Freudian realm, in the way that, to take the figure back to the point where linguistics is constituting it 'anew', Lacan preserves it in the sanctuary of the phallos (ø) 'sheltered' from *castration's lack!*
>
> (Cixous, 1976: 884)

4 'For we think back through our mothers if we are women. It is useless to go to the great men writers for help, however much one may go to them for pleasure. Lamb, Browne, Thackeray, Newman, Sterne, Dickens, de Quincey – whoever it may be – never helped a woman yet though she may have learnt a few tricks of them and adapted them to her use' (Woolf, 1977: 72–3).
5 Cixous may not regard her admiration for Joyce, Kleist and Genet in these terms, but from a gynocritical perspective all of these authors belong to the canon of male writing constructed and preserved by the academy. Indeed the academy's celebration of their subversive and revolutionary potential could be read as a strategy of privileging one type of subversion, a type which, because it derives from a male 'author', is less challenging than less daring work by women. See Jardine, 1985: 65–105 for modernism's ambivalent occupation of the space of the feminine.
    Hazard Adams, in an unusual reading of Cixous, cites her identification of the feminine in the work of male writers as an example of the 'antithetical' tendency of Cixous's aesthetic:

> There are no such things as male and female writing – from an antithetical point of view. Efforts to establish the latter, as in the work of Hélène Cixous, for example, have ended in identifying the work of certain writings by men as feminine. This in itself begins, in spite of its original aim, to break down the distinction as a power distinction. Indeed, it ends by dividing things between the purely literary and everything else representing the strife of power relations. Cixous's search begins to look like a search for the antithetical.
>
> (Adams, 1988: 755–6)

This would be more persuasive if Adams identified those works of Cixous to which he refers and identified how and where he has located the origin and end of Cixous's project.

6 It raises immediately the problem of western feminism 'colonizing' the work of women with very different cultural and political agendas.

7 The *Short History of the World*, unfortunately, not the science fiction.

8 Darko Suvin (1979) corrects this last term, borrowed from Brecht, to 'estrangement' as a more precise translation, but the wider reverberations of the term 'alienation' are useful here.

The term 'speculative fiction' is used in preference to 'science fiction'. It is a more accurate term for Lessing's fiction in general. It also resolves the problems of genre definition posed by the more allegorical novels, such as *The Marriages Between Zones Three, Four and Five*, and the 'inner space' fiction, such as *Briefing for a Descent into Hell*.

9 'What is not-I, not masculine, is most probably feminine' (Jung, 1971: Part 1, 27).

10 It is interesting that feminine madness takes a similar form in Ford Madox Ford's *The Good Soldier* (1972).

3 HISTORY AND WOMEN'S TIME

1 Where possible, quotes and references to the work of Julia Kristeva will be from the translated versions in *The Kristeva Reader* (1986). This serves the purpose of simplifying references and of directing the reader towards a source which is widely available. It has the disadvantage of obscuring the development of Kristeva's work over time. Where necessary, reference to this development will be made in the text. Appendix 1 gives a list of all the Kristeva texts referred to, their original publication dates and the dates of publication of English translations.

2 For analysis of history and its relation to the feminine and to feminism from a variety of very different perspectives, see: Ezell, 1990; Marcus, 1989; Newton, 1989; Ostriker, 1987; Robinson, 1990; Todd, 1988 and Tompkins, 1986.

3 The OED offers the more logical but less interesting options of 'an error in computing time, or fixing dates; the erroneous reference of an event, circumstance or custom to a wrong date' or 'anything done or existing out of date; *hence* anything which was proper to a former age, but is, or, if it existed, would be, out of harmony with the present'.

4 See Suvin, 1979 and Scholes, 1975 for the definition of speculative fiction in terms of the interaction of alienating or unfamiliar elements with cognitive or familiar ones.

5 The current study will not deal in detail with the Kristevan concept of negation.

6 See Kristeva, 1982: 245 for a discussion of the relation between 'style' and the death drives in Céline.

7 I am distinguishing here between escape, an attempt to become free of reality's constraints, and escapism, an attempt to evade reality.

8 Muriel Spark may be attempting to forestall an attack on these grounds against Mary Shelley – and the Gothic elements in Spark's own fiction – when she repudiates the term 'Gothic' as signifying the merely sensational rather than the disturbingly different (Spark, 1988).

9 Lessing may be adapting Jung's acausal principle of synchronicity as an alternative to deterministic, causal principles of plot. This falls outside the scope of the present study.

10 In a particularly condensed version of her encoding of modernist within feminist discourse, Jardine quotes Kristeva quoting Joyce:

'Father's time, mother's species', as Joyce put it; and indeed, when evoking the name and destiny of woman, one thinks more of the *space* generating and forming the human species than of *time*, becoming or history. The modern sciences of subjectivity, of its genealogy and accidents, confirm in their own way this intuition, which is perhaps itself the result of socio-historic conjecture.
(Kristeva, 1986: 190; quoted in Jardine, 1985: 89)

11 Angela Carter indicated her use of Brontë and referred me to the ballad 'The demon lover', in response to queries made by me in June 1987. For the variant texts of 'The demon lover' see Child, 1965: vol. 4, 360–9.

12 The play of images, the imaginary, Marianne's dream.

13 Though curiously does not comment on the superficially more obvious parallels to the biblical tale of Tamar, Amnon and Absalom (2 Samuel 13: 1–37).

14 See *The Waste Land*, lines 338–42:

If there were only water amongst the rock
Dead mountain mouth of carious teeth that cannot spit
Here one can neither stand nor lie nor sit
There is not even silence in the mountains
But dry sterile thunder without rain

15 See Brown, 1983 for an analysis of Lessing's use of the Grail legend and *The Waste Land*.

16 'The essential point in all this is that the form does not suppress the meaning, it only impoverishes it' (Barthes, 1972: 120).

17 See Ortner, 1974 for an analysis of the way in which 'Woman' functions in western culture as mediator between nature and culture.

18 Here it is Marianne, not Jewel, who is identified with the 'totemic animal' (Gilbert and Gubar, 1979: 272).

19 Kristeva specifies this as a new generation within the women's movement, which, in contrast to the first equality-orientated movement which sought '*insertion* into history', is engaged, through 'exploration of the dynamic of signs', in 'the radical *refusal* of the subjective limitations imposed by this history's time' (1986: 195).

20 See Jardine, 1985; also Meaney, 1991.

21 I am grateful to Angela Carter for pointing out the novel's

engagement with the work of Rousseau and her comments on its significance in the novel's exploration of a variety of utopias and dystopias.

22 Which he characterizes as 'group marriage'.

23 I am indebted here to Anne Owens Weekes whose 1987 paper, 'The breakdown of contract in *Castle Rackrent*', clarified a number of the implications of the concept of 'contract' for any discussion of women's social and sexual relations.

24 My emphasis.

25 Althusser's reading is based on a recognition of the amorphous nature of these RPs or Recipient Parties (to the contract). RP1 is initially defined as the individual or individuals, RP2 as the community, though, as will be seen above, this is not a fixed relation.

26 'Consider the womb . . . domain of futurity in which the embryo forms itself from the flesh and blood of the mother; the unguessable reaches of the sea are a symbol of it' (Carter, 1979: 107–8).

4 (UN)LIKE SUBJECTS

1 The relevant chapter is entitled 'Spaces for further research'.

2 Ruins which correspond to the state of her marriage to Casaubon.

3 Who also features briefly in *Wise Children*.

4 These are his 'legitimate' children, Saskia and Imogen.

5 Carter is obviously making reference to the 1935 version directed by Max Reinhardt and William Dieterle.

6 In the ballads of the demon lover and of the ship carpenter's wife, the lover typically comes back from the dead to tempt the woman away with him. See Child, 1965: vol. 4, 360–9. Peregrine's resurrection is not literal. He was merely believed dead and presented in Dora's prior narrative as such.

7 Carter, like Kristeva, is obviously influenced by Mikhail Bakhtin's work on the novel and carnival. An essay originally published in 1969, 'Word, dialogue and novel' (Kristeva, 1986: 34–61), illuminates Kristeva's emphasis on the concepts of the dialogical and intertextuality in Bakhtin's work and her understanding of these concepts and of carnival in relation to modernism. Bakhtin's work was a major influence in Kristeva's formulation of the central issues in *The Revolution in Poetic Language*.

8 See chapters 1 and 3.

9 Homans reads in the later entries in Gaskell's diary an anxiety on the author's part that the birth of her daughter Meta may have resulted in the loss of her own adoptive mother whose fatal stroke may have been brought on by caring for Marianne during her mother's confinement (Homans, 1986: 167–8).

10 Homans interprets this and similar comments as evidence of 'the writer's assumption that the diary is legible or worth reading, only if one or the other of its two subjects is dead', but this is an over-

literal reading which ignores the insight elsewhere in Homans's text into the recurrent depiction in women's writing of access to the symbolic and social as a death of the mother. Gaskell's first child died, but her anxiety that she may 'lose' her daughter must surely be read in the textual context of that child's language acquisition and increasing autonomy.

11 See Kershner, 1989.

12 See Jardine, 1985; a similar process may be observed in Eugene O'Neill's play for the mother, *Long Day's Journey into Night* (see Meaney, 1991).

13 As Stephen Heath has pointed out, Joyce was proudly conscious of the 'scorching' effect of his writing (Heath, 1984: 32).

14 The translation found in *The Kristeva Reader*, that by Leon S. Roudiez, does not follow the column divisions within 'Stabat Mater' as they appear in *Histoires d'amour*, possibly for unavoidable practical reasons. While Roudiez's translation is not otherwise changed, the division and structure of the columns here and in the rest of this chapter follow *Histoires d'amour* (as closely as is practically possible) and not the translation.

15 Kristeva's original '*enivre*' (intoxicate) is already somewhat ambiguous, though it could be said that in adopting 'enthrall' Leon Roudiez's translation enhances the original.

16 Gallop discusses the essay under the title 'Heréthique de l'amour', the title given to it on its first publication in *Tel Quel* 74 (Winter 1977): 30–49. The title 'Stabat Mater' was adopted when the essay was reprinted in *Histoires d'amour*, a collection of essays published in 1983.

17 Warner is acknowledged as a major source by Kristeva (1986: 186, note).

18 Dora and Nora, in *Wise Children*, are the Chance sisters.

19 Already 'VERBE FLESH' in Kristeva's version (1983).

20 See chapter 1 for a discussion of the interplay of voices and confusion of identity in 'And the one doesn't stir without the other'.

21 Jardine's quotations are from Kristeva, 1981: 238.

22 The concept of primacy of any kind is obviously intensely problematic here and the effect of Kristeva's and Gallop's strategy is to undermine the possibility of any relationship or situation achieving the status of primary agent in the construction of identity. None the less it can be argued that 'Stabat Mater' and *The Daughter's Seduction* postulate a consciously fictive primacy for a relationship which has traditionally been not so much secondary as invisible.

23 Gallop is parodying Kristeva's comment, 'The vulgar but oh how effective trap of "feminism": to recognize ourselves, to make of us The Truth . . . so as to keep us from functioning as unconscious truth' (Kristeva, 1986: 155).

24 Gallop here reverses the schema within 'Stabat Mater' itself where the left-hand column was the (aberrant) maternal voice, while the right-hand was the more normative scientific one. An analysis, so alert to Kristeva's 'fraudian' slips and nagged by the suspicion that

Kristeva's 'privileges a relation called "heterosexuality"' (127), is surely not unselfconscious in describing the mother as the 'right path to take' and the path to lesbianism as 'the one left'.

25 In the 'active', 'effective' women 'playing supermen' (Kristeva, 1974: 42–3; quoted by Gallop, 1982: 129–30).

26 Irigaray's essay explicitly attacks Freud's 'The psychogenesis of a case of homosexuality in a woman', but she characteristically refuses to name Lévi-Strauss, whose comments on the exchange of women (1977: vol. 2, 61, 83) she ironically paraphrases here.

27 'For a mother on the other hand, the other as arbitrary (the child) is taken for granted. As far as she is concerned – impossible, that is just the way it is: it is reduced to the implacable. The other is inevitable, she seems to say' (Kristeva, 1986: 184–5).

5 UNKNOWING THE TRUE-REAL

1 There are parallels here with Carter's appropriation of Joyce and Shakespeare in *Wise Children*. See chapter 4.

2 For an outline of the reservations about Irigaray's work as ahistorical see Moi, 1985: 147–9. These objections have been answered at length by Margaret Whitford (1991).

3 Gillian C. Gill uses Stephen MacKenna's late nineteenth-century translation of Plotinus in her translation of *Speculum of the Other Woman*. MacKenna's translation may occasionally sacrifice accuracy to felicity of expression, but it would be unnecessarily confusing and complex to introduce a different translation of Plotinus in discussing '*Une Mère de glace*'.

Even without the problem of accuracy of translation of Plotinus, Leon Roudiez finds it impossible to use any of the available English versions of the *Enneads* directly in his translation of Kristeva. (He does acknowledge 'occasional stylistic borrowings' from Guthrie's 1918 *Complete Works of Plotinus*.) The problem for Roudiez is the discrepancy between French and English translations of Plotinus. He adopts the expedient of himself directly translating Kristeva's quotes from Plotinus.

The difficulties of any attempt to discuss both Irigaray's and Kristeva's readings of Plotinus together in English is obvious. Since it is the two contemporary readings of him, and not Plotinus himself, which are relevant to this study, I have adopted the simplest way out of the maze of editions and translations, i.e. to quote Plotinus from the Gill translation of Irigaray and the Roudiez translation of Kristeva. I have used some additional material from Plotinus' Third Ennead, sixth tractate, which is the text Irigaray transposes. Since the material is thus more closely related to Irigaray's treatment of Plotinus than Kristeva's, I have followed Gill in using MacKenna's translation.

4 Liriope's name associates her with the lily, a water-flower, a connection which foreshadows her son's metamorphosis into a narcissus.

5 Gill explains that she retains the French title in order to maintain 'the play on the homonyms *mer/mère*, sea/mother and the double meaning of the word *glace*, ice/mirror' (Irigaray, 1985a: 168 note).

6 On the orders of Diana in Actaeon's case.

7 Freud is citing Romberg (1840) and deduces from the latter's observations that 'If this is so – if the memory of the psychical trauma must be regarded as operating as a contemporary agent . . . and if nevertheless the patient has no consciousness of such memories or their emergence – then we must admit that *unconscious ideas exist and are operative*' (Freud, 1981a: vol. 2, 221; original emphases).

8 Harrison's project is to force the texts of both these awkward women to submit this operation to the service of 'reality' as (his) tradition defines it.

9 The comment is made by Lacan's editor and translator, Alan Sheridan.

10 Irigaray's prefatory comment suggests one reason why dreams figure so prominently in the fiction of Lessing, Carter and Spark and why Carter in *Heroes and Villains* and Spark in *The Hothouse by the East River* suggest that the narrative framework is that of a dream: 'Woman's desire can find expression only in dreams' (Irigaray, 1985a: 125).

11 These demonic women share certain characteristics with the male 'demon lovers' of Lessing's and Carter's fiction, though these female demons have none of the nurturing potential of their male counterparts. All are agents of a transgression which leads to death. Margaret, their closest counterpart in *Symposium*, is directly identified as a demon lover figure by her mad uncle, who greets her with the entire first verse of the ballad (version F, from *Minstrelsy of the Scottish Border*; Child, 1965: vol. 4, 367).

6 THE ABJECT AND THE ABSENCE OF THE IDEAL

1 Compare Longinus: 'A lofty passage does not convince the reason of the reader, but the Sublime takes him out of himself . . . the Sublime, acting with an imperious and irresistible force, sways every reader whether he will or no' (1890: 2).

2 In 'The true-real' Kristeva has a long section on 'Truth as separation' (1986: 222–7): 'Separation, rejection, displacement, gap [*béance*] – isn't it in this way that language constitutes itself and operates in the radical discoveries of Freud? . . . *truth* is nothing more than language as a mechanism of displacement, negation and denegation' (224).

3 See Kristeva, 1988: 267–79 for a discussion of the relationship between the instability of identity (4) in amatory discourse and in metaphor. 'Let us call metaphor, in the general sense of a *conveyance of meaning*, the economy that modifies language when subject and object of the utterance act muddle their borders' (268).

4 The pursuit of the end of night is a reference to the *Journey to the End of the Night* (1934), the Céline text which is central to the elabor-

ation of abjection in *Powers of Horror*. For the problems involved in focusing on this anti-Semitic writer, see Conclusion.

5 Compare Longinus: 'A sublime thought, if happily timed, illumines an entire subject with the vividness of a lightning-flash, and exhibits the whole power of the orator in a moment of time' (1890: 3).

6 Lyotard does acknowledge the revolutionary potential of the women's movement, specifically in undermining 'claims to construct meaning, to speak the Truth' (1989: 120). None the less, it is difficult to read 'One of the things at stake in women's struggles' (the article in which that acknowledgement occurs) without irritation. There are fairly commonplace and inoffensive warnings against the dangers implicit in too great an emphasis on feminine difference. More strikingly, there seems to be an underlying fear that such difference does exist and a desire to pre-empt its articulation of itself (see chapter 4) and to integrate it into his own anti-narrative of the end of philosophy.

7 See chapter 5 for a discussion of the techniques of negation and qualification in *The Cloud of Unknowing* and *The Hothouse by the East River*.

8 The 'Sabbath Notebooks' is Nicholas's unpublished polemical work.

9 Santayana makes explicit reference to Aristotle.

10 'Whatever is any sort terrible, or is conversant about terrible objects, or operates in a manner analogous to terror, is a source of the *sublime*; that is, it is productive of the strongest emotion which the mind is capable of feeling' (Burke, 1852 [1759]: 585).

11 Spark, 1967: 173.

12 Burke gives 'black he stood as night' for 1.670b (1852 [1759]: 600).

13 'In the classical image of Zeus bearing Athene from his brain, where we have already recognized an example of "sublimation", we now note that the "sublimation" has been rendered by means of an image of the type that Freud termed "transference upward": as the woman gives birth from the womb, so the father from his brain. Creation by the power of the word is another instance of such a transfer to the male womb: the mouth the vagina, the word the birth' (Campbell, 1974: vol. 3, 157).

14 In *Powers of Horror*, the flash where abject and sublime are united has apparently superseded the flash where opposite terms were discharged like thunder (9).

Bibliography

In most cases, widely available paperback editions of the fiction have been used. This simplifies referencing to Lessing's *Children of Violence* series in particular, since there is no uniform series of first editions. The second edition of *The Golden Notebook* is the edition referred to throughout, in order to avail of the author's Preface to that edition. For more detailed bibliographical information on the writings of Julia Kristeva referred to in this text, the reader is referred to Appendix 1. In general, translated works are listed under the name of the author, not the translator. An exception is made for the different translations of Plotinus which, because of the discrepancies between them, constitute a special case (see chapter 5, note 3).

Adams, H. (1988) 'Canons: literary criteria/power criteria', *Critical Inquiry*, 14: 748–64.
Adorno, T. W. and Horkheimer, M. (1973) *see* Horkheimer.
Althusser, L. (1972) *Politics and History: Montesquieu, Rousseau, Hegel and Marx*, trans. Ben Brewster, London: NLB.
Atherton, J. (1974) *The Books at the Wake: A Study of Literary Allusions in James Joyce's Finnegans Wake*, New York: Paul P. Appel.
Awkward, M. (1989) 'Appropriative gestures: theory and Afro-American literary criticism', in L. Kauffman (ed.) *Gender and Theory: Dialogues in Feminist Criticism*, New York and Oxford: Blackwell, pp. 238–46.
Bakhtin, M. (1981) *The Dialogic Imagination: Four Essays*, trans. C. Emerson and M. Holquist, Austin, Tex.: University of Texas Press.
—— (1984) *Problems of Dostoevsky's Poetics*, trans. C. Emerson, Manchester: Manchester University Press.
Barthes, R. (1972) *Mythologies*, trans. A. Lavers, London: Cape.
—— (1975) *S/Z*, trans. R. Miller, London: Cape.
Beckett, S. (1959) *Molloy*, London: Calder.
Bersani, L. (1976) *A Future for Astyanax*, Boston, MA: Little, Brown.
Bessière, I. (1974) *Le Récit Fantastique: la poétique de l'incertain*, Paris: Librairie Larousse.
Bradbury, M. (1972) 'Muriel Spark's fingernails', *Critical Quarterly* 14: 241–50.

Brecht, B. (1973) *Brecht on Theatre: The Development of an Aesthetic*, trans. J. Willett, London: Eyre Methuen.

Brontë, C. (1966 [1847]) *Jane Eyre*, ed. Q. D. Leavis, Harmondsworth, Mx: Penguin.

Brontë, E. (1965 [1847]) *Wuthering Heights*, ed. David Daiches, Harmondsworth, Mx: Penguin.

Brown, S. G. (1983) 'That vanished mind: *The Waste Land* and the Grail legend as metaphor in the novels of Doris Lessing', PhD thesis, Rutgers State University of New Jersey and New Brunswick (Literature, Modern).

Burke, E. (1852 [1759]) 'A philosophical enquiry into the origin of our ideas of the sublime and beautiful', *The Works and Correspondence of Edmund Burke*, vol. II, London, Rivington.

Burrow, J. A. (1977) 'Fantasy and language in *The Cloud of Unknowing*', Essays in Criticism 4: 283–98.

Campbell, J. (1974) *The Masks of God: Occidental Mythology*, London: Souvenir.

Carter, A. (1967) *The Magic Toyshop*, London: Heinemann.

—— (1969) *Heroes and Villains*, London: Heinemann; reprinted (1981) Harmondsworth, Mx: Penguin.

—— (1971) *Love*, London: Hart-Davis.

—— (1972) *The Infernal Desire Machines of Doctor Hoffman*, London: Hart-Davis.

—— (1977) *The Passion of New Eve*, London: Victor Gollancz; reprinted (1982) London: Virago.

—— (1979) *The Sadeian Woman: An Exercise in Cultural History*, London: Virago.

—— (1984) *Nights at the Circus*, London: Chatto & Windus/Hogarth Press; reprinted (1985) London: Pan.

—— (1991) *Wise Children*, London: Chatto & Windus.

Céline, L. F. (1934) *Journey to the End of the Night*, trans. J. H. P. Marks, Boston, MA: Little, Brown.

Chesler, P. (1972) *Women and Madness*, New York: Avon.

Child, F. J. (ed.) (1965) *English and Scottish Popular Ballads*, vol. 4, New York: Dover.

Christian, B. (1989) 'The race for theory', in L. Kauffman (ed.) *Gender and Theory: Dialogues in Feminist Criticism*, New York and Oxford: Blackwell, pp. 225–37.

Cixous, H. (1969) *Dedans*, Paris: Grasset.

—— (1974) 'The character of character', *New Literary History* 5: 384–402.

—— (1976) 'The laugh of the Medusa', trans. K. and P. Cohen, *Signs* 1(1): 875–99. First published as (1975) 'Le rire de la Meduse', *L'Arc* 61: 39–54.

—— (1981) 'Castration or decapitation?', trans. A. Kuhn, *Signs* 7(1): 41–55. First published as (1976) 'Le sexe ou la tête', *Les Cahiers du GRIF* 13: 5–15.

—— (1990) *Reading with Clarice Lispector*, ed., trans. and with an introduction by Verena Andermatt Conley, Hemel Hempstead, Herts: Harvester Wheatsheaf.

—— and Clément, C. (1986) *The Newly Born Woman*, trans. Betsy Wing, Manchester: Manchester University Press. First published as (1975) *La Jeune Née*, Paris: Union Générale d'Éditions.

Conrad, J. (1973 [1902]) *Heart of Darkness*, ed. P. O'Prey, Harmondsworth, Mx: Penguin.

Daly, M. (1973) *Beyond God the Father: Toward a Philosophy of Women's Liberation*, Boston, MA: Beacon Press.

—— (1979) *Gyn/Ecology*, London: Women's Press.

de Beauvoir, S. (1972) *The Second Sex*, trans. H. M. Parshley, Harmondsworth, Mx: Penguin.

Derrida, J. (1974) *Glas*, Paris: Editions Galilée.

—— (1981) 'Freud and the scene of Writing', in *Writing and Difference*, London: Routledge, pp. 196–231.

de Sade, D. A. F., Marquis (1965a) *Philosophy in the Bedroom*, trans. R. Seaver and A. Wainhouse, New York: Grove Press.

—— (1965b) *Juliette*, trans. R. Seaver and A. Wainhouse, New York: Grove Press; and trans. P. Bowles, London: Calder & Boyars.

Douglas, M. (1984) *Purity and Danger: An Analysis of the Concepts of Pollution and Taboo*, London and New York: Ark.

Draine, B. (1984) *Substance Under Pressure: Artistic Coherence and Evolving Form in the Novels of Doris Lessing*, Madison, WI and London: University of Wisconsin Press.

du Plessis, R. (1985) *Writing Beyond the Ending: Narrative Strategies of Twentieth-Century Women Writers*, Bloomington, IN: Indiana University Press.

—— (1986) 'In search of the Etruscans', in E. Showalter (ed.) *The New Feminist Criticism*, London: Virago, pp. 271–91.

Ecker, G. (ed.) (1985) *Feminist Aesthetics*, trans. H. Anderson, London: Women's Press.

Edelman, L. (1989) 'At risk in the sublime: the politics of gender and theory', in L. Kauffman (ed.) *Gender and Theory: Dialogues in Feminist Criticism*, New York and Oxford: Blackwell, pp. 213–24.

Eliot, G. (1981 [1860]) *The Mill on the Floss*, ed. G. S. Haight, Oxford: Clarendon.

—— (1986 [1871–2]) *Middlemarch*, ed. D. Carroll, Oxford: Clarendon.

Eliot, T. S. (1961) *Selected Poems*, London: Faber.

Ellman, M. (1968) *Thinking About Women*, New York: Harcourt, Brace, Jovanovich.

Engels, F. (1972) *The Origin of the Family, Private Property and the State*, rev. edn, ed. E. B. Leacock, trans. A. West, London: Lawrence & Wishart.

Ezell, M. J. M. (1990) 'The myth of Judith Shakespeare: creating the canon of women's literature'. *New Literary History* 21(3): 579–92.

Felman, S. (1975) 'Women and madness: the critical phallacy', *Diacritics* 5:2–10.

Ford, F. Madox (1972) *The Good Soldier*, London: Heinemann.

Freud, S. (1955) *Standard Edition of the Complete Psychological Works*, ed. J. Strachey, vol. 18, *Beyond the Pleasure Principle, Group Psychology and*

Other Works, London: Hogarth Press for the Institute of Psycho-analysis.

—— (1981a) *Standard Edition of the Complete Psychological Works*, ed. J. Strachey, vol. 2, *Studies on Hysteria* (with Josef Breuer), London: Hogarth Press for the Institute of Psychoanalysis.

—— (1981b) *Standard Edition of the Complete Psychological Works*, ed. J. Strachey, vol. 22, *New Introductory Lectures on Psycho-Analysis and Other Works*, London: Hogarth Press for the Institute of Psychoanalysis.

Friedan, B. (1963) *The Feminine Mystique*, New York: Dell.

Gallop, J. (1982) *Feminism and Psychoanalysis: The Daughter's Seduction*, London: Macmillan.

Gaskell, E. (1923) *My Diary: The Early Years of My Daughter Marianne*, London: privately printed by Clement Shorter.

Gauthier, X. (1981) 'Is there such a thing as women's writing?', trans. M. A. August, in E. Marks and I. de Courtivron (eds) *New French Feminisms: An Anthology*, Brighton, Sx: Harvester, pp. 161–4.

Gilbert, S. (1986) Introduction to H. Cixous and C. Clément, *The Newly Born Woman*, Manchester: Manchester University Press, pp. ix–xviii.

Gilbert, S. and Gubar, S. (1979) *The Madwoman in the Attic: The Woman Writer and the Nineteenth-Century Literary Imagination*, New Haven, CT: Yale University Press.

Guthrie, K. S. (trans.) (1918) *Complete Works of Plotinus*, London: Bell.

Habermas, J. (1976) *The Legitimation Crisis*, trans. T. MacCarthy, London: Heinemann.

Hanrahan, M. (1989) 'Dedans', paper given at 'Etudes Féminines: Women's Writing and Literary Studies in Theory and Practice', University of Liverpool, May.

Harrison, B. (1976) 'Muriel Spark and Jane Austen', in G. Josipovici (ed.) *The Modern English Novel: the Reader, the Writer and the Work*, London: Open Books, pp. 225–51.

Hawking, S. (1988) *A Brief History of Time*, London: Transworld.

Heath, S. (1984) 'Ambiviolences: notes for reading Joyce', in D. Attridge and D. Ferrer (eds) *Post-Structuralist Joyce: Essays from the French*, Cambridge: Cambridge University Press, pp. 31–68.

Hesiod (1982) 'The theogany', in *The Homeric Hymns and Homerica*, trans. H. G. E. White, London: Heinemann, 78–154.

Holderness, G. (1991) ' "What ish my nation?": Shakespeare and national identities', *Textual Practices* 5(1): 74–93.

Homans, M. (1980) *Women Writers and Poetic Identity: Dorothy Wordworth, Emily Brontë and Emily Dickinson*, Princeton, NJ: Princeton University Press.

—— (1986) *Bearing the Word: Language and Female Experience in Nineteenth-Century Women's Writing*, Chicago and London: University of Chicago Press.

Horkheimer, M. and Adorno, T. W. (1973) *The Dialectics of Enlightenment*, trans. J. Cumming, London: Allen Lane.

Irigaray, L. (1974) *Speculum de l'autre femme*, Paris: Editions de Minuit.

—— (1981) 'And the one doesn't stir without the other', trans. H. V.

Wenzel, *Signs* 7(1): 60–7. First published as (1979) *Et l'une ne bouge pas sans l'autre*, Paris: Editions de Minuit.

—— (1985a) *Speculum of the Other Woman*, trans. G. C. Gill, Ithaca, NY: Cornell University Press. First published as (1974) *Speculum de l'autre femme*, Paris: Editions de Minuit.

—— (1985b) *This Sex Which is Not One*, trans. C. Porter with C. Burke, Ithaca, NY: Cornell University Press. First published as (1977) *Ce Sexe qui n'en est pas un*, Paris: Editions de Minuit.

Jackson, R. (1971) *Fantasy: the Literature of Subversion*, London: Methuen.

Jacobus, M. (ed.) (1979) *Women Writing and Writing about Women*, London: Croom Helm.

—— (1986) *Reading Women: Essays in Feminist Criticism*, London: Routledge & Kegan Paul.

Jardine, A. (1985) *Gynesis: Configurations of Woman and Modernity*, Ithaca, NY and London: Cornell University Press.

Jonson, B. (1983) *Volpone*, ed. R. B. Parker, Manchester: Manchester University Press.

Joyce, J. (1966 [1957]) *Letters*, ed. Stuart Gilbert, vol. 1, London: Faber.

—— (1992a [1939]) *Finnegans Wake*, ed. Seamus Deane, Harmondsworth, Mx: Penguin.

—— (1992b [1922]) *Ulysses*, ed. Declan Kiberd, Harmondsworth, Mx: Penguin.

Jung, C. G. (1971) *The Collected Works of C. G. Jung*, ed. H. Read, M. Fordham and G. Adler, vol. 9, *Aion: Researches into the Phenomenology of the Self*, London: Routledge.

Kant, Immanuel (1892 [1790]) *Critique of Judgement* ed. and trans. H. Bernard, London: Macmillan.

Kemp, P. (1974) *Muriel Spark*, London: Elek.

Kermode, F. (1963) 'The house of fiction: interviews with seven English novelists', *Partisan Review* 30(1): 61–83.

—— (1967 [1966]) *The Sense of an Ending: Studies in the Theory of Fiction*, London: Oxford University Press.

—— (1971) 'Muriel Spark', in *Modern Essays*, London: Fontana, pp. 267–83.

Kershner, R. B. (1989) *Joyce, Bakhtin and Popular Literature: Chronicles of Disorder*, Chapel Hill, NC: University of North Carolina Press.

Kristeva, J. (1977) *About Chinese Women*, trans. A. Barrows, London: Boyars. First published as (1974) *Des Chinoises*, Paris: Des Femmes.

—— (1979) *La Folle Verité*, Paris: Editions du Seuil.

—— (1981) *Desire in Language*, ed. L. S. Roudiez, trans. A. Jardine, I. A. Gora and L. S. Roudiez, Oxford: Blackwell.

—— (1982) *Powers of Horror: An Essay on Abjection*, trans. L. S. Roudiez, New York: Columbia University Press. First published as (1980) *Pouvoirs de l'horreur*, Paris: Editions du Seuil.

—— (1984) *The Revolution in Poetic Language*, trans. M. Waller, New York: Columbia University Press. First published as (1974) *La Révolution du langage poétique*, Paris: Editions du Seuil.

—— (1986) *The Kristeva Reader*, ed. T. Moi, Oxford: Blackwell.

—— (1987) *Soleil Noir: Dépression et Mélancolie*, Paris: Gallimard.

—— (1988) *Tales of Love*, trans. L. S. Roudiez, New York and Guildford, Sy: Columbia University Press. First published as (1983) *Histoires d'amour*, Paris: Denoël.

—— (1989) *Black Sun: Depression and Melancholy*, trans. L. S. Roudiez, New York: Columbia University Press. First published as *Soleil Noir: Dépression et Mélancolie*, Paris: Gallimard.

—— (1991) *Strangers to Ourselves*, trans. L. S. Roudiez, London: Harvester Wheatsheaf. First published as (1988) *Etrangers à nous-mêmes*, Paris: Fayard.

Lacan, J. (1977) *Écrits*, ed. and trans. A. Sheridan, New York: Norton.

—— (1982) *Feminine Sexuality: Jacques Lacan and the Ecole Freudienne*, ed. J. Mitchell and J. Rose, London: Macmillan.

Laing, R. D. (1960) *The Divided Self*, London: Tavistock.

—— (1967) *The Politics of Experience and the Bird of Paradise*, Harmondsworth, Mx: Penguin.

—— and Esterson, A. (1970) *Sanity, Madness and the Family*, Harmondsworth, Mx: Penguin.

Lawrence, K. (1990) 'Joyce and feminism', *The Cambridge Companion to James Joyce*, ed. Derek Attridge, Cambridge: Cambridge University Press, pp. 237–58.

Lessing, D. (1950) *The Grass is Singing*, London: Michael Joseph.

—— (1952–69) *Children of Violence*:

(1952) *Martha Quest*, London: Michael Joseph; reprinted (1983) London: Granada.

(1954) *A Proper Marriage*, London: Michael Joseph; reprinted (1984) London: Granada.

(1958) *A Ripple from the Storm*, London: Michael Joseph; reprinted (1969) London: Granada (Panther).

(1965) *Landlocked*, London: MacGibbon & Kee; reprinted (1967) London: Granada (Panther).

(1969) *The Four-Gated City*, London: MacGibbon & Kee; reprinted (1983) London: Granada.

—— (1962) *The Golden Notebook*, London: Michael Joseph; 2nd edn (1972) London: Granada (see the introduction to this bibliography).

—— (1964) *African Stories*, London: Michael Joseph.

—— (1971) *Briefing for a Descent into Hell*, London: Cape; reprinted (1977) London: Granada (Panther).

—— (1972) see (1962) *The Golden Notebook*.

—— (1973) *The Summer Before the Dark*, London: Cape; reprinted (1975) Harmondsworth, Mx: Penguin.

—— (1974) *Memoirs of a Survivor*, London: Octagon Press; reprinted (1976) London: Picador.

—— (1979–83) *Canopus in Argos: Archives*:

(1979) *Re: Colonized Planet 5 Shikasta*, London: Cape.

(1980) *The Marriages Between Zones Three, Four and Five*, London: Cape.

(1981) *The Sirian Experiments*, London: Cape.

(1982) *The Making of the Representative for Planet 8*, London: Cape.

(1983) *The Sentimental Agents in the Volyen Empire*, London: Cape.

—— (1985a) *The Diaries of Jane Somers*, Harmondsworth, Mx: Penguin. First published under the pseudonym 'Jane Somers' as (1983) *The Diary of Jane Somers*, London: Michael Joseph and as (1984) *If the Old Could Only*, London: Michael Joseph.

—— (1985b) *The Good Terrorist*, London: Cape.

—— (1988) *The Fifth Child*, London: Cape.

Lévi-Strauss, C. (1977) *Structural Anthropology*, vol. 2, trans. M. Layton, London: Allen Lane.

Lodge, D. (1971) *The Novelist at the Crossroads*, London: Routledge.

Longinus (1890) *On the Sublime*, trans. H. L. Havell, London: Macmillan.

Lyotard, J.-F. (1984) *The Postmodern Condition: A Report on Knowledge*, trans. G. Bennington and B. Massumi, Manchester: Manchester University Press.

—— (1989) 'One of the things at stake in women's struggles', in *The Lyotard Reader*, ed. Andrew Benjamin, Oxford: Blackwell, pp. 111–21.

MacKenna, S. rev. edn, (ed. and trans.) (1956) *Plotinus: The Enneads*, London: Faber.

Marcus, J. (1989) 'The asylums of Antaeus: women, war and madness', in H. A. Veeser (ed.) *The New Historicism*, London: Routledge, pp. 132–51.

Marcuse, H. (1978) *The Aesthetic Dimension*, trans. H. Marcus and E. Sherover, Boston, MA: Beacon Press.

Marks, E. and de Courtivron, I. (eds) (1981) *New French Feminisms: An Anthology*, Brighton, Sx: Harvester.

Meaney, G. (1991) '*Long Day's Journey into Night*: modernism, postmodernism and maternal loss', *Irish University Review* 21(2) (Autumn): 204–18.

Millett, K. (1970) *Sexual Politics*, New York: Doubleday.

Milton, J. (1931) *Paradise Lost*, in *The Works of John Milton*, ed. F. A. Patterson, 2(1), New York: Columbia University Press.

Mitchell, J. (1974) *Psychoanalysis and Feminism*, Harmondsworth, Mx: Penguin.

Moi, T. (1985) *Sexual/Textual Politics*, London and New York: Methuen.

Mulvey, L. (1990) 'Afterthoughts on visual pleasure and narrative cinema' in E. Ann Kaplan (ed.) *Psychoanalysis and Cinema*, London: Routledge.

Newton, J. L. (1989) 'History as usual? Feminism and the new historicism', in H. A. Veeser (ed.) *The New Historicism*, London: Routledge, pp. 152–67.

Ortner, S. B. (1974) 'Is female to male as nature is to culture?', in S. Z. Rosaldo and L. Lamphere (eds) *Women, Culture and Society*, Stanford, CA: Stanford University Press.

Ostriker, A. (1987) 'Dancing at the devil's party', *Critical Inquiry* 13: 579–96.

Ovid (1955) *Metamorphoses*, trans. M. M. Innes, Harmondsworth, Mx: Penguin.

Owens Weekes, A. (1987) 'The breakdown of contract in *Castle Rackrent*', paper given at the Third International Congress on Women, 'Visions and Revisions', Dublin, July.

Plato (1974) *The Republic*, trans. H. D. P. Lee, Harmondsworth, Mx: Penguin.

Plotinus (1918) *Complete Works*, ed. and trans. K. S. Guthrie, London: Bell.

—— (1956) *Plotinus: The Enneads*, rev. edn, ed. and trans. S. MacKenna, London: Faber.

Pratt, A. (1972) 'Women and nature in modern fiction', *Contemporary Literature* 13: 476–90.

Rand, R. (1987) 'Ozone: an essay on Keats', in R. Machin and C. Norris (eds) *Post-Structuralist Readings of English Poetry*, Cambridge: Cambridge University Press, pp. 294–307.

Rigney, B. H. (1978) *Madness and Sexual Politics in the Feminist Novel: Studies in Brontë, Woolf, Lessing and Atwood*, Madison, WI and London: University of Wisconsin Press.

Robinson, L. S. (1990) 'Sometimes, always, never: their women's history and ours', *New Literary History* 21: 377–94.

Romberg, M. H. (1840) *Lehrbrich der Nerven*, Berlin: Krankheiten des Menschen.

Rose, H. J. (1959) *A Handbook of Greek Mythology*, 6th edn, London: Methuen.

Rousseau, J.-J. (1973) *The Social Contract and Discourses*, rev. edn, trans. G. D. H. Cole, London and Melbourne: Dent (Everyman).

Rubenstein, R. (1979) *The Novelistic Vision of Doris Lessing*, Urbana, IL, Chicago and London: University of Illinois Press.

Russ, J. (1973) 'The subjunctivity of science fiction', *Extrapolation* 15(1): 51–9.

—— (1984) *How to Suppress Women's Writing*, London: Women's Press.

Samuel, I and II (1977) commentary P. R. Ackroyd, Cambridge: Cambridge University Press.

Santayana, G. (1979) 'The nature of beauty', in M. Rader (ed.) *A Modern Book of Aesthetics*, New York and London: Holt, Rinehart & Winston, pp. 162–81.

Scholes, R. (1975) *Structural Fabulation*, London: University of Notre Dame Press.

Sellers, S. (ed.) (1988) *Writing Differences: Readings from the Seminar of Hélène Cixous*, Milton Keynes: Open University Press.

Showalter, R. (1982 [1978]) *A Literature of Their Own*, rev. edn, London: Virago.

—— (1984) 'Women's time, women's space', *Tulsa Studies in Women's Literature* 3: 29–43.

—— (ed.) (1986) *The New Feminist Criticism*, London: Virago.

—— (1987) *The Female Malady: Women, Madness and English Culture, 1830–1980*, London: Virago.

—— (ed.) (1989) *Speaking of Gender*, New York and London: Routledge.

Signs: Journal of Women in Culture and Society 1 (1976).

Smith, B. (1986) 'Towards a Black feminist criticism', in E. Showalter (ed.) *The New Feminist Criticism*, London: Virago, pp. 168–85.

Spark, M. (1957) *The Comforters*, London: Macmillan; reprinted (1963) Harmondsworth, Mx: Penguin.

—— (1963a) *The Girls of Slender Means*, London: Macmillan; reprinted (1966) Harmondsworth, Mx: Penguin.

—— (1963b) Interview with Frank Kermode, 'The house of fiction: interviews with seven English novelists', *Partisan Review* 30(1): 61–83.

—— (1967) *The Mandelbaum Gate*, Harmondsworth, Mx: Penguin. First published (1965) in the *New Yorker*, 15 May, 10 July, 24 July, 7 August, and London: Macmillan.

—— (1968) *The Public Image*, London: Macmillan; reprinted (1970) Harmondsworth, Mx: Penguin..

—— (1970) *The Driver's Seat*, London: Macmillan. First published in *The New Yorker*, 16 May.

—— (1971a) Interview with Philip Toynbee in *Observer Colour Supplement*, 7 November.

—— (1971b) 'The desegregation of art', the Blashfield Foundation Address, *Proceedings of the American Academy of Arts and Letters*.

—— (1971c) *Not to Disturb*, London: Macmillan; reprinted (1974) Harmondsworth, Mx: Penguin..

—— (1973) *The Hothouse by the East River*, London, Macmillan; reprinted (1982) St Albans, Herts; Granada.

—— (1981) *Loitering with Intent*, London, Bodley Head; reprinted (1982) St Albans, Herts: Granada (Triad).

—— (1984) *The Only Problem*, London: Bodley Head; reprinted (1985) St Albans, Herts: Granada (Triad).

—— (1988) *Mary Shelley: Child of Light*, rev. edn, London: Constable. First published (1951) as *Child of Light*, Hadleigh, London: Tower Bridge Publications.

—— (1990) *Symposium*, London: Constable.

Spivak, G. C. (1981) 'French feminism in an international frame', *Yale French Studies* 62: 154–84.

—— (1987) *In Other Worlds: Essays in Cultural Politics*, New York and London: Methuen.

Stone, M. (1979) *The Paradise Papers*, London: Virago.

Suvin, D. (1979) *Metamorphoses of Science Fiction: On the Poetics and History of a Literary Genre*, New Haven, CT and London: Yale University Press.

Szasz, T. (1973) *Ideology and Insanity: Essays on the Psychiatric Dehumanization of Man*, London: Calder & Boyars.

—— (1987) *Insanity: The Idea and Its Consequences*, New York: Wiley.

Tiger, V. (1987) 'Doris Lessing's revision of feminist utopias', paper given at the Third International Congress on Women, 'Visions and Revisions', Dublin, July.

Todd, J. (1988) *Feminist Literary History*, Oxford: Blackwell.

Tompkins, J. (1986) 'Indians: textualism, morality and the problems of history', *Critical Inquiry* 13: 101–19.

Vlastos, M. (1976) 'Doris Lessing and R. D. Laing: psychopolitics and prophecy', *PMLA* 91 (2): 245–58.

Warner, M. (1976) *Alone of All Her Sex: the Myth and Cult of the Virgin Mary*, London: Weidenfeld & Nicolson.

Wells, H. G. (1987) *An Illustrated Short History of the World* 2nd edn, Exeter, Devon: Webb & Bower.

Whitford, M. (1991) *Luce Irigaray: Philosophy in the Feminine*, London: Routledge.

Wittig, M. (1969) *Les Guérillères*, Paris: Editions de Minuit.

Wollstonecraft, M. (1975) *The Vindication of the Rights of Woman*, ed. M. Brody, Harmondsworth, Mx: Penguin.

Wolters, C. (ed.) (1978 [1961]) *The Cloud of Unknowing and other works*, Harmondsworth, Mx: Penguin.

Woolf, V. (1966) 'George Eliot', in *Collected Essays of Virginia Woolf*, vol. 1, London: Hogarth Press.

—— (1977 [1928]) *A Room of One's Own*, London: Grafton.

Wordsworth, W. (1969) *Poetical Works of William Wordsworth*, rev. edn, ed. T. Hutchinson, London: Oxford University Press.

Yaeger, P. (1989) 'Toward a female sublime', in L. Kauffman (ed.) *Gender and Theory: Dialogues in Feminist Criticism*, New York and Oxford: Blackwell, pp. 191–212.

Appendix 1

Julia Kristeva:
a chronology of cited texts

The following chronology refers exclusively to the writings of Kristeva cited in the text. In the case of English translations of Kristeva's work, the date and identification of the French text are included in parentheses after details of the English text. So, for example:

> 1977b: *About Chinese Women*, trans. A. Barrows, London: Boyars (1974a).

indicates that 1977b is a translation of 1974a. In the case of *The Kristeva Reader* the list of dates refers to the original French publication of texts included in full or in part in Moi's selection *which are referred to in this work*. Conversely, the date and identification of English translations of part or all of the French texts is given in parentheses after details of those texts.

1969: *Séméiotiké: Recherches pour une sémanalyse*, Paris: Editions du Seuil (1981a, 1986).

1974a: *Des Chinoises*, Paris: Des Femmes (1977b, 1986).

1974b: *La Révolution du langage poétique*, Paris: Editions du Seuil (1984, 1986).

1977a: 'Heréthique de l'amour', *Tel Quel* 74 (Winter): 30–49. Reprinted (1983) as 'Stabat Mater' in *Histoires d'amour* (1986, 1988a).

1977b: *About Chinese Women*, trans. A. Barrows, London: Boyars (1974a).

1977c: *Polylogue*, Paris: Editions du Seuil (1981a).

1979a: 'Le vréel', in *La Folle Verité*, Paris: Editions du Seuil (1986).

1979b: 'Le temps des femmes', *34/44: Cahiers de recherche de sciences des textes et documents* 5: 5–19 (1981b, 1986).

1980: *Pouvoirs de l'horreur*, Paris: Editions du Seuil (1982).

1981a: *Desire in Language*, ed. L. S. Roudiez, trans. A. Jardine, T. A. Gora and L. S. Roudiez, Oxford: Blackwell (1969, 1977c).

1981b: 'Women's time', *Signs* 7(1): 13–35, trans. A. Jardine and H. Blake (1979b).

1982: *Powers of Horror: An Essay on Abjection*, trans. L. S. Roudiez, New York: Columbia University Press (1980).

1983: *Histoires d'amour*, Paris: Denoël (1986, 1988).

1984: *The Revolution in Poetic Language*, trans. M. Waller, New York: Columbia University Press (1974b).

1986: *The Kristeva Reader*, ed. T. Moi, Oxford: Blackwell (1974a, 1974b, 1977a, 1979a, 1979b, 1983).

1987: *Soleil Noir: Dépression et Mélancolie*, Paris: Gallimard (1989).

1988a: *Tales of Love*, trans. L. S. Roudiez, New York and Guildford, Sy: Columbia University Press (1983).

1988b: *Etrangers à nous-mêmes*, Paris: Fayard (1991).

1989: *Black Sun: Depression and Melancholy*, trans. L. S. Roudiez, New York: Columbia University Press (1987).

1991: *Strangers to Ourselves*, trans. L. S. Roudiez, London: Harvester Wheatsheaf (1988b).

Index